Contents

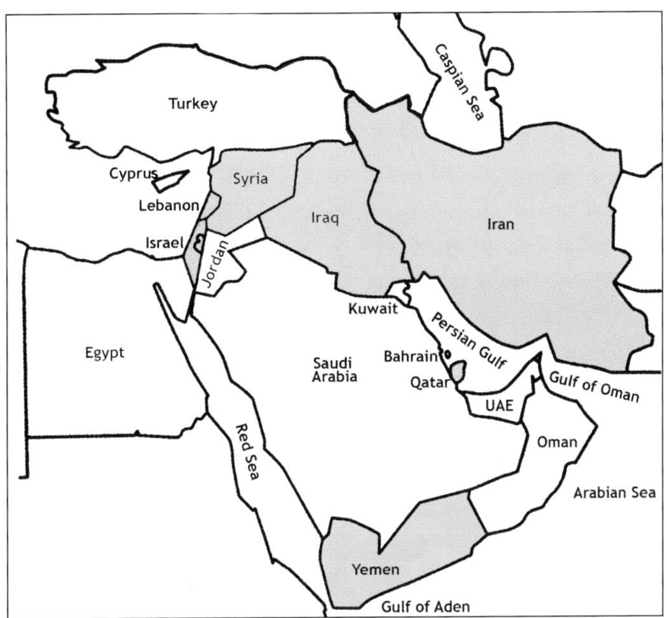

Helion & Company Limited
Unit 8 Amherst Business Centre, Budbrooke
Road, Warwick CV34 5WE, England
Tel. 01926 499 619
Email: info@helion.co.uk Website: www.helion.co.uk X (formerly
Twitter): @helionbooks Visit our blog http://blog.helion.co.uk/

Published by Helion & Company 2026
Designed and typeset by Mach 3 Solutions (www.mach3solutions.co.uk)
Cover designed by Paul Hewitt, Battlefield Design
(www.battlefield-design.co.uk)

Text © Bill Norton 2026
Artworks by: David Bocquelet, Luca Canossa, Tom
Cooper, Anderson Subtil, Daniel Uhr 2026
Maps George Anderson © Helion & Company 2025

Every reasonable effort has been made to trace copyright holders
and to obtain their permission for the use of copyright material.

The author and publisher apologise for any errors or omissions in
this work, and would be grateful if notified of any corrections that
should be incorporated in future reprints or editions of this book.

ISBN: 978-1-806722-94-5

British Library Cataloguing-in-Publication Data.
A catalogue record for this book is available from the British Library.

For details of other military history titles published by Helion
& Company Limited contact the above address, or visit
our website: http://www.helion.co.uk. We always welcome
receiving book proposals from prospective authors.

Front cover artwork: A 107 Squadron F-16I is depicted dropping an Air LORA air-launched ballistic missile. This was one of three such weapon types employed by the Israel Air and Space Force during air attacks on Iran in 2024 and 2025. With the super-heavy weapon and centreline tank, only wingtip AIM-9M missiles are carried – an old system indicating the low likelihood of an air-to-air engagement. The artwork shows the aircraft over ar-Ramadi, in al-Anbar province, Iraq. (Artwork by Daniel Uhr © Helion & Company 2026)

Back cover artwork: The Caterpillar D9 bulldozer was modified in Israel as a rugged army vehicle. Added armour was concentrated around the cab that included armoured glass. Optional is a machine gun atop the cab and grenade launchers. This D9R has added grating around the cab and an overhead canopy to defeat UAV-delivered explosives. The Combat Engineers used the 'Dubi' or 'Doobi' in combat areas to defeat IEDs and knock down buildings in which enemy personnel were operating. The D9 use in civilian areas was the subject of controversy. (Artwork by David Bocquelet)

Three IASF units operated the stealth F-35I airplanes (conventional variant) from Nevatim. The low-observable characteristics may have been useful for some missions, but electronic warfare probably weighed more heavily in penetrating defended airspace. Consequently, flights with external stores to increase the strike potency was performed, a capability Israel matured during the war. (Artwork by Tom Cooper)

ABBREVIATIONS AND ACRONYMS

AAM	air-to-air missile		km	kilometre(s)
AB	air base		kts	knots (nautical air miles per hour)
ABM	anti-ballistic missile		lb	pound(s)
AEW	airborne early warning		m	metre(s)
AI	artificial intelligence		MANPADS	man-portable air defence systems
APC	armoured personnel carrier		mi	mile(s)
CFT	conformal fuel tank		mm	millimetre(s)
CGS	Chief-of-General-Staff		MoD	Ministry of Defense
COGAT	Coordination of Government Activities in the Territories		NGO	non-governmental organisations
			NPT	Non-Proliferation Treaty
C-UAS	counter-uncrewed air system		OWA	one-way attack UAV
DMZ	demilitarised zone		PA	Palestinian Authority
EO	electro-optical		PGM	precision-guided munition
EU	European Union		PIJ	Palestinian Islamic Jihad
EW	electronic warfare		PLO	Palestine Liberation Organization
ft	foot, feet		PM	Prime Minister
GHF	Gaza Humanitarian Foundation		RPG	rocket-propelled grenade
GPS	Global Positioning System		SAM	surface-to-air missile
IAEA	International Atomic Energy Agency		SDB	small diameter bombs
IAP	international airport		SIGINT	signals intelligence
IASF	Israel Air and Space Force		TEL	transporter erector-launcher
ICC	International Criminal Court		THAAD	Terminal High Altitude Area Defense
ICJ	International Court of Justice		UAE	United Arab Emirates
IDF	Israel Defense Forces		UAV	uncrewed air vehicle
IDF/AF	Israel Defence Forces/Air Force		UK	United Kingdom
IED	improvised explosive device		UN	United Nations
IN	Israeli Navy		UNGA	UN General Assembly
IRGC	Islamic Revolutionary Guard Corps		UNRWA	United Nations Relief and Works Agency
ISF	International Stabilization Force		UNSC	Security Council
JCPoA	Joint Comprehensive Plan of Action		USA, US	United States of America
JDAM	Joint Direct Attack Munition		USAF	United States Air Force
kg	kilogram(s)		UNIFIL	United Nations Interim Force in Lebanon

PREFACE

The 7 October 2023 attack on Israel by terrorists from the Gaza Strip was the worst such event in Israel's complex history.[1] It marked the beginning of the longest war in the state's existence with the highest casualties and infrastructure damage, and another tough period for the Palestinians under Israeli military occupation. The Israel Defense Forces (IDF) was employed in strikes across the Middle East to an extent never before witnessed. The political climate became more polarised and the future more obscure. It continued a century-old conflict for which many across the world have strong opinions. This book focuses on the military aspects of this war and its place in the wider Arab-Israeli conflict that had been in play since 1947. However, geopolitical underpinnings are examined to appreciate motives and consequences. It is limited to the span of a single Helion @War volume and draws largely upon international news reporting as the events unfolded.

I have worked to make this account accurate by balancing reports that often had a political 'bend' towards one perspective or another. The employment of open media for 'messaging' by the involved parties targeting specific demographics to win backing or enforce preconceptions was in full bloom during the war. Battle lines in the 'culture wars' were more starkly drawn than ever. Any errors that may have crept in and disinformation unwittingly repeated are entirely my own responsibility. I worked on my own with no agenda but to relate the events clearly and objectively. I am well aware of the animus regarding the

events summarised in this book, with aspects of the conflict persisting beyond those two years of intense combat. Some believe Arabs, Muslims and others are persistently working to unfairly defame Israel whilst there is also a belief Israel has worked, with its supporters, to promote an inaccurate narrative of innocent rebuttal to this malalignment and defence of its military actions (called *Hasbara*), both camps perceived to be a generations-long conspiracy of disinformation. I make no assessment of such claims. I have had no personal connection to the events or participants. I worked for an honest and impartial account avoiding stereotypes and loaded labels or phrases. I had no intention to demean or diminish the stance, motives or behaviour of any group or individual. That I will still offend is understood, but it is not intentional.

Place names and the names of persons are those most commonly referenced, as are translations. Written for the distant future reader, past tense is employed throughout.

I thank all those who assisted with research material, additional information and confirmation of facts, and providing photographs.

Those readers who would care to comment on these and my other publications, or offer additional research material, may contact me at nortowj1@gmail.com.

Bill Norton
Tehachapi, California, March 2026

1

HISTORICAL BACKGROUND

The central issues of the Arab-Israeli conflict have been land and people displaced from it by the creation of Israel and its wars with surrounding states. A *brief* history emphasising those aspects sets the events of 2023–2025 into context.

EARLY VIOLENCE

Persons of the Jewish diaspora set out in the early 1880s to re-establish a Jewish homeland in the Biblical land of their ancestors, then known as Palestine.[1] These Zionists were primarily from Eastern Europe where they lived under periodic pogroms. They began to buy land in Palestine and create towns and settlements among the pastoral Arabs, principally Muslim. The Jews and Arab saw each other as alien. Both were deeply religious but shared little else in common, including language, and lived largely in separate communities. Palestine was then ruled by the Ottoman-Turks who were displaced during the First World War by the British.

The United Kingdom (UK) assumed a Mandate to govern the country until its self-determination could be resolved. This became a fraught responsibility as the Arabs grew increasingly disgruntled with the growing population of Jews who were altering the cultural landscape. The Zionist goal to turn all of Palestine into a Jewish state and likely displace most of the Arab inhabitants was no secret. In time the Arabs began embracing national ambitions and anti-Semitic leanings. The UK, seeking to placate the region's Arabs for foreign policy objectives, constrained Jewish immigration. However, the factions felt it was backing the national ambitions of one to the detriment of the other. Efforts to bring the sides together in some joint governance always failed in the face of mutual distrust and competing goals.

As the Jewish community, the Yishuv, grew the Arabs could see they would eventually become a poor, segregated minority. There was suspicion the Jews would tear down Muslim holy sites, primarily in Jerusalem, to build their own on sacred land.[2] There were days of rioting on three occasions during the 1920s in which hundreds of Jews were killed and their property attacked. The communities became openly hostile. The Arabs revolted against the Mandate and the Jewish presence in 1936–1939. The British Army put this down with great effort. Hundreds more were killed and the opponents grew to hate each other. The Yishuv could see they were living on a volcano and there would likely be no coexisting in harmony with the Arabs as they moved steadily towards Zionist goals. The Zionists were convinced, then and now, that their cause was historically if not religiously righteous and outweighed any Arab protest or perceived immorality as to their treatment. The Yishuv's small and illegal self-protection force was grown into a militia, the Haganah. They had also begun a practice of retaliatory raids of Arab villages following attacks.

Before and during the Second World War the Yishuv began to smuggle in Jews displaced by rampant anti-Semitism in Europe, beyond immigration quotas. Word of the Holocaust made this an imperative and the Haganah,[3] with an extremist faction, began a terror campaign against the British. By 1947 the UK, dismayed by the military and monetary toll of the Mandate, asked the United Nations (UN) to decide a path forward.

A UN committee offered a plan to partition Palestine into peaceful and economically co-dependent Arab and Jewish states based on demographics and economic factors. Jerusalem was to be an international city, this working counter to plans of the two sides to make Jerusalem the capital of their respective states. At the time the Yishuv, 33 percent of Palestine's population, owned approximately seven percent of the land. Yet, the plan allotted them 57 percent of Palestine. The Jewish state would also consist of 44 percent Arabs. The Arabs rejected the plan as unfair and another imposition on their national aspirations by imperialist powers. The

Likely a staged photograph (especially as it includes a woman and a preponderance of rare machine guns) shows Palestinian Arab irregulars in an ambush position during the Arab Revolt. (Public Domain)

Yishuv welcomed the plan, but fully expected circumstances would expand its share of land.

The UN General Assembly (UNGA) voted on 29 November 1947 to adopt the partition plan. The UN charter did not encompass powers to partition any region or create new states, so the resolution was a recommendation to the Security Council (UNSC) for implementation. Arabs across the region were incensed and promised armed opposition. Consequently, Palestine descended into civil war as the British evacuated. Arab combatants were largely from abroad, most locals choosing not to actively participate. However, these militias were poorly armed, trained and led. The fighting was sometimes vicious, with excesses on both sides. By spring 1948 the Haganah had defeated them and gained important territory.

1948–1949 PALESTINE WAR

The State of Israel was proclaimed on 14 May 1948 with no clearly defined borders. The next day, as expected, elements of the armies of Egypt, Syria, Transjordan and Iraq crossed into the country ostensibly to save their Palestinian brethren from an historic injustice and prevent Israel from taking root. However, the campaign was uncoordinated, poorly planned and led, and with ulterior motives to seize land. The Yishuv had secretly negotiated with Transjordan to not oppose its seizure of Judea and Samaria, where few Jewish settlements lay. As this was the majority of the land identified for a Palestinian state, Israel was actively working against its establishment. However, the Transjordanians and Israelis came to blows over Jerusalem, fighting to a stalemate with the city divided. The other fronts saw exhausting fighting for nearly a month before a truce was arranged. There were four more bouts of brief fighting through March 1949 – in total seven weeks of sustained combat – each with Israeli successes for firmly held territorial boundaries. After summer 1948 the new Israel Defense Forces was clearly superior, greatly aided by volunteers and Jewish funds from abroad, the latter supporting weapons smuggling. It occupied portions of southern Lebanon and northeastern Sinai until pressured to withdraw.

Armistices were negotiated through intermediaries with each combatant except Iraq. In the end Israel held 79 percent of the former Palestine with 60 percent of the land proposed for a Palestinian state. Transjordan held what they would soon name the West Bank and Egypt the Gaza Strip. Palestine disappeared from the map.[4] All parties were dissatisfied with the armistices alone, especially with the Palestinian refugee (see later) and state issue remaining unresolved. Israel wanted resolution to be part of a final settlement whilst the Arabs insisted it precede the other. The war had been a disaster (*Nakba*) for the Arab world, and a 'Second Round' appeared likely. When it suited the current political narrative, both sides would point out they were technically still at war. Each continued to paint the other as racial and religious foes. The Arabs imposed punitive measures such as the Arab Boycott against Israeli business and constrained passage to the country.

The unfinished state of the war sustained the Arab-Israeli conflict. The UN worked to keep this from escalating and so had an organisation on the ground to resolve disputes. There were many such and the UNSC seemed forever mediating thousands of complaints, unlike other regions.

PALESTINIAN REFUGEES

As the country dissolved into civil war, and then an invasion, the Palestinian civilians sought safety. Sixty percent of those in areas dominated by Jewish forces, 725,000 people, fled some 400 neighbourhoods, towns and villages, expecting to return once calm was restored. Of these people 55 percent left due to general Jewish/Israeli military actions (sometimes just their appearance), 15 percent from direct terror attacks and atrocities,[5] 10 percent general fear, 11 percent followed their neighbours, five percent answering Arab instructions, two percent due to Haganah-spread rumours of imminent expulsion, and two percent Israeli-ordered evictions.[6] Thus, 84 percent of the exodus was because of Jewish/Israeli actions, directly or indirectly.

Israeli commanders were authorised to clear out villages that might pose a risk to operations if Arab forces were stationed there. Accounts relate many instances of this being done, tens of thousands evicted under government orders. One particular massacre created fear and rumours. Arab massacres of Jews tended to be grislier. Consequently, soldiers were not inclined to deal with Arabs compassionately. Zionist leadership had long felt an Arab minority of no more than 15 percent was essential for a viable Jewish state. After the war it stood at 20 percent. This was not coincidental.

Approximately 80 percent of refugees went to other parts of Palestine and the rest to surrounding countries. About two-thirds melded into the population whilst the rest became homeless. The refugees and those remaining in what was left of Palestine became known as Palestinians. Those in Israel became Israeli Arabs.

The unhoused refugees were destitute, initially hungry and desperate, and some dying of exposure. The international community moved to assist whilst their fate was being determined. Tent camps were erected until concrete structures could be built, and these became 58 permanent communities. By 1958 there were 387,664 refugees in these camps with services offered by the United Nations Relief and Works

David Ben-Gurion, leader of the Jewish community in Palestine, is seen proclaiming creation of the State of Israel on 14 May 1948. (Public Domain)

This map shows the territorial state of the country after the Palestine War and 1949 armistices. (Map by George Anderson)

Palestinian Arab men are seen held by Israeli forces during July 1948 as they are loaded into lorries in preparation for being expelled from the country. (National Library of Israel)

Agency (UNRWA). These were dreary places with little work. Israel steadfastly resisted all measures permitting these people to return.

It is often asked why the Arab countries in which these people ended up did not simply adopt and settle them, giving them citizenship. Some believe an Arab is an Arab is an Arab. However, nationalities and regions define groups that do not always meld harmoniously. Such foreigners could serve as the nucleus of a movement to destabilise the government, these then usually fragile and not popularly elected. It was believed most of the refugees would not want to integrate, though some argued that suggesting to them there was hope of returning home was tragically misleading. Furthermore, all of these countries were struggling financially at the time. Apart from Egypt, all were new nations still establishing basic administration and services. Jordan (the renamed Transjordan) and Lebanon, particularly, could be described as poor, and Syria barely better off. The demands of the refuges were overwhelming, and the flood was at first resisted until finally relenting. Additionally, the expectation during the first years was these people would be resettled inside Israel (itself poor), reclaiming their homes and property. When this was clearly not going to happen anytime soon, the UN stepped in to support the refugees and so the nations did not need to find the resources. As with any nation, citizenship is jealously guarded. Jordan granted citizenship to Palestinians in the West Bank, but this was largely a measure to earn their acceptance of the new governing situation. That over decades and generations these countries continued to host refugee camps in part as accusatory symbols for what they insisted was Israeli racism, colonialism and expansionism cannot be denied. However, the story is far more complex.

Even before the war's end some refugees filtered back to reclaim homes or collect belongings, visit family, harvest crops and graze animals. This influx amounted to tens of thousands living illegally inside Israel, unacceptable as it sought to establish undisputed borders, ensure their Arab minority did not grow, and guarantee property for Jewish immigrants. The Army and Border Police patrolled the frontiers to round-up and expelling infiltrators. Unoccupied villages were razed and crops burned. The problem reached such dimensions that shoot-on-sight orders were issued.

The problem persisted following the war. Conditions inside refugee camps were so grim that some infiltrators stole from Israeli settlements and took revenge for their plight. Dozens of Israelis killed and wounded each year in thousands of infiltration incidents.

The shoot-on-sight order persistent. More crossers then came armed and the violence escalated. Thieving gangs were formed, and perhaps 10 percent of infiltrators came to cause mayhem. Israeli reprisal raids were launched, disproportionate to the crimes, as a means of deterrence. The violence escalated again. Scores of Palestinians were commonly killed and their homes blown-up. Israel was also active pushing some Israeli Arab communities across the borders and expropriated additional property to reduce trouble and open areas for immigrants, the last perhaps in 1956. The State plus Jewish individuals and businesses soon owned or directly controlled

Israeli paratroopers are seen during the Qalqilya police station raid, 10/11 October 1956. (IDF Spokesman)

93 percent of the land. At that time Israel's Arab inhabitants were marginalised and surveilled,[7] and some 80 percent under Military Administration until this was abolished in 1965. Israeli leadership feared they could be a fifth column in time of war. During the 1956 war (later) more than 48 civilians were summarily shot for violating a curfew they were unaware of.

Surrounding states, principally Egypt and Jordan worked to inhibit the infiltration, but the borders were too porous. Israel then attacked national forces during reprisals to prompt a greater effort, but this was counterproductive. Hundreds of Arab security personnel were killed, and the region was in an uproar. Egypt then armed groups of Palestinians sent into Israel on terror forays. This was the origin of the Fedayeen (those who sacrifice) and the beginning of Palestinian irregulars to follow.

A total 200–300 Israelis were killed and 500–1,000 wounded by infiltrators. Israeli security personnel killed 2,700–5,000 infiltrators, most unarmed civilians.[8]

QUARTER CENTURY OF WARS

Israel prioritised defence and spent heavily. They were seized with a sense of power following founding of the state. The new image of the 'fighting Jew' contrasted heroically with centuries of impotency. Some in leadership wanted to sustain this image and give the new generation examples of Israeli warriors. Consequently, they encouraged an aggressive spirit and strong if not excessive military responses to provocations. In time the Israeli military tradition, with so many serving in the Army, became an important 'glue' within society that few could imagine living without.

The infiltrators, Fedayeen terrorism and IDF reprisal raids sustained tensions on the borders for many years. Israel also insisted the demilitarised zones (DMZ) on the borders identified in the armistices were its territory, contrary to the wording of the documents, and worked to assert sovereignty. There were persistent armed exchanges. Israel was widely perceived as an unruly neighbour, UN observers finding it the instigator of much of the troubles.[9]

Nations began building their armed forces to meet the threats, the Arabs turning principally to the Soviet Union. In Egypt the popular President Gamal Abdul Nasser sought to unite the Arab world; a potential that alarmed Israel. These factors led Israel to launch a 'preventive' war against Egypt in October 1956, in collusion with France and the UK who sought to ensure an international character of the Suez Canal. Israel succeeded in capturing the Gaza Strip and Sinai Peninsula. In Gaza the efforts to eradicate the Fedayeen and Palestinian soldiers of the Egyptian Army caused excesses. Some 500 Palestinian civilians were killed.[10] Israel initially sought to hold Sinai and Gaza indefinitely, but American pressure dissuaded it. Plans for the Strip had evidently included reducing the population from 200,000 to 80,000 by expulsions to make it more manageable.[11] Israel unilaterally abrogated the armistice with Egypt.

Arab states continued working to isolate Israel and supported Fedayeen activity. Israel, as usual, reacted forcefully, to include espionage and reprisals, particularly harming Palestinians, which brought Arab responses. In spring 1967 the Arab world was seized by another war psychosis, propelled by politically motivated anti-Israeli rhetoric. This reached such a state that a war to 'drive the Jews into the sea' appeared imminent. Israel struck first, consistent with its pre-emption strategy, and in six days won a resounding victory. It defeated Egypt to hold the Sinai and Gaza, Syria to hold the Golan Heights, and Jordan to take the West Bank. The Golan included a high outpost on Mount Hermon. Egypt blocked the Suez Canal, significantly disrupting sea commerce, making the conflict an issue the world-over. Approximately 235,000 Palestinians (approximately 20 percent) fled or were expelled. At least five refugee camps were destroyed, the residents driven out. Ten more camps were soon established elsewhere. Many of these people settled in Jordan where more than half the population became Palestinian. A diaspora of Palestinians living and working outside the region developed.

Israel initially offered to swap the occupied territory for peace treaties. The Arabs balked, not about the settle on Israeli terms. Israel soon reclaimed abandoned settlements and Jewish neighbourhoods

Displaced from their homes in Palestine, more Palestinian dislocations occurred from territories occupied by Israel during the 1967 war. (Israel GPO)

Israeli troops are seen during their operation in Jerusalem, June 1967. (IDF Spokesman)

from the past and established new ones in these territories, also relocating military camps there. The clear intent was to hold some of the land indefinitely as a buffer to further Arab military adventure. However, Zionist zeal lent an intent to remain forever. Jerusalem was unified and effectively annexed by the end of June 1967.[12] A military occupation was imposed on the territories, its forces reacting when necessary to keep the population's resentment contained.

The UN passed Resolution 242 on 22 November 1967 as the basis for resolving the conflict. This opened with a general statement recognising the 'inadmissibility of the acquisition of territory by war' and calling for a 'just settlement of the refugee problem.' It called for Israeli withdrawal 'from territories occupied in the recent conflict.' Focusing on this aspect and the lack of a call for peace treaties, Egypt and Jordan accepted. Syria, Iraq and Saudi Arabia rejected it. Having assured that the document did not explicitly call for withdrawal from *all* territories, Israel nominally accepted 242 on 1 May 1968 and then explicitly on 26 May 1970. However, subsequent Israeli governments declared they were not bound by this.

Syria and Egypt were determined to recover the lands lost to Israel. They needed a clear defeat of Israeli arms and the Palestinian issue addressed before seeking final resolution. Israel was determined to hold Sinai and the Heights as bargaining chips. Jordan had no hope of reclaiming the West Bank. A War of Attrition soon emerged, the Arabs seeking to weaken the IDF ahead of a war to recover the occupied territories. Especially the Israel Defence Forces/Air Force (IDF/AF) became a vital tool, bombing far beyond the borders. The United States of America (USA) came to support Israel monetarily (eventually billions of dollars per year) and with arms to a growing and vital extent. This derived from a strong American Jewish political influence and social identification with Israel. The war and

subsequent actions lent an image in foreign press accounts of IDF 'supermen' who acted with daring and dedication. The Israeli side of the story generally reached the outside world whilst Arab accounts, peppered with obvious misinformation and dissonant rhetoric, were largely dismissed. (Israel was always better at the propaganda game.) The result was to paint the Arabs as inept and lacking resolve, and the Israelis as exceptionally clever and capable. Neither were entirely true depictions.

Israel found itself engaged on all sides and isolated as never before. With the perception as an international pariah, they were adopted more clandestine methods to meet aims. It became known for bold if borderline illegal intelligence gathering operations and daring self-defence actions. Their attitude became that the world community did not treat Israel fairly and so Israel did not need to play fair. Although Israel insisted it should be held to a higher standard than surrounding states, it as often expressed resentment of the double-standard. Additionally, Israel has long lionised those who broke laws in the interest of state security, making such actions less likely to be rejected. Israelis insisted they were encircled by hostile Arab states, supporting Palestinian terrorists, determined to eradicate them. Its neighbours insisted they were persistently tormented by an aggressive Israel supported by a preponderance of US arms.

The War of Attrition saw indecisive fighting on all fronts. This included a Palestinian insurgency from initially Jordan and then Syria and Lebanon. This was principally led by the Palestine Liberation Organization (PLO), founded in 1964 and with funding from numerous Arab states, but many similar groups emerged. Not being potent enough to challenge the IDF directly, the insurgency consisted largely of terror attacks seeking to compel a change in Israeli policies. This was a hopeless endeavour and the insurgency in the West Bank was put down by 1970. Israeli operations in Syria and Lebanon sought to keep attacks from those quarters in check. 'Israeli incursions' became a frequently heard phrase as the IDF made forays across the border to temporarily diminish threats.

The Palestinian irregulars in Jordan became a 'state-within-a-state', challenging the authority of the government as it struggled to contain them and end IDF reprisals. A civil war emerged in September 1970, 'Black September' seeing the Palestinians defeated. Many combatants left for Lebanon where the delicate ethnic balance was disrupted, becoming a hotbed for terrorism. Terrorist outrages sullied the Palestinian cause with the blood of innocents. Especially the murder of Israeli athletes at the 1972 Olympic Summer Games was widely denounced. Israel reacted by seeking those involved throughout Europe in a campaign of murder, with Palestinians doing the same against Israeli targets.

Egypt and Syria succeeded in launching a surprise attack against Israeli forces in Sinai and the Golan Heights on 6 October 1973. The war was hard fought, but the IDF gained the upper hand before a firm ceasefire. The superpowers were brought to the brink of armed conflict in supporting their associates and an Arab oil embargo affected the world economy. As in all of these wars there were Palestinian formations fighting under the colours of Arab nations. Since 1948 Palestinians always had a military tradition and many thousands of individuals gained martial experience. The War of Attrition and October War were fought over occupied territory, but the Arab combatants continued to pay lip-service to the Palestinian cause.

Egypt sought to end the conflict with Israel and a peace treaty requiring American mediation emerged in 1979. Whilst Egypt sought some Israeli concessions for the Palestinians, these terms eventually fell away. The Palestinians were incensed that Egypt would sign a peace treaty with Israel leaving their fate still undecided. It was a signal for renewed Palestinian attacks. The treaty also relinquished any Egyptian claim to Gaza. Jordan did the same for the West Bank in 1988 prior to the 1994 peace treaty with Israel. This sought to allow the PLO to take responsibility for their destiny. Meagre negotiations with Syria made little progress and Israel annexed the Heights in 1981.

WAR AGAINST TERRORISM

As the occupation continued Jewish settlements grew on land confiscated by Israel citing defence justifications. Some Palestinian residents were evicted for military imperatives that suited settlement ends and, in some cases, existing structures were demolished. Some of the settlers were Nahal paramilitary and the locations were meant to support security purposes but, by design, they evolved into permanent civilian communities. Infrastructure was improved, lending the appearance of permanence, running roads, power, telephone, and water to the settlements. Initially, much of this occurred without a clearly considered government policy and sometimes without approval. The government lacked resolve to oppose settlements or remove 'pioneers', and even funded some of the activities. However, in time, official settlement programs emerged. The Palestinians were justifiably infuriated that land which they had owned for generations was being seized by a military administration allowing little legal recourse, adding to those from which they had been evicted in 1948 and 1967. The government would sometimes eject Israelis creating illegal outposts, but when they repeatedly returned the presence would usually be accepted. Power was extended, a road cut, and the Army included it in its

The Israeli settlement of Kfar Eldad goes up in the West Bank in 2019 on confiscated land, one property already with a lawn. (Open source)

patrols. The cycle continued. Decisions on property boundaries and resources by the military administration, especially allocation of scarce water, nearly always benefitted Israelis. As always, the military ruled over movement and commerce.

Palestinian terrorism, supported by sympathetic groups, became the principal threat to Israel. The PLO and other militant organisations sought an end to the occupation and elimination of Israel by actions outside the territories whilst assisting those inside. Insurgency attacks from Lebanon and international terrorism, whilst inducing pressure from other states, seemed their only means of compelling Israel to change course. Although meant to highlight the plight of the Palestinian people, garnering sympathy and aid, murderous outrages were not endearing. Yet, the acts were usually cheered by many common Palestinians and held up as heroic in Arab society.

Militant Palestinian actions and IDF reactions so disrupted the socio-political structure of Lebanon that a civil war resulted. Israel aided the sectarian militias fighting the Muslims and Palestinians, helping to fuel the violence and dysfunction. The PLO grew to a substantial non-state military force with enormous stockpiles of modern weapons and trained as battlefield formations. An Israeli invasion in 1978 pushed the PLO beyond the Litani River, but they filtered back. Palestinian attacks on Israel attracted repeated IDF airstrikes and ground incursions. A full-scale Israeli invasion on 6 June 1982 saw the IDF immediately exceed stated goals and encircled Beirut on the 13th plus fighting Syrian forces. It blockaded the city whilst bombing and shelling large portions. The devastation and human suffering drew the ire of the USA and much of the UN. Israel was compelled after two months to ease the blockade and allow 10,000 PLO combatants to evacuate the country. However, the IDF facilitated

At top, an Israeli Kfir aircraft bombs targets in Lebanon in June 1982. Below are the remains of the Beirut sports stadium bombed on 4 June and with surrounding buildings badly damaged. Many areas of Beirut would be reduced to this in the coming weeks. (top Efim Sandler collection, bottom Phan Robert Feary)

Christian militias entering two Palestinian refugee camps in the city where they massacred a thousand or more civilians. Israel was held culpable and the Minister of Defense indicted for complicity. Israel was directly responsible for as many as 13,000 collateral deaths during the war that significantly damaged Lebanon. Regardless, they became numb to international condemnations of what it saw as legitimate and essential defence actions. It then spent 18 years occupying portions of southern Lebanon where IDF personnel were subjected to repeated attack by Palestinian and Shia Muslim guerrillas.[13]

This marked the end of 'big Mid East wars', the IDF more than a match for any combination of regional forces. Facing no peer adversary in the region, military operations became asymmetrical in nature – the IDF greatly superior in all respects. Yet, the Palestinian and Islamic militias saw benefit in bringing Israel to battle on occasion for political ends. Consequently, Israel's focus became counter-terrorism and military occupation of the territories. Even with the PLO displaced, Israel continued to go after it.

The Shia Muslim militia group Hezbollah rose to oppose the Israeli occupation in Lebanon, its continued military dominance, and its fundamental existence. Hezbollah ultimately displaced nearly all other militias in the south, with arms, funding and training from Iran. Repeated Hezbollah rocketing of northern Israel and attacks on IDF patrols would commonly draw army fire and airstrikes, some being major operations that commonly took more civilian lives than combatants. Air power was a poor counterterror tool, but it minimised IDF casualties at the expense of collateral harm. Israel withdrew from Lebanon in 2000, willing to battle Hezbollah from across the border. The rise of Islamic fundamentalist militias elsewhere, with Israel as its avowed enemy, was another concerning trend.

After the 1979 Islamic Revolution in Iran that nation assigned Israel as its principal foe, after its sponsor the United States, owing to its defence activities decried as repressing Muslim peoples and as a remaining imperialist entity. Elevating Israel as a villain to partially blame for Iran's woes was a tactic of the theocratic government to distract from its authoritarianism. As national policy, Iran supported those opposing Israel to include transporting enormous quantities of arms to the area and training militias whilst being careful not

Israel's continued effort to degrade the Palestinian combat capabilities was expressed notably in the 1 October 1985 exceptionally long-range attack on PLO headquarters buildings in Tunis. This image shows bomb detonations that destroyed or heavily damaged the structures, killing 73 and leaving more injured. This was the IDF/AF's first exceptionally long-range attack. (Author's collection)

to attack Israel directly. It also aided militant Islamic groups that sought to undermine Western influence. Assisting in this was Syria that benefitted from Iranian assistance during the civil war that erupted in 2011. Iran built up a large arsenal of ballistic missiles capable of striking Israel and established a nuclear program that had the potential for yielding atomic weapons. Israel railed against all this as rising to an existential threat the world was ignoring.

The 1990–1991 Gulf War saw Iraq fire 38 ballistic missiles at Israel as a distraction from the Coalition campaign in Kuwait. Little damage resulted and the Coalition successfully impeded any direct Israeli response. However, the experience propelled creation of an anti-ballistic missile (ABM) capability. The Arrow 2 system was for high altitude interception and the Arrow 3 an exo-atmospheric interceptor. The middle air defence tier was David's Sling. Iron Dome was the lower tier, countering short-range rockets and mortar shells. All was integrated with command-and-control centres plus radar. This multilayered air defence system became the densest in the world given the small area it covered.

Israel's overriding security concerns became preventing terror attacks from and within the territories, containing civil unrest, and protecting Israeli citizens who settled in occupied areas. There was also an Israeli underground of terrorists plaguing Arab residents. Many thousands of IDF soldiers served each month in the tense areas, much resented by the Palestinians. Their pent-up frustration was vented to a civil uprising (Intifadah) beginning in 1987 and lasting several years. Apart from civil resistance to the occupation there were murderous terrorist attacks that cost Israel 160 soldiers and civilians. It responded with harsh repression, arrests and expulsions, home demolitions, and sometimes live-fire incidents. The crackdown cost Palestinians nearly 1,100 killed.

THE PEACE PROCESS

International efforts to broker the conflict's resolution were many over the decades, marking it as one of the most intractable yet worrisome of the world's armed struggles. As with all such accomplishments between Israel and the Arabs, progress was possible only during rare alignment of willing leaders on both sides plus in the USA, sufficient national consensus, and a relative military calm. The 1978 Camp David Accords, mediated by the USA, provided a framework for reaching a two-state solution – Israel and a Palestinian state coexisting side-by-side. Direct talks yielded two Oslo agreements signed in 1993 and 1995. The PLO recognised Israel and vowed to remove words in its charter calling for its eradication. Israel recognised the PLO as the representative of the Palestinian people. The Palestinian Authority (PA) was created for limited self-rule in the West Bank and Gaza Strip with bilateral relations with Israel.

The agreement divided, at least temporarily, the West Bank and Gaza Strip into a patchwork of three types of areas. Area A (21 percent of the land) was under Palestinian administration and security arrangements, Area B (18 percent) under PA authority but joint security, and Area C (61 percent) solely under Israeli administration and security. This was to see phased IDF withdrawals, stand-up of PA self-governance and police force, and settlement activity reined-in by Israel.

The Accords (passing the Knesset [Israel's parliament] by one vote) were interim arrangements whilst permanent status negotiations continued, addressing such knotty issues as Jerusalem, settlements, refugees' return, and seemingly unattainable security arrangements satisfying Israel. The goal was final resolution of the conflict by 4 May 1999. In the meantime the PA held elections and deployed its police. Friendly nations aided them, particularly in construction projects, to help ensure they did not slip back into militancy. This

Israel's troops confront Palestinian protesters in the Gaza Strip during 1987, the civilians waving a Palestinian flag. The action was part of the Palestinian civil uprising resisting the military occupation during the Intifadah. (Efi Sharir, Israel Press and Photo Agency, Dan Hadani collection)

From left to right Israeli PM Yitzhak Rabin, USA President Bill Clinton and PLO Chairman Yasser Arafat celebrate the signing of the Oslo I Accords on 13 September 1993 at the White House – the most hopeful event in the desolate history of Israeli-Palestinian relations. (Public Domain)

An Israel Defence Forces/Air Force F-4E Phantom fighter-bomber flies over Jerusalem in 1971. Phantoms were key warplanes during combat in that decade, seen frequently over Arab nations delivering punishing strikes. The flight over the capital (Temple Mount and Dome of the Rock shrine visible) could be seen as an expression of determination to hold the whole of the disputed city to include the annexed East Jerusalem. (Jay Miller collection)

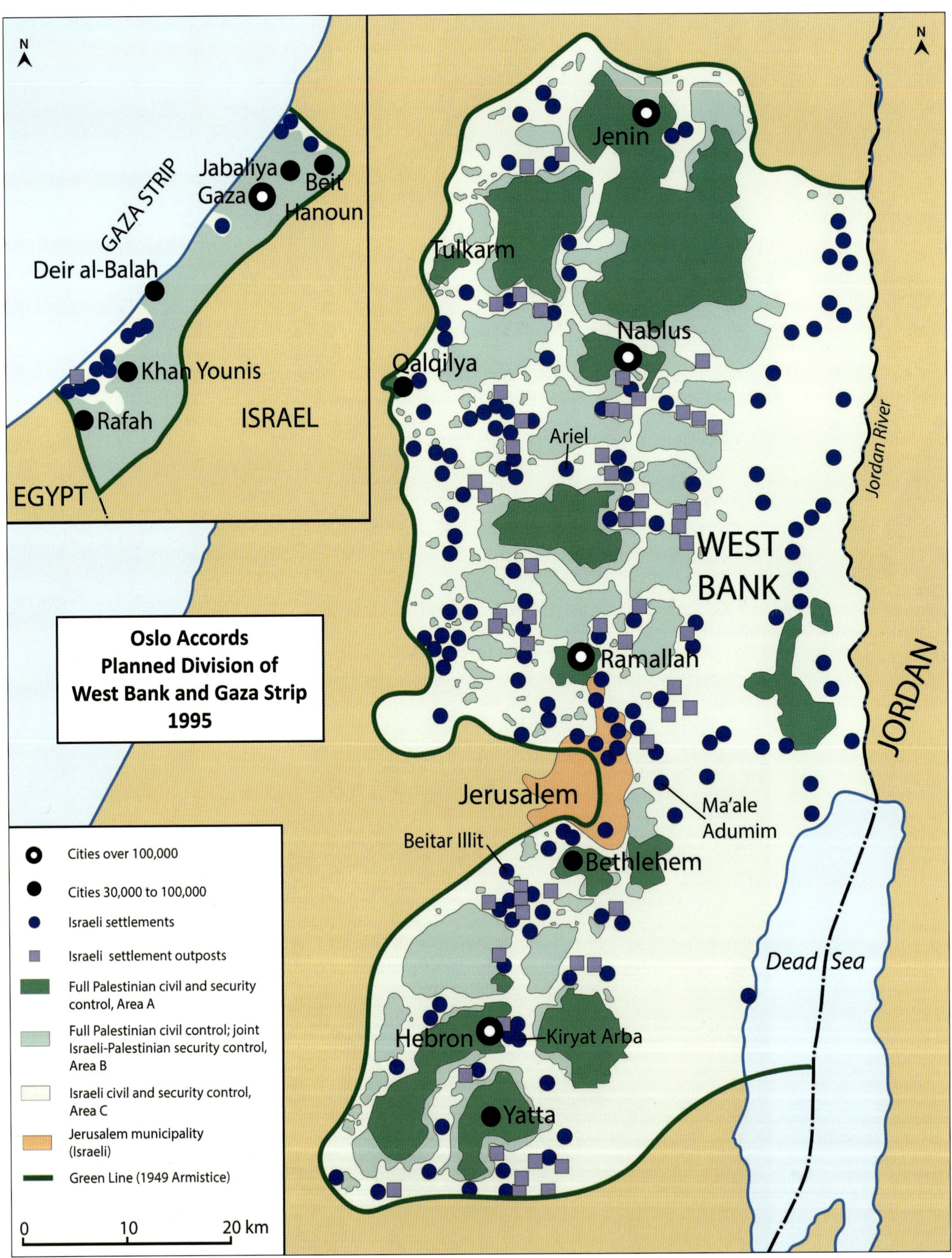

The Oslo Accords created the rump of a Palestinian state in the West Bank and Gaza Strip, but was a patchwork of Palestinian, Israeli and jointly controlled areas. This broke down after a few years under terrorist and IDF pressures, with the Israel expropriating more lands. (Map by George Anderson)

included building an airport and port in Gaza. There were land and air corridors between the two parts of the embryonic state, across Israeli territory.

The Israeli Prime Minister, and signer of the Accords, Yitzhak Rabin, was assassinated on 4 November 1995 by a radicalised Jewish settler angered by Israel surrendering any territory. There were other outrages by extremist Israeli elements, more than matched by Palestinian attacks. Israeli elections the following year brought the far-right Likud party to the majority, with Benjamin Netanyahu in the Prime Minister (PM) seat, who delayed withdrawals and permitted settlement activity and other incitements to continue. Efforts to revive peace process momentum ultimately failed in the face of the changing political complexion in Israel and inability of the PA to contain violence against the occupation that remained very much in place.

With failure of final status talks the Palestinians saw only a bleak future ahead. Consequently, a second and more violent Intifadah arose in 2000, lasting several years. Instigators of the Second Intifadah considered that constant pressure on Israel could compel their acquiescence as it appeared to have done for their withdrawing from southern Lebanon in the face of persistent Hezbollah attacks. However, the uprising most likely began spontaneously. An attempt to quell the unrest quickly through a strong Israeli show of force only drove violence to greater extremes. Israel began to suffer suicide bombings and other attacks originating from the territories, with hundreds of civilian casualties.

At the beginning of 2001 the Israeli government declared that a state of armed conflict existed with the PA. After more horrific suicide bomb attacks the IDF conducted major incursions into West Bank areas during March–May 2002 to destroy terrorist cells and resources. All towns were reoccupied temporarily which saw IDF tanks and helicopter gunships striking Palestinian infrastructure. On 18 May 2001 the IDF/AF began bombing targets in the West Bank and Gaza Strip for the first time in over 30 years. Some neighbourhoods were flattened and thousands rendered homeless. Intending to induce the PA to restrain terrorist elements, and placating Israeli public demands for action, destruction of government infrastructure and security apparatus worked against this goal and into the hands of extremists. The IDF suffered 30 killed and the Palestinians nearly 500, mostly noncombatants, with thousands more detained.

Apart from hitting militant or terrorist sites, the Israelis also adopted 'targeted killing' to eliminate arch terrorists and instigator leaders. The frequency of such operations rose with the growth of guerrilla forces in Lebanon and the need to interrupt terrorist attacks from the territories. Air action was employed where use of ground personnel was judged too hazardous, but soon became the preferred method. It demanded precision to reduce collateral damage and casualties, and was usually executed with helicopter-fired missiles until uncrewed air vehicles (UAV) were armed. Eventually the crews were tracking and targeting individuals inside specific rooms of buildings, in moving vehicles, and even walking on the street. When ground personnel were employed the violence could be intense to ensure safety of Israeli personnel. Hundreds of persons were killed in these extrajudicial executions. It introduced another source of Palestinian fury given that strikes could occur anytime and anywhere, and frequently claimed collateral casualties. They knew they were under constant Israeli surveillance.

One measure against terrorist infiltration was Israeli construction over decades of a 710km (440mi) long Separation Barrier between its territory and the West Bank. This took several forms, but

An Israeli bus shows the aftermath of a suicide bombing on 12 April 2002 during the Second Intifadah. Numerous such murderous events prompted a harsh Israeli response and the violence took thousands of lives. (Zvika Golan, IDF Spokesman)

A Palestinian child in the Dheisheh refugee camp, in July 2002, hurls a rock at an IDF Magach tank during the Second Intifadah. (Public Domain)

most commonly tall concrete walls with watchtowers, electronic monitoring, razor wire and checkpoints at gates. Although ostensibly to be built along the recognised frontier established in the 1949 armistice (Green Line), it instead cut deeply into Palestinian areas at many points so as to encompass Israeli neighbourhoods and settlements. It created a de facto annexation of 9.4 percent of the West Bank. The International Court of Justice (ICJ, a UN body) assessed in 2004 that the barrier was unlawful, and the UN General Assembly voted by large margin calling for its removal. Israel rejected and ignored all adverse judgements and criticism. The barrier greatly reduced terrorist infiltrations and was very popular with Israelis who did not have to look 'over their shoulders' so frequently. It assisted them in not seeing Palestinians who called it the Apartheid Wall.

Israeli leaders occasionally made what they considered generous offers for a self-governing Palestinian entity on a fraction of the West Bank and Gaza. As these usually denied full sovereignty and a capital in East Jerusalem, did not address right of return, ensured settlements remained if not grew, and assured Israel overarching military dominance, they were never satisfactory. Outside efforts at peace-making along similar lines also never gained traction. It was also clear an agreement by one Israeli government might be disavowed by the next.

The heart of the Jenin refugee camp was reduced to rubble during the 2002 fighting, this image from 13 April 2002. (IDF)

The PA's battered presidential compound in Ramallah is seen occupied by an IDF Merkava tank and Achzarit APC in April 2002. The PA President, Yasser Arafat, was besieged there for months. (Institute for Palestine Studies)

The path of the Separation Barrier with respect to the Green Line around the West Bank and in Jerusalem depicts intrusions segregating 9.4 percent of the land to Israeli control and constituting de facto annexation. (Map by George Anderson)

A small portion of the Separation Barrier is seen at the Qalandia refugee camp in 2014 with a checkpoint and observation tower visible. (L-BBE)

GAZA TUMULT

During the Second Intifadah, the organisation Hamas began firing homemade rockets across the Gaza border, along with breaches of the border fence to attack IDF patrols and attempt to take hostages. Founded in 1987, Hamas (an Arabic acronym for Islamic Resistance Movement) was a Shia religious movement that evolved into a political party with an armed wing (Izz al Din al-Qassam Brigades). It promoted continued armed struggle with Israel and had been a principal instigator of Second Intifadah violence. Other radical factions joining Hamas in Gaza included the Palestinian Islamic Jihad (PIJ). Hamas was principally funded and armed by Iran and so its rockets increased in destructive power and range as weapons and fighters were smuggled in. Volume increased steadily from a few rockets per year to hundreds then thousands fired. Israel worked to inhibit smuggling of weapons into the Strip including sea intercept, possibly air attacks in Sinai with Egyptian acquiescence,[14] and long-range airstrikes in Sudan.

After the February 2005 ceasefire ending the Second Intifadah, Hamas did not fire rockets for more than a year. As in southern Lebanon, the IDF presence in the Gaza Strip had seemed only to fuel the growth of radical elements. Deciding to control Gaza from beyond the border and focus on the West Bank, Israel completed a unilateral disengagement in September 2005, withdrawing the Army (50,000 soldiers) and uprooting 21 settlements with their 8,000 residents.[15] As with the Egyptian peace treaty and evacuation of communities in Sinai, there was resistance and national anguish at abandoning settlements.

In the PA's 2006 elections the Hamas faction gained a plurality of seats in parliament. Israel and most other nations stated they needed some indication the PA would remain nonviolent despite the recognised terrorist organisation being in ascendance. Hamas rejected this and economic assistance was subsequently suspended whilst Israel imposed sanctions. Palestinian areas began to suffer, and a PA unity government failed to satisfy foreign powers. A struggle then ensued between Fatah and Hamas factions over control of the security apparatus.[16] In 2007 there was armed conflict in Gaza ending with Fatah being expelled. The PA was subsequently split with neither party recognising the other's authority. Only Fatah was engaged by Israel and most other nations. Although the PA and Hamas formed a unity government in 2014, Israel worked against its success. The PA was then accused of aligning with terrorists.

Israel would not negotiate with Hamas, and the Fatah-backed PA did not represent the entire Palestinian population. With no single party with which to negotiate it became an excuse for Israel to halt further progress made towards the two-state solution. It held to some aspects of the Accords, generally respecting Palestinian areas, but 'fudged' the rest when it suited its interests. To them a status quo was desirable, permitting settlement and security activities to continue, but there was a price to pay.

Israel imposed a blockade of Gaza to stem the flow of arms and dual-purpose materials, though also barring exports. It effectively continued the occupation (as judged by multiple legal bodies) by controlling all movement of people, goods and services in and out of the Strip via its border crossings and sea patrols. The IDF destroyed the airport in 2001. It maintained close surveillance of activities within the Strip. Egypt carefully controlled movements across its frontier as well. By mutual agreement in 2005 Israel and Egypt created the 14km (9mi) long and 100m (330ft) wide Philadelphi Corridor on the Gaza/Egyptian border. All this was criticised internationally as collective punishment, Hamas making up a tiny

A homemade Qassam rocket, the earliest Hamas type, is seen on the simple launcher. The coarse angle adjustment and crude orientation method emphasises such poor accuracy that they could only serve as terror weapons. (IDF)

Israeli security personnel are seen assaulting the compound of the Kfar Darom settlement on 18 August 2005 in the Gaza Strip to evict the resisting Jewish residents, similar to what happened in the Sinai during the final withdrawal in 1982. The Gaza disengagement was a traumatic event for many Israelis, hardening attitudes towards any similar actions in the West Bank. (IDF)

minority of the populace,[17] and Gaza likened to the world's largest open-air prison with most of the inhabitants indigent and suffering high unemployment.

The hardships in Gaza brought on by the blockade sparked spontaneous weekly mass protests along the Gaza border in 2018. The spectacle of Israeli troops arrayed along the fence with many thousands of peaceful protesters on the other side was compelling. In time Hamas took control of these and there was some low-level violence such as throwing rocks, breaching the fence, rolling burning tires towards the fence, throwing Molotov cocktails, and sending incendiaries into Israel beneath balloons and kites. Cultivated fields and forests were set ablaze. When Israel started firing on the crowds (ordered to shoot at legs), to drive people away from the fence, the visuals were disturbing. In 20 months they killed 189 people and wounded 13,000, only a small percentage militants. One soldier was slightly injured.

An Israeli Shaldag Mk.3 patrol vessel is seen under speed. Such vessels patrolled the Gaza coastline to intercept smugglers, insurgents, and maintain the blockade. At the bow is a 25mm Typhoon gun and at stern 20mm Oerlikon. (Oded Breyer from Israel Shipyards)

The perception of Gaza as the world's largest open-air prison is illustrated in this 5 October 2018 image of protests along the border fence by unarmed civilians. The image of IDF personnel arrayed on the opposite side and eventually opening fire did not play well. (IDF Spokesman)

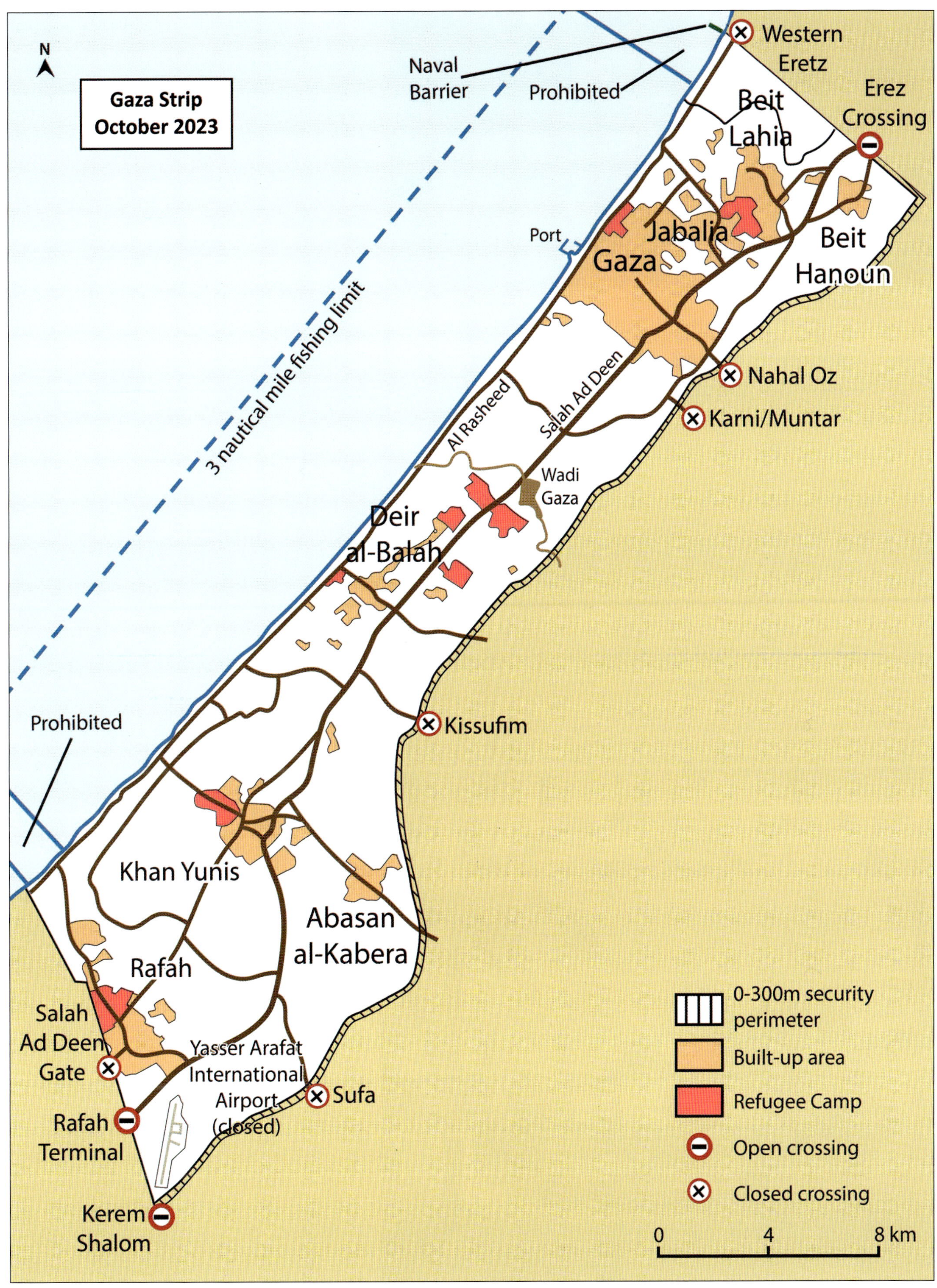

Gaza as it stood on 7 October 2023, essentially the entire enclave became a battlefield. The fishing limit was effectively reduced to zero.
(Map by George Anderson)

An airstrike inside the Gaza Strip during 12 May 2021 targets a building that fell after several bomb impacts. Considerable collateral damage within the dense neighbourhood is also evident in this frame-grab of drone footage. (IDF Spokesman)

Rockets remained the favourite Hamas means of retaliating against Israel or making a statement, along with small unit tactics. However, UAVs and unmanned submersibles were also employed. When the provocations reached intolerable volume the Israelis retaliated with overwhelming power, especially shelling, bombing, precision missile attacks, targeted killings, and occasional forays by ground forces. Gazans definitely felt besieged and Israeli harassed.

A ceasefire ended after six months with exchanges that prompted the IDF's Operation Cast Lead on 27 December 2008. An intense bombing campaign was joined by a ground incursion before Israel called an end on 18 January. Some 46,000 buildings had been destroyed, 100,000 people rendered homeless, and around 1,300 Gazans killed at a cost of 13 Israeli deaths.

A typical sight for 25 years was rocket smoke trails rising from the Gaza Strip en route to impacts in Israel. The inexpensive rockets launched by Muslim and Palestinian irregulars tormented a generation of Israeli residents on the receiving end on that and the Lebanese borders. (Human Rights Watch)

Tanks in the garden – and IDF Achzarit APC halts among Gaza homes during the 2014 invasion. (IDF)

More provocations in November 2012 led to Israel eliminating the Hamas military chief via a targeted killing. Rockets flying in reaction drew a wave of airstrikes. Operation Pillar of Defense ended after eight days during which hundreds of rockets flew and bombs dropped, taking scores of lives. Iron Dome interceptors were drawn down alarmingly and so supply was ramped-up. Seven weeks of intense combat with ground incursion during summer 2014 (Operation Protective Edge) claimed some 2,200 Gazans for 72 Israeli deaths. Thousands of buildings were destroyed and many more damaged. The IDF had mobilised 40,000 reservists and what was expected to be a three-day ground operation became three weeks.[18] A wave of Palestinian protests and violence in May 2021, with Hamas firing rockets in sympathy, got the expected IDF response. Operation Guardian of the Walls was 15 days of bombing, hundreds more people and buildings falling. Amongst these were many small clashes. Israeli generals referred to the cyclical violence as 'mowing the lawn'; repetitive drudgery.[19] The IDF commonly had a list of hundreds or thousands of potential targets. Ceasefires would occasionally have prisoner exchanges with militants returned to the fight in a 'vicious cycle.'

Hamas had made tunnels a major resource for smuggling, protection from detection and bombing, and supporting combat tactics. This became a vast network under the Strip and beneath the borders. Israel assessed that there were more than 150 under the Philadelphi Corridor alone. Some were wide enough for vehicles and others had well-appointed quarters. Arms caches and factories plus command-and-control centres were included. Those under the borders accommodated smuggling and also surprise raids to assault IDF patrols, capture hostages, and plant explosives beneath positions. Some 1,300 tunnels were dug, some more sophisticated than others, and running more than 480km (300mi) to earn the name 'Gaza Metro'. Given the density of the urban areas in the Strip they were by necessity under thousands of buildings, many sensitive, though some of this was intentional to support tactical needs. They were found beneath schools, hospitals and UNRWA facilities, with entrances in some of these. The IDF struggled to devise the best means to detect and destroy the tunnels. Air-delivered bombs were only partially successful. The builders dug deeper, up to 60–70m (200–330ft).

In time Hamas rockets fired into Israel numbered tens of thousands, the first targeting Tel Aviv and other central Israelis cities in 2021. The fire saw much reduced effectiveness with deployment of Iron Dome in 2011. The system projected impact points and engaged only those likely to fall in populated areas. Israel built thousands of protective shelters all over the country where people could take refuge when rockets were inbound. It also introduced a cellphone app giving alerts for the individual's location. As in Lebanon, low-cost Hamas drones grew in use, though usually quickly shot down. However, the frequency increased as a 'war of drones' gradually developed. Israeli airstrikes in the Strip were common. Much effort was expended devising the best combination of systems to locate then quickly strike rocket and mortar teams before they moved. Paramilitary and Hamas administration buildings, tunnels, weapons factories and storage facilities, rocket launch sites, and leadership were common Israel Air and Space Force (IASF) targets. Sonic boom intimidation was also employed. Much effort was made to avoid harming civilians in airstrikes, but hundreds died and thousands were injured. Apart from telephone calls and text messaging, and leaflet drops, some buildings were first hit with a 'roof-knocker' flash-bang charge on a light rocket to alert the residents to evacuate immediately before the missile or bomb arrived.

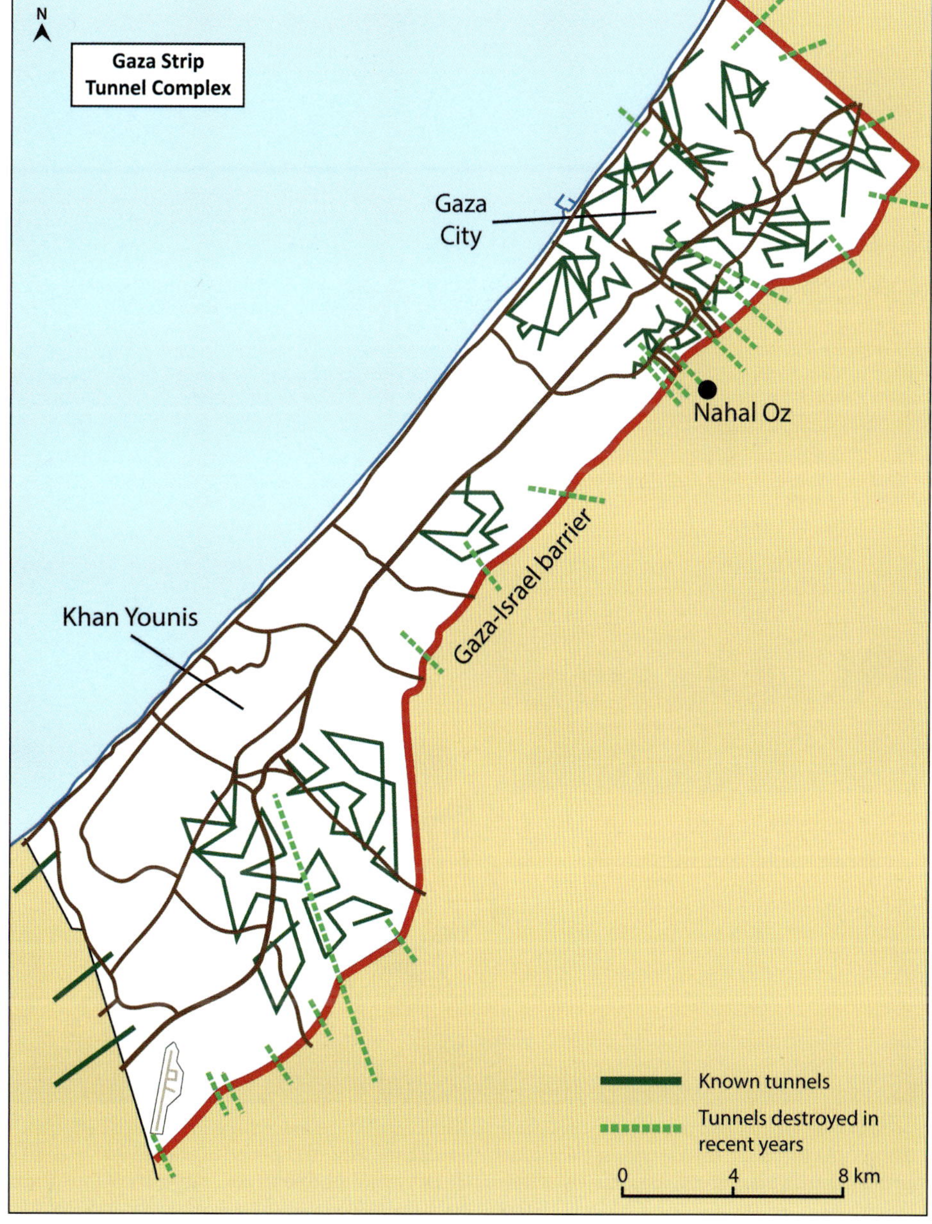

The map shows only a known portion of the expansive Hamas tunnel complex under the Gaza Strip and beneath the borders as depicted in a 2015 IDF publication. Hundreds of smaller branches are not included. (Map by George Anderson)

In answer to rockets and mortars, the Iron Dome system (bottom) was fielded and immediately effective in almost nullifying the threats. At top Iron Dome Tamir interceptors are seen engaging Hamas rockets during the May 2021 period of intense exchanges. The booster smoke trails end after the motor burns out but illustrate the high manoeuvrability of the missile as it intercepts the target. The bursts of smoke at detonation are seen, presumably beside the enemy rocket that is invisible at that altitude. (Israel Air and Space Force)

It was a rare month during this period when there was not some military action that kept animosities elevated. Israel worked to deter and diminish Hamas that worked, despite the pounding, to maintain its relevance whilst planning more decisive action. Palestinians hailed Hamas for at least doing *something*. The PA had kept militancy in the West Bank tamped down for nearly 20 years and all they got for the trouble was unrelenting repression and more Israeli settlements.

A major upgrade to Israeli fencing along the Gaza border was completed in 2021. This ran most of the 65km (40mi) length and took 3.5 years to complete at a cost of $1.1 billion. Wire fencing 6–9m (20–30ft) tall gave way to a concrete wall on the northern border, running from the sea to the Erez Crossing. Aerosats (balloons) with cameras were tethered at several points. Sensors and cameras worked to detect intruders and tunnelling. A command-and-control centre had soldiers and artificial intelligence (AI) programs monitored these 'Smart Fence' features around-the-clock. Patrols supplemented the sensors and some towers had remotely controlled machine guns. An underground wall to unspecified depth discouraged (but did not defeat) tunnelling. A 200m (650ft) sea wall was built at the northern border to discourage infiltration by swimmers. (A sea tunnel was discovered that permitted swimmers to enter the water unseen.) Forces were nearby to respond if the barrier was breached. The new 'Iron Wall' gave Israelis a sense of security.

Israel's disproportionate retaliations included repeatedly bombing Gaza infrastructure to encourage the populace to urge Hamas restraint. These strategies generally had the opposite effect. Israel invariably looked the bully in protecting its citizens by attempting to induce Hamas restraint through massive destruction with more deaths and resentment. There seemed no ending the threats to Israeli civilians, especially from indiscriminate rocket fire, and sudden death to Gazans from Israeli reactions. For the Palestinians, the occupation was intolerable and they felt Israelis had to share the insecurity.

One of the gun towers in the Israeli barrier surrounding the Gaza Strip is seen with the protective clamshell retracted. The heavy machine gun was directed and fired remotely via video camera. (Public Domain)

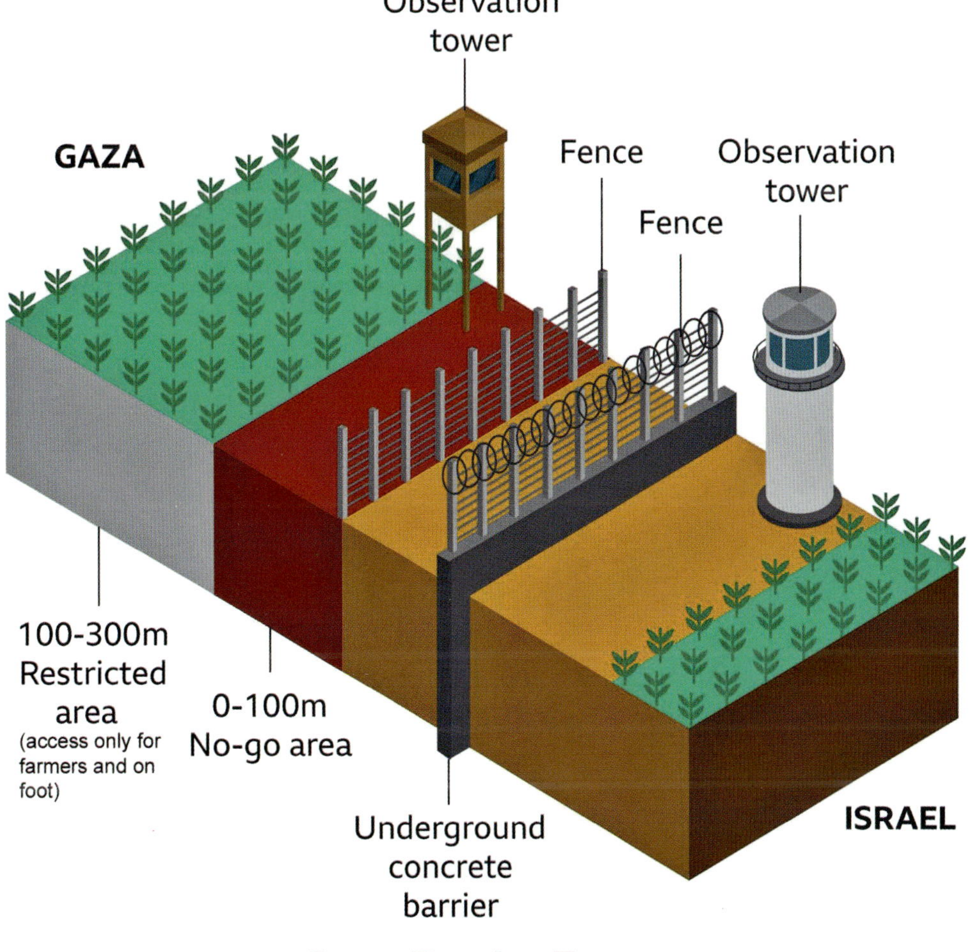

Figure 1: Details of Israel's border fence along the land side of the Gaza frontier are shown. The wire fencing was replaced with concrete walls at points. (UN Office for the Coordination of Humanitarian Affairs)

EVOLVING NORTHERN THREATS

Hezbollah maintained the confrontation with Israel and the responding IDF actions in Lebanon numbered in the hundreds. They ramped up during periods when the group sent scores of rockets across the border or there were other provocations such as attempting to abduct IDF personnel.

In summer 2006 the conflict escalated again to war. A month of air operations ensued along with minor ground forces incursions and Israel blockaded the country. The Air Force was running out of targets, yet the volume of rocket fire barely slackened. The Army was largely unprepared to meet Hezbollah on its own ground and its performance was lacklustre. A quarter million Israelis were temporarily displaced and the same number spent long periods in bomb shelters. Because Hezbollah was then part of the Lebanese government, attacks on state infrastructure ensued with vast destruction wrought across the country and approximately one million Lebanese fled. Yet, few of the expected benefits were realised. Israel was strongly condemned for what appeared to be, for a second time, gravely damaging Lebanon and imposing great suffering well beyond affecting Hezbollah. Given this and the thousands killed, it seemed little was gained.

The ceasefire resolution required the IDF to withdraw, foreign powers to cease sending arms to Hezbollah, the organisation to disarm, and the Lebanese Army to occupy the entire south along with a greater role for UN peacekeeping forces in preventing Hezbollah from firing rockets. There were no measures to enforce these terms and, apart from the IDF pulling out, they were either not enforced or proved temporary. Hezbollah spun the war's outcome into victory, but took time to recover militarily. There were only rare rocket attacks through 2023.

The years-long Syrian civil war made it the breeding ground for radical and violent groups. Syria continued supporting Hezbollah and its activities in southern Lebanon with financing and weapons supplied by Iran. Israel reacted whenever a potentially destabilising weapons system was known to be in transit to or introduced inside Lebanon. It made clear there were lines across which Hezbollah and its patrons could not cross without risking punishment. These included long-range missiles, those with precision guidance systems, and unconventional munitions.

Beginning in 2012 Iran began sending tens of thousands of 'volunteers' to Syria to help prop-up the government in the civil war, confront some Sunni enemies, and provide arms and training to Hezbollah. Prominent was the Islamic Revolutionary Guard Corps (IRGC), and particularly its Quds Force auxiliary principally responsible for covert operations. This was seen as a grave development by Israel. A campaign of airstrikes began in 2013 to contain the threat and destroy equipment en route to Hezbollah judged unacceptable. This included continually degrading Syrian chemical and ballistic missile development/production capacity. The introduction of Russian aviation and antiaircraft system in 2015 to support Syria complicated Israeli mission planning.

On 10 February 2018 an Iranian-controlled drone, armed with an explosive device, entered Israeli airspace from Syria and was shot down. Israel immediately responded with heavy airstrikes on the drone launch/control and training site. An F-16I was hit by a surface-to-air missile (SAM) and came down inside Israel after the aircrew ejected. This was the first combat loss since 1983, discounting UAVs. The shootdown was then followed by more IASF attacks on SAM batteries and other air defence sites.

A neighbourhood in Beirut is badly damaged following Israeli airstrikes during the Second Lebanon War, July 2006. (Public domain)

This exchange marked a significant change in scope and extent of Israeli attacks inside Syria as they reacted to particularly Iranian provocations. Concern with this enemy answering more vigorously with ballistic missile volleys from Iran had to be cautiously set aside. Over the next year or so the Air Force struck targets inside the country on some 200 occasions. Israel would usually not confirm or deny its role in these events so as not to give Syria the need to react as a face-saving measure. The scale of attacks, with hundreds of casualties and extensive property damage (including civilian), would usually have provoked a war. However, even with Russian and Iranian combat elements in the country, Syria was no match for Israel.

Israel continued to concentrate on hitting Iranian assets and forces, degrading their capabilities and hopefully convincing Tehran to withdraw its forces. On the night of 9/10 May 2018 Quds Force fired 20 rockets into the Golan, the first direct Iranian attack on Israeli soil. The IASF responded the same night with the heaviest series of retaliatory airstrikes into Syria since October 1973. In January 2019 the Iranians fired a medium-range ballistic missile aimed across Mount Hermon into Israel. It was destroyed by anti-missile defences. From the beginning of this period Israel targeted Hezbollah and Iranian senior leadership inside Syria, especially around Damascus. Israeli-Iranian hostile acts extended well beyond the Syrian-Lebanese skies.

Many of the attacks in Syria were evidently conducted using standoff weapons released from over Lebanon or the Golan, and some intercepted by air defences. Aircraft overflying Syria, reaching targets in all corners of the country, were occasionally engaged by SAMs but not interceptors. The IASF ability to evade and counter air defences during hundreds of missions was a measure of very effective electronic intelligence and jamming capabilities, plus cyber warfare. These were also said to have been used in strikes in Iraq, likely hitting Iranian proxy militants. All missions were commonly supported by electronic warfare (EW) aircraft and UAVs. Sometimes multiple targets were hit with simultaneous missions, as was the Israeli want, to make the most of resources committed and swamping defences.

An attack inside Iran attributed to Israel in June 2019 struck a building assembling components for the nuclear program.[20] The drone dropped the explosive and was guided back to a recovery site. In mid-February 2022 six quadcopters struck a UAV collection warehouse near Kermanshah, northwestern Iran, possibly destroying hundreds. Iran believed Mossad (Israel's foreign intelligence service) operated the UAVs from Kurdish territory in Iraq (Kurdistan). The country responded on 13 March by firing ballistic missiles at a residence near the USA consulate in Erbil they believed to be housing a Mossad unit. The attack also followed the killing of two IRGC colonels by Israeli airstrikes inside Syria. There was also a cyber-attack on Israeli government websites. Another quadcopter hit occurred on 25 May 2022. On 28 January 2023 a lab in Isfahan, developing warheads for missiles and drones, was attacked by three 'micro drones' believed to be quadcopters with 5–10kg (11–22lb) explosive charges. The roof of the building was shielded by 'anti-drone netting' and so minimal damage resulted. Iran linked the attack to Israel given similarity of the drones to those believed to be used by Mossad in Beirut and other attacks within Iran since 2021.

NUCLEAR WEAPONS

Early in its history Israel began a nuclear program and soon had a secret weapons project. Diplomatically isolated and feeling threatened by Arab states, with memory of the Holocaust fresh in Jewish consciousness, Israel judged it needed such a deterrent factor. The project required much clandestine effort and theft. It is believed Israel was manufacturing atomic bombs by 1968 and had a ballistic missile delivery system by 1971. It may have prepared to employ them during the October 1973 war. These developments were known to the USA and suspected by others, but attempts to restrain Israel were without 'teeth.' Israel consistently misled and lied about such activities and did not join the nuclear Non-Proliferation Treaty (NPT). The warheads and Jericho missiles were improved over the decades.

A 201 Squadron F-16I takes off heavily loaded for a strike mission with a standoff Delilah missiles and targeting pods. Probably all combat aircraft contributed during the 10 years of airstrikes inside Syria during the 2010s and into 2025, but standoff weapons were helpful in reducing risk to aircraft when hitting heavily defended targets. (Ofer Zidon collection)

The fact leading powers countenanced Israel possessing undeclared nuclear weapons, yet Arab and Muslim states were persistently pressured not to pursue same was irksome to many. When Iraq built a nuclear reactor capable of producing fissile material, Israel bombed it in 1981. The same was done in Syria during 2007. The potential for Iran acquiring nuclear weapons then became a concern. Their extensive and costly nuclear program, for a country with vast oil reserves, included just one power generation plant and uranium enrichment beyond that necessary for the plant, plus intentionally deceiving the International Atomic Energy Agency (IAEA). Israel warned the world of this threat for a decade and prepared to eliminate it if necessary. One outcome of Israel's Jericho work was a space access capability that included 'spy' satellites permitting monitoring of developments in Iran.

The USA and five other nations plus the European Union (EU) signed the Joint Comprehensive Plan of Action (JCPoA) with Iran in 2015 to constrain the nuclear program in exchange for lifting some sanctions and embargoes. The IAEA assessed that Iran was holding to the agreement, though Israel and others found room to disagree. The next American President, Donald Trump, unilaterally withdrew the USA from this agreement in 2018, causing its collapse. Iran subsequently enriched uranium to greater levels and stockpiled same whilst curtailing cooperation with the IAEA. Trump acted, in part, at the urging of Benjamin Netanyahu who objected to JCPoA not also limiting Iran's anti-Israeli actions in the region and ballistic missile work. That Iran might provide lower than weapons grade nuclear material to terrorists to assemble a 'dirty bomb' could not be dismissed.

Israel began planning and training for strikes in Iran during 2008. This included long-range flights over the Mediterranean and refuelling from US Air Force (USAF) aerial tankers. Weapons procurement, including aircraft and long-range air-launched weapons, development of EW capabilities, and maturation of ABM systems, supported these plans. When they approached the Americans about supporting such a campaign they received very firm pushback.[21] Netanyahu then unsuccessfully sought to strike in 2010, but the defence establishment demurred arguing the results would set the program back just a few years. Israeli cyber-attacks and espionage helped slow any Iranian nuclear weapons development. Netanyahu argued over years for a united front against the Iranian threat, standing before the UNGA and the US Congress with flipcharts depicting the danger. In his view the alleged nascent nuclear threat, the destabilising military assistance to militants, and radical Islamic influence was a threat to Western civilisation.

THE PERPETUAL OCCUPATION

In recent decades there are very few countries carrying on a military occupation, and none as long as Israel – 2017 marking the 50th year of its occupation of lands captured in June 1967, much of this identified in the Oslo Accords as the rump of a Palestinian state. However, moves towards realising the two-state solution had ground to a halt in the face of Hamas terrorism and successive far-right Israeli governments that embraced the ambition for a 'Greater Israel' with boundaries encompassing all the occupied land and more. These governments forestalled negotiations indefinitely and relentlessly surveilled the Palestinians. They enabled settlements to expand to a point their removal appeared untenable. After more than half a century, many observers concluded that this had always been the goal.

A segment of the settlers were militant, defending their 'right' to live there and pushing for the government to allow more to join them. If this

The Dassault MD-620, developed for Israel and becoming the basis for the Jericho missile, is seen in firing position during a fit check (and lacking mid-body fins) on a transporter-erector-launcher at the plant in France. (Dassault via Albert Grandolini)

meant taking from the Palestinians, so be it. Whether agreeing with occupation or not, large segments of the Israeli public could not foresee peaceful coexistence with an adjacent Palestinian state.

By 2024 approximately three-quarters of a million Israelis lived in the occupied areas, or around one in 10 Jewish citizens. They inhabited 146 settlements in the West Bank and 14 Jewish neighbourhoods in Jerusalem and one in Hebron. Multiple international judicial judgements over the decades assessed the occupation and settlements as illegal.[22] Instead of the long-stated principle of trading land for peace, Israeli governments were evidently willing only to trade peace for land and continue 'living by the sword.'

One of the outcomes of this generations-long conflict was that Israelis came to see anyone who resisted the occupation, violently or non-violently ('political activism'), as a terrorist. If they were detained by the police or military and led away for interrogation and detention, they must be terrorists or 'Hamas operatives.' A teenager throwing a rock and a writer publishing disparaging words about Israel were terrorists. It became a pejorative and provocative word, much overused.

Combating 'terrorism' and containing resistance to the occupations was seen as demanding unconventional methods. Israel passed a law in 2002 legalising indefinite internment without charges or legal counsel for unlawful combatants of non-state actors. This extended to anyone deemed a threat, armed or otherwise. Children, pregnant women and the elderly were detained. Provisions of the practice contravene international law. Approximately 20 percent of the Palestinian population under Israeli jurisdiction (around 800,000, 40 percent of males) came to be detained or imprisoned at some point in their lives, equating to approximately 70 percent of families having a member detained. Everyone knew someone in this grouping and were aware of others who had been killed or wounded. For those that stood trial the conviction rate, by military courts, was 90–95 percent. They complained of poor treatment in detention and prisons. After 7 October 2023 the Knesset passed additional laws restricting protests, freedom of expression, and other common rights, bound to increase resentment and breed more opposition.

CHANGING PERCEPTIONS

After 75 years as a state, and demonstrably not the 'underdog' it portrayed itself as, many throughout the world felt Israel had been 'cut enough slack' and needed to act more responsibly. Images of Israel bombing the Gaza Strip every four or five years, justified or not, expansion of Jewish settlements in the West Bank and neighbourhoods in East Jerusalem, and continued military repression of the occupied population for security objectives, undermined Israel's avowed character as a democratic and peace-seeking nation.

Whereas previously service in the IDF had been viewed by many outside Israel as a commendable distinction, it was increasingly becoming seen as dishonourable. Likewise, the IASF's actions over the Strip also brought condemnation for its evident severity and high civilian suffering, its lustre tarnished with the phrase 'they bomb Gaza.'

A UN Special Committee had investigated and documented occupation practices for decades, though always denied access to the area by Israel. A thorough investigation of the occupation reported by Human Rights Watch in 2021 reached similar conclusions that it was a form of apartheid with 'systematic oppression of Palestinians and inhumane acts'. The Israeli government and a vast segment of the citizenry were enraged by the assessment, but it reflected what much of the informed world population also perceived. It was not lost on people that it was such racist practices by others that had compelled the Jews to seek a state of their own a century before. The conclusions were echoed again in a 23 September 2025 report of an inquiry by the UN Human Rights Commission. It concluded that land confiscation, population displacement, discrimination in land and housing, and construction and expansion of settlements was seeking a clear Jewish majority in the West Bank.[23] It claimed destruction of some buildings under claims they were terrorist

Israeli security personnel detain two Palestinian men in an all-to-familiar process to contain resistance to the occupation. (The Palestine Information Center)

havens, or erected without permits (nearly impossible to obtain), plus explicit and implicit support for settler violence, were clear intimidation and collective punishment. It was also pointed out, for Israeli Arabs, 'successive Israeli Governments have implemented laws and policies to diminish Palestinian space, including through confining Palestinian localities and hindering Palestinians with Israeli citizenship from moving and integrating into Jewish localities'. The discrimination was deepening with 'informal barriers resulting from wider, primarily socio-economic inequalities'. Israel and its supporters dismissed all of this as misleading and the UN as inherently anti-Israeli. To this and associated disputes, the UN General Secretary, Kofi Annan, wondered aloud, 'Can the whole world be wrong and only Israel is right?'[24]

Of the globe's nations by the end 2024 approximately 75 percent recognised the Palestinians as a national entity denied a promised state by the continuing conflict. In November 2012 a UN vote won the Palestinians status as a non-member observer state. In 2024 Ireland, Norway, Slovenia and Spain formally recognised the State of Palestine, bringing Israeli diplomatic retaliation. Israel insisted this was all wrong-headed and anti-Israeli. They emphasised Palestinian statehood could only be arrived at between the parties and not imposed by external declarations (not the intent). However, nearly two decades of Israel impeding the two-state solution did not suggest this was a fruitful course.

Israelis had different concepts of Zionism following founding of the state. To some it was strengthening Israel and encouraging more Jews to immigrate to the country. This might demand more land for housing. Increasing the Jewish character of the nation was another, at the inevitable expense of non-Jewish inhabitants. Expanding the boundaries of the state to encompass more of the historical 'Land of Israel' or 'Land of our Forefathers' was an ambition bringing Israel into direct conflict with Palestinians and the international community. Israel was founded as a secular country and, whilst intended as a homeland for Jews, was overtly welcoming of all people. It was only in 2018 that a Basic Law was passed, championed by far-right nationalists, which stated unequivocally that Israel was the nation-state of the Jewish people. Nearly 70 percent of Jews still lived outside of Israel and some 25 percent of Israeli inhabitants were non-Jewish (and many of those noncitizens).

'Bibi' Netanyahu and the Likud, elected multiple times since 1996, embodied the Greater Israel ambitions and worked diligently to realise them. Israelis went to the polls five times in 3.5 years in the 2010s seeking to elect a government. Either the voting was too close to call, the win was too narrow for a government be formed, or the government collapsed. Returning to the premiership in December 2022, Netanyahu's effort to reform the judiciary was seen by many as a means to gather more unchecked authority under the PM, undermining Israeli democracy. It would limit the court's authority to contain the PM's ability to enact unilateral government changes, to include replacing leading figures for more uniform policies. These practices and ambitions generated numerous disruptions of Israeli governing norms, creating the equivalent of a constitutional crisis. Many citizens were repelled by what they saw as a swing to authoritarianism. There were weekly mass protests, unlike anything previously seen in the country. Add to this the continuing rise of influence by religious and settler extremists, instability in the increasingly divided nation meant even challenges like defence did not get full attention.

A Palestinian building under construction in the West Bank is being reduced by Israeli equipment as security personnel patrol nearby.
(The Palestine Information Center)

A 4 March 2023 mass demonstration in Tel Aviv illustrates the sustained opposition to PM Netanyahu's policies. (Amir Terkel)

Some Sunni Arab states normalised relations with Israel since September 2020 – the Abraham Accords – as a measure against Iran and because 'it is good for business'. These were Sudan, Morocco and Bahrain, plus a free trade agreement with the United Arab Emirates (UAE). Negotiations were underway with Saudi Arabia in 2023 to the same end. These Arab states set aside prior expectations that such normalisation would only follow resolution of the Palestinian issue. The greater urgency was a unified front against Shiite Iran and any nascent nuclear weapons program. Some in the Palestinian sphere feared this trend undermined backing for the two-state solution. However, the sense was that the Palestinians were not helping themselves and there seemed no end to the imbroglio. Many observers concluded the PA was doing its level best to contain radicals and violence against Israelis despite provocations but was not receiving suitable credit for the effort. A majority of the Palestinian public supported the continued armed struggle against the occupation, though eliminating Israel and reclaiming property within the country had become a minority ambition. Palestinians contemplating a sovereign state were leery of living, largely unarmed, beside Israelis who had repeatedly shown their contempt and the high likelihood of attacking and invading a Palestinian state at will.

Beginning in 2018 Israel worked with Qatar to pass money to Hamas. Israel considered permitting more Gazans to cross the border to work. The hope was that the organisation would focus on social programs instead of military endeavours. However, there was no accounting for how the money was spent and much seems to have gone to military preparations. The belief was that Hamas was contained and deterred militarily. The last major war with Hamas (with ground incursion) was in 2014 – an unusually long period. Subsequent outbursts had been smaller and not required calling up reservists. Netanyahu wanted to avoid high casualties and bogging the Army down in Gaza for months or years when there were more significant threats in Syria and Iran.[25] Some in the government felt Hamas should be suppressed pre-emptively, Defense Minister Avigdor Liberman resigned in 2018 over the issue. It seemed to them Israel was buying a period of relative quiet whilst Hamas, not having 'changed its spots', made ready.

Netanyahu's government rhetoric grew increasingly strident. He had two members of his coalition who were particularly extremist. National Security Minister Itamar Ben-Gvir, with control of the Border Police, had previously been convicted for inciting racism and supporting a terrorist organisation. Finance Minister Bezalel Smotrich also had a role in the Defense Ministry for governing the West Bank. Both men had made inflammatory statements empowering settler terrorism. They advocated expelling Arabs and annexing the West Bank. Netanyahu's supporters called him King of Israel, but this was a title of derision for his detractors. The PM had been indicted on corruption charges.[26] Word of the Qatari money flow also caused a scandal. There was suspicion it was also meant to create further division between Hamas and the PA to keep the Palestinians weak.

Israel was a famously factious and fractious society at the best of times, but the temperature was rising. The IDF was not immune from the growing polarisation. Over 1,100 IASF personnel and 10,000 reservists signed a letter stating they would not serve under a Netanyahu government if the judicial reform law passed. Some soldiers acted beyond orders in line with their religious or political beliefs. There was non-uniform application of policy and adherence to rules-of-engagement. Disputes within commands could be divisive, personnel walking way. This, however, had always been a characteristic of the IDF and had not undermined mission execution.

Many Israelis assessed their concessions in the peace process had cost them thousands of lives. They did not speculate how many more would have fallen without those concessions, or the outcome if both parties had held to the agreements. When it came to the confrontation with the Palestinians, the sense for many in Israel was that they would never be satisfied and would always seek to destroy Israel. For the Palestinians the sense was that Israel would always seek to take their land and repress them. Both sides taught their children these viewpoints, with the inevitable consequences. Palestinians asked why Israel was being permitted to act unlawfully without consequences. Israelis asked why the world criticised them when they were just acting to protect themselves from terrorism that could spread elsewhere without their actions. Outsiders wondered who would stop Israel and how.

One can imagine Netanyahu and his ministers reflecting on the past and concluding nothing anyone had ever done had significantly restrained Israel unless weak Israeli governments had chosen to be restrained. Israel had the strongest and most capable military in the region and should use it to push back or eliminate threats regardless of international reaction.[27] Netanyahu knew all the lines not to cross to avoid precipitating large-scale combat with Israel's adversaries and provoke an international outcry bringing great pressure on Israel. He would intentionally cross all of them.

National Security Minister Itamar Ben-Gvir (left) and Finance Minister Bezalel Smotrich (right) were lightning rods of controversy in the Netanyahu government of 2022 and later. Both were ultra-nationalists with extremist attitudes towards Palestinians and settlements. At every turn they called for war against Israel's enemy, repeatedly threatened to bring down Netanyahu's coalition if the war did not continue. (Public Domain)

2

HAMAS ATTACK AND INITIAL RESPONSE

By 2023 Hamas had a military organisation of around 30,000 fighters in 24 battalions, though many were semi-trained militiamen. A shock unit was called Nakba. Common weapons were antitank missiles, rocket-propelled grenades (RPG), grenades and mortars, and firearms. Their arsenal of rockets was believed to number around 15,000, some with range up to 250km (155mi). Mortar bombs may have numbered around 5,000. Antiaircraft weapons were dated former-Soviet man-portable air defence systems (MANPADS, shoulder-fired anti-aircraft missiles), easily countered. They had been preparing since 2016 for a large-scale terror operation inside Israel. (Intelligence agencies had obtained a copy of the plan in April 2022 but did not take it seriously.[1]) More tunnels were built. In spring 2023 they began specific training, some out in the open where they were observed by the Israelis, desensitising them. This included drills on a mock-up of a Merkava tank, barrier walls, and nearby IDF outposts, use of quadcopters, and how to process hostages. Copies of a handbook were provided describing tactics, and including maps and descriptions of targets in the Gaza Envelope (within about 7km/4mi), and Hebrew phrases. Knowing they were being observed, some activities and intentionally leaked information were to mislead. Religious motivation was widely used, but claims the men were religious fanatics consumed with an irrational thirst for Jewish blood does not appear justified.

Hamas eventually selected 7 October as the date of the attack, just a day beyond the 50th anniversary of the Egyptian-Syrian surprise attack beginning the October 1973 war, a shock Israel had worked to ensure could never occur again. It was also the Sabbath and a Jewish holiday. The true plans for the attack were known to just a few top leaders.

Israel's guard had been lowered with hubris lending assurance Palestinian militant organisations were thoroughly penetrated by intelligence services and no significant terror operation could be initiated without sufficient warning. However, Israel had no human intelligence (spies) within Hamas.[2] Preparedness had been allowed to slip with exercises and readily available weapons having been reduced. Security forces were not structured to respond to a mass penetration of the border fence and there were no war plans for destroying Hamas via a campaign

Members of the Qassam Brigades drill in Gaza City. Their light attire and AK-47 assault rifles were common. (Hadi Mohammad)

Palestinian fighters pose at a tunnel nexus under the Gaza Strip, lending insight into the construction. There were several varieties of tunnels, so this is but one example. (Public Domain)

inside the Strip. Indications of the impending operation were missed, misinterpreted or dismissed. The result was the deadliest single attack on Israeli soil and, subsequently, the longest war with the highest death toll.

The year 2023 began with heightened tensions. Minister Ben-Gvir, with a group of followers, visited the Temple Mount during a Jewish day remembering the fall of the Second Temple and so was symbolic of aspirations to reclaim the site. Being a government official, the visit breached prior agreements with the Muslim authorities and was intentionally inflammatory. A rocket flew from Gaza in reaction. The first rockets in years from Lebanon came on 6 April 2023 after Israeli police entered the Al-Aqsa Mosque to arrest protesters. On 2 May Palestinian activist Khader Adnan died in an Israeli prison after an 87-day hunger strike. This sparked four days of exchanges between Hamas and Israel. After a week Israel eliminated PIJ commanders, and more violence ensued. It was becoming a year of more-than-usual rhetoric and fire.

7 OCTOBER 2023 CATACLYSM

On the day of the attack several observation aerostats were nonfunctional. The program that collated data from various sources to warn of unusual activity had also gone down. Although this was not uncommon, it was subsequently believed Hamas may have taken down the program via a cyber-attack. Even as warning signs multiplied, the general conclusion was it was a Hamas drill or a small incursion may be attempted. Some extra measures were taken, but it proved too little too late. An additional Dvora patrol boat was put to sea in time to intercept any sea assault. Two Apache helicopter gunships were summoned from the northern border, but this was delayed. One more Hermes 450 drone was put up (the request had been four). With the holiday weekend, the four battalions stationed along the Gaza border were minimally manned.

The Hamas operation, Al-Aqsa Flood, was heralded by a cascade of some 4,300 rockets and mortar rounds beginning at 0629 hours, approximately 3,000 in the first four hours – an unprecedented volume of fire. This was in salvos of 140 at a time. In the next week they likely expended 5,500 rounds. All this overwhelmed Iron Dome and some rounds fell on populated targets. (Two Iron Dome launch sites were overrun and a reload team intercepted.) Impacts were as far north as 80km (50mi) and 12 people were killed with dozens wounded. A new 114mm short-range Rojam rocket was small and flew at low trajectory, almost impossible for Iron Dome to intercept.

The rocket fire may have been intended as a distraction from the ground assault. Approximately 3,800 fighters and perhaps 2,200 noncombatants entered Israel in vehicles – mostly pickup trucks and motorbikes – and on foot at 119 points through the breached border fence, via paraglider, and by boat. (No tunnels were used in penetrating into Israel that day.) Their targets were carefully selected

A staged demonstration shows Hamas personnel loading a launcher with rockets. These might be Grad rockets or just mock-ups, but certainly one of the large types with long range. (Hamas)

based on intelligence assessments and the teams assigned accordingly.[3] A second wave followed the first, exploiting success or filling-in where there had been failures, and a third later in the day. They continued coming over that day and the next until the fence was secured.

Personnel spread out and assaulted military outposts, police stations and civilian communities alike. They attacked aerostats and communication towers, and feeds to cameras were cut to blind the enemy. Water, electricity and telephone services were impaired. Drones were used to hit watchtowers and their weapon positions. The tower-mounted remote-controlled machine guns were taken out by explosives dropped by quadcopters or powering severed. Several tanks were overwhelmed or hit by missiles, their crews killed or captured. More than 20 local communities plus a music festival were assaulted. The goal was indiscriminate killing, but was accompanied by sexual assault, torture and mutilation. (Subsequently, some stories of the atrocities were exaggerated and this repeated in the press, though not as government policy.) Dozens of fires were set and some people holed up in their secure rooms were trapped and perished. Some road intersections were held to ambush traffic that included security forces' response.

Seven IDF bases and outposts in proximity to the border were attacked. Not prepared for such an onslaught, instead of working to coordinate responses they were fighting for their lives. Gaza Division was reduced to impotency, with command and control collapsing. It was 0743 before the first specific instructions to IDF units went out, though without

A CCTV image of the 7 October attack in Beeri show Hamas gunmen on motorcycles rampaging through the streets early that morning, shooting at everyone. The car at left has had the left side windows shot out, likely killing the occupants. (Public Domain)

A photo taken 90 minutes into the 7 October 2023 Hamas attack on Israel shows a burned-out Israeli Merkava tank beside a border fence breach made by the tractor in the background. The main gun's muzzle still has the cover in place. (Yousef Masoud)

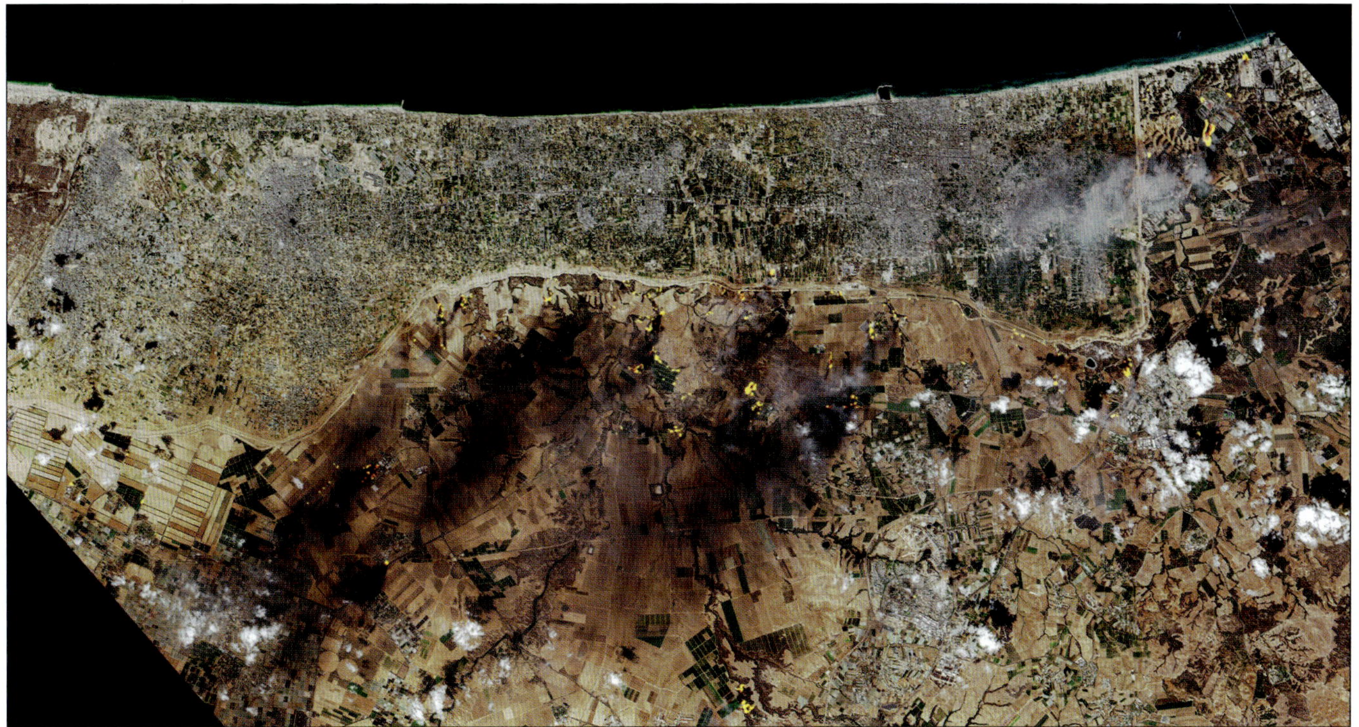

A satellite photograph of the Gaza Envelope on 7 October, visible light with infrared overlay, emphasis the fires burning and smoke generated during the Hamas attack. (Public Domain)

a clear picture of the situation they would face. At 1100 coherent units began to arrive and it was 1600 before they had decisive forces on hand. In addition to weapons, the enemy took radios, cellphones and computers such that they could track and anticipate Israeli reactions. Response from beyond the Division was delayed and situational awareness degraded for some 18 hours. It was more than an hour before IDF action, initially with helicopters seeking to identify the extent of the penetration and engage militants with gunfire. Helicopters also transported troops to the area and lifted survivors to safety and hospitals. However, with risk from Hamas fighters in the area, some with MANPADS, it was important to have the landing zone secured by ground forces before alighting. Hamas employed GPS jamming, and the IDF did the same, denying the common navigation means.

A 124 Squadron Black Hawk takes on a litter-borne casualty in a medivac scenario. This was played out scores of times during response to the 7 October 2023 Hamas terror attack. The extreme mass casualty event strained emergency services to their limits and it was 'all hands on deck' for three days. Fortunately, flight time to hospitals was relatively short in the small country. (IDF/AF)

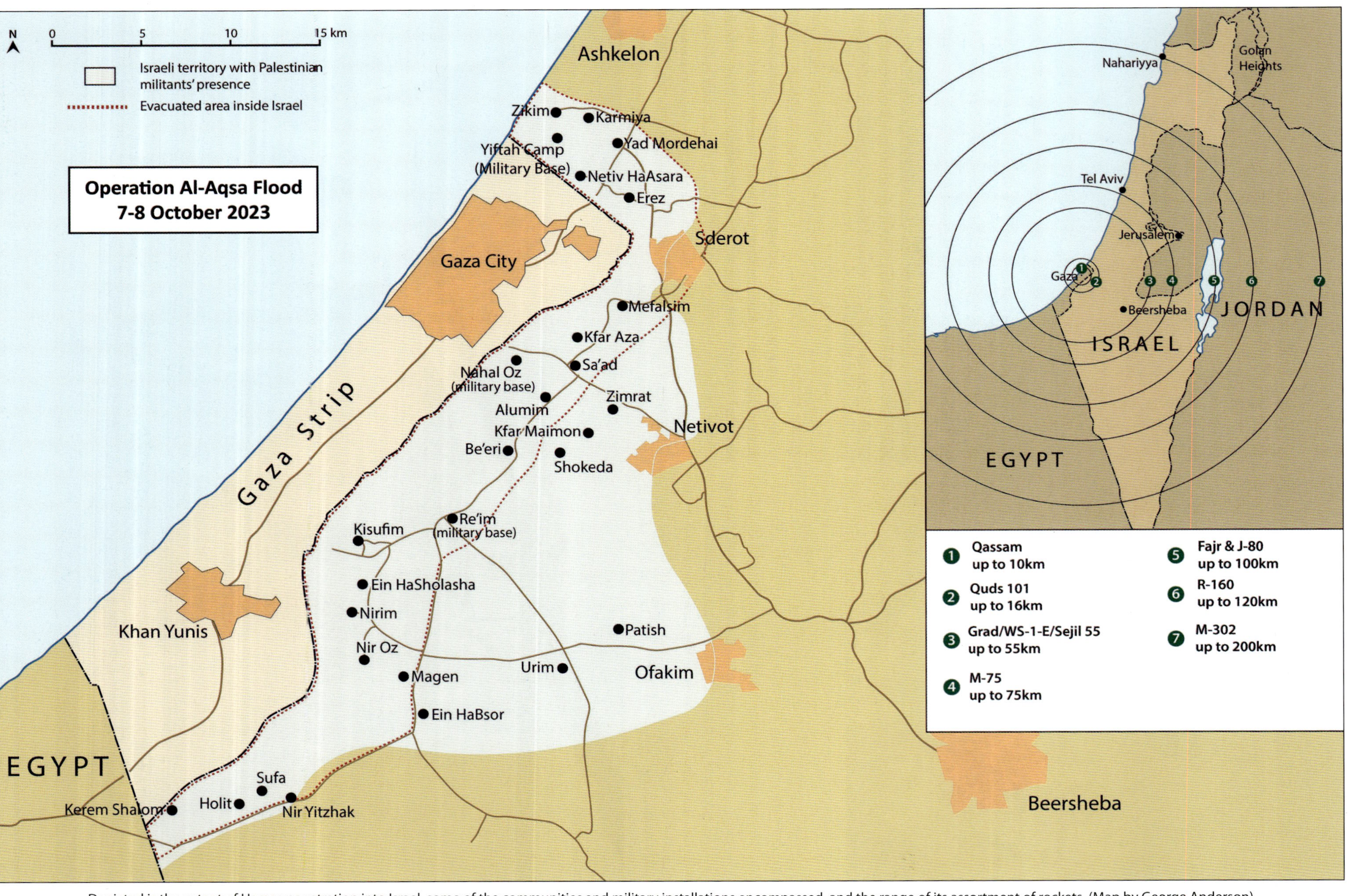

Depicted is the extent of Hamas penetration into Israel, some of the communities and military installations encompassed, and the range of its assortment of rockets. (Map by George Anderson)

Over the span of the day the military and police response increased, but usually without clear orders, or any at all. Not all were trained in counterterror tactics and urban warfare. Citizen-soldiers and off-duty police showed up to assist without being summoned and so added to the disorder.[4] Some IDF units gathered and moved without orders.[5] Some civilians spent nearly two days in shelters before it was safe to emerge.[6]

Through the 11th Israeli forces tracked down and eliminated terrorists hold up in fortified positions and prepared to be 'martyred', having penetrated up to 18km (11mi). Killed were 1,609 and 200 captured. Helicopter gunships and Hermes 450 drones contributed (the Hermes executing 283 strikes missions on the 7th), the UAVs also tracking movements. In some cases the attacks were on Israeli civilian and IDF locations where the terrorists had gone to ground. Attacking targets inside Israel was a new experience.

The terrorists killed 1,194 of whom 815 were civilians, whilst wounding 3,400. Not all of these were Israelis or Jews, and not all occurred on 7 October but over a span of days, and not all the attackers were Hamas. Abducted were 251 people (some dead), again not all Jewish Israelis. Surveillance and signals intelligence (SIGINT) aircraft were at work immediately seeking evidence of hostage whereabouts, aided by a UK airborne asset.

Hamas and Hezbollah had made taking hostages priority objectives. Israeli negotiations for their release over years had always been an anguishing task, usually seeing prisoners with 'blood on their hands' released in exchanges. Consequently, attempts on 7 October to impede the transport of hostages into Gaza, mostly by gunship fire, saw several of the civilians killed and injured. This was in accordance with the Hannibal Directive that Defense Minister Yoav Gallant ordered into effect that day. Later revelation of this caused some heated discord given that the government had secretly decided it was better to kill its citizens to prevent them falling hostage. The Directive dated from 1986 and mention of it in the press was forbidden. It had been invoked several times previously.[7] The IDF decided not to follow the terrorists transporting hostages into Gaza 'in hot pursuit' to avoid falling into traps.

Arabs around the world were praising the Hamas operation for giving Israelis 'a taste of their own medicine'. That the attack was savage was undeniable. However, Hamas saw little difference between a Palestinian child blown apart by a $10,000 smart bomb and an Israeli child blown apart by a $100 grenade. One is called a legitimate self-defence military operation and the other is labelled terrorism. Regardless, both children are innocent victims of the conflict in which such actions were commonplace efforts at influencing behaviour of those in positions of authority.

The attack was a profound shock to the nation. Israelis had been confident the 'Iron Wall', backed by IDF personnel stationed nearby, was virtually impregnable. As word of the penetration and deaths emerged, there was anger and resolve to respond as never before.

Air travel into and out of Israel ceased as airports closed under the threat of rocket fire. Stranded passengers took boats to Cyprus to catch flights. The national airline, El Al, resumed operations for periods of time, but foreign carriers were months before returning. Even then occasional inbound rockets and even impacts within the perimeter of Ben-Gurion International Airport (IAP) prompted shutdowns. Extended combat with Hezbollah and Iran (see later) would have travellers grounded for months.

An Israeli National Unity Cabinet with a 'War Cabinet' was formed on the 11th, bringing in the opposition, to oversee the response without the usual political rancour. Five divisions were gathered opposite Gaza, three held in the north, and one in the West Bank. The stated goal of Operation Swords of Iron was to free the hostages and completely eliminate Hamas from the Gaza Strip as a governing and military entity. Israel laid siege to the Strip to include access to the sea for fishing and services from Israel greatly reduced or denied. As Gallant said, 'There will be no electricity, no food, no fuel, everything is closed'. Gaza had some of their own sources of these, but very limited. Communication services were curtailed, greatly reducing the ability for word to get out about conditions in the Strip apart from what Israel released. Call-up of approximately 360,000 reservists was the largest since October 1973. Air Force aircraft went abroad to bring some of these personnel home. All these soldiers appearing in a short period took time to sort and organise.

Netanyahu seemed transformed by the events and freed to execute security ambitions previously held back because of IDF cautions of risks and warnings of high casualties, or opposition emphasis on political fallout. He also had to erase his culpability in the failures leading to 7 October by producing a resounding victory and re-establish his defence credentials by addressing threats to Israel aside from Gaza. Having experienced the largest slaughter of Jews in a single day since the Holocaust, Netanyahu stated bluntly he sought revenge and to reduce Gaza to rubble – making these moral values and military objectives in notable departures from the past. Hamas was cast as evil and the war against them a fight of Light against Darkness for which, presumably, anything was justified. Gallant said all restraints were lifted and a defence spokesman added that emphasis was to be on damage inflicted and not precision. This total war implied any pretence of proportionality was dismissed.[8] Gallant insisted the blockade was justified given that the IDF was fighting 'human animals', an irresponsible phrase that encouraged dehumanisation of the Strip's inhabitants and seeing everyone as a terrorist. 'There are no innocents' was often heard. Netanyahu referenced the Amalek when addressing an assembly of soldiers, referring to a Biblical story of God ordering the Israelites to exterminate their enemy the Amalekites and any memory of them – a story familiar to anyone passing through the Israeli education system. Military personnel embraced all these words in a disturbing departure for a professional army.

During at least the first phase of the war in Gaza supporters of Israel insisted the IDF was acting with such restraint to ensure civilians were not unnecessarily harmed – 'one hand tied behind its back' – that it was placing soldiers at additional risk and lengthening the time required to locate hostages. Such voices had largely fallen silent by the second year of combat. Apart from attempting to clear civilians from areas of imminent operations with methods previously described, it was never clear which rules-of-engagement were considered so extraordinary. Movement of formations were observed and reported so that the enemy prepared. So, loss of the element of surprise was common. One IDF officer described how his team engaged anyone in the warzone, even if unarmed, unless they were obvious noncombatants.[9] Numerous accounts heard in the media were of soldiers disturbed by what they experienced, describing operations that seemed devoid of rules-of-engagement.[10] Former Chief-of-General-Staff (CGS), General Halevi, remarked in September 2025 that the Ministry of Defense (MoD) lawyers had never restricted his actions or orders during the time he oversaw the war, though many outside his command had previously accused them of unnecessarily hampering the Army's operations.

INITIAL IDF OPERATIONS IN GAZA

Israeli bombing in the Gaza Strip began immediately with hundreds of targets hit, many for the psychological impact of the destruction being wrought. The IASF attacked 436 targets on the first day. (Table 1 summarises the Air Force's order of battle.) On the night of 13 October these were 750 targets and on the 22nd 320 targets. On the 13th the IDF said that all civilians in the north should move south of Wadi Gaza within the next 24 hours for their own safety. The UN warned that this was impossible to achieve given the mass of people, some 1.1 million. In the first month and a half artillery fired 10,000 shells into the enclave. Some small-scale raids by ground personnel were executed. It was 27 October before the ground operation got underway, the delay owing to continuing government debate but offering the opportunity for training in addition to gathering forces and materiel. Israel had put into motion resupply from the USA whilst also going to 24/7 work for items produced within the country, expecting high expenditure of munitions.[11]

Table 1: IASF Combat Aircraft Summary

Attack
39 F-35I (ongoing delivery), 116, 117, 140 Squadrons
25 F-15I, 69 Squadron
97 F-16I, 107, 119, 201, 253 Squadrons
48 F-15 (14 A, 6 B, 16 C, 12 D), 106, 133 Squadrons
79 F-16 (30 C, 49 D), 101, 105, 109 Squadrons
53 AH-64 (36 AI, 17 DI), 113, 190 Squadron
-- Hermes 450S UAV (optionally armed), 161 Squadron
-- Hermes 900 UAV (optionally armed), 147, 166 Squadrons (147 formed 7 April 2024)
-- Heron TP UAV (optionally armed), 210 Squadron
Electronic Warfare
3 G.V Shavit (SIGINT), 122 Squadron
2 G-550 Eitam (airborne early warning, AEW*), same squadron
1 G-550 Oron (AEW/SIGINT), same squadron
(2) Yas'ur 2025, alternative mission configuration
-- Hermes 900 and Heron TP UAVs, alternative mission configuration
Reconnaissance/Surveillance
several camera pods for F-15 and F-16
3 Super King Air with EO** balls, 100 Squadron
≈20 Hermes 450S (losses continuously replaced), squadron as above
8–10 Hermes 900 (losses continuously replaced), squadron as above
10–15 Heron UAV (losses continuously replaced), 200 Squadron
10 Heron TP (losses continuously replaced), squadron as above
18–20 Orbiter 4 UAV (losses continuously replaced), 144 Squadron
5? RA-01 UAV (new and designation uncertain)
3 Aerostats
Aerial Refuelling
6 Boeing 707 (boom), 120 Squadron
5 KC-130H (hose-drogue), 131 Squadron
Maritime Patrol
4 Heron 1 UAV, flight of 200 Squadron
Heavy Transport and Assault
4 Boeing 707 cargo/passenger, hospital, squadron as above
7 C-130J, 103 Squadron
3 C-130H (with KC-130H), squadron as above
26 Yas'ur (21 Yas'ur 2025, 5 Yas'ur 2000) upgraded S-65 and CH-53, 114, 118 Squadrons
48 Black Hawk (9 UH-60A, 39 S-70A/UH-60L), 123, 124 Squadrons
Maritime Helicopter
3 AS.565MA (withdrawn 2 September 2025), 193 Squadron
Ballistic Missile
50-100 Jericho III in one wing
* AEW = airborne early warning, ** EO = electro-optical

Israel's defense minister Yoav Gallant greets the USA Defense Secretary Lloyd Austin in Tel Aviv on 18 December 2023. Close allies, America provided Israel additional funds and munitions to meet the crisis. (USA DoD, Chad, J. McNeeley)

Israel's air base and airport locations are depicted. (Map by Tom Cooper)

The campaign, when it got underway, essentially proceeded from north to south, seeking out and eliminating Hamas elements, infrastructure, and arms caches. Initially the 162nd Division proceeded south along the coast whilst the 36th struck out west to meet them near the port, effectively encircling the northern segment of the Strip. They were soon joined by the 98th Division, other brigades acting independently. Eventually five divisions with 20 brigades, in excess of 30,000 personnel, were committed. A road was cut from the border to the sea south of Gaza City, the 6km (4mi) long Netzarim Corridor, to bisect and control the battlespace. This was named after an Israeli settlement existing before the 2005 pullout. A buffer zone was created beside the road with buildings knocked down and rubble cleared.

Civilians fled before the onslaught, urged on by leaflet drops and media warnings. (No mention of 'roof-knockers' is found in accounts of the war.) There were reports early on of Hamas trying to prevent people from leaving certain areas, for whatever reason, but the flood was irresistible. Given the dense living conditions and the confined combat area, civilian suffering was unavoidable. Yet, the IDF's performance saw a new fury and so became the most severe example of the destruction and death wrought by urban combat waged over an extended period.

By January 2024 there had been 29,000 bombs, shells and missiles delivered into the Strip and by June 70,000 tonnes. With the targeted militants operating amongst the population, the potential for collateral damage and casualties was recognised as inevitable. Urban combatants are compelled by circumstances to operate from within the community. Given Hamas's meagre antiaircraft capabilities, operating in open areas would be tantamount to putting up billboards declaring 'Israeli pilots bomb here!' So, accusations of fighters intentionally using the populace as 'human shields' is not entirely justified.[12] Additionally, the Gaza Strip is among the most densely populated regions on the planet and fighters have few options but to move amongst the civilians. In the case of Hamas, however, there were many instances in which they insisted civilians remained in an area or deliberated ensured they were in front of their operations to discourage Israeli strikes. They always assumed they were under observation when in the open, if not targeted. Hamas also openly stated that the blood of 'martyrs' was essential in the destruction of Israel and the liberation of Palestine. The populace was to make sacrifices, even if not consenting.

Israel controlled the movement of relief supplies into the enclave to intercept contraband and ensure the safety of those conducting that mission. This and other impediments meant these supplies never met need. Some Israeli citizens actively interfered with the relief supply effort to include obstructing trucks travelling from Jordan. Israel was accused of obstructing the operation as a form of collective punishment or war by means of deadly deprivation of noncombatants (a war crime). In time, civilian deaths mounted to the tens of thousands, medical aid became meagre and injured died for want of care. Sanitation was hard hit, clean water and food scarce. People began to suffer malnutrition, to contract preventable diseases, and die of exposure. (The UN and other agencies warned of imminent starvation throughout 2024, but this did not evidently set in.) Transport aircraft from the USAF, the Royal Jordanian Air Force and the UAE performed airdrops of aid as one measure to provide relief.

The ground campaign was a tough effort to locate and eliminate militant personnel and assets building-by-building and tunnel-by-tunnel. The enemy fought back as best they could with gunfire, mortar bombs, anti-

At top a USAF C-130 is prepared for a bundle airdrop over the Gaza Strip and below bundles descend under parachute. (US Central Command and Government of Egypt)

An IDF Merkava Mk 4 tank and Namer APC pause on a Gaza street during an advance on 23 November 2023. Note the cope cage above the Merkava's turret, that the vehicles are buttoned-up, and that all the surrounding buildings have had their windows blown out by bomb concussions. (IDF Spokesman)

tank missiles, improvised explosive devices (IED), booby-traps, and even drones dropping grenades and converted RPG warheads. (Soldiers commented on the altering battlefield, the IEDs now chasing them instead of lying in wait.) The IDF began to fit metal 'cope cages' (canopies) atop vehicles to protect them from such falling ordnance. They also began using 'autonomous explosive-armoured vehicles' in the city to neutralise explosive devices. Enemy fighters moved between partially destroyed buildings and tunnels to avoid direct contact with IDF units. They would also emerge from tunnels to fire anti-tank missiles or run to attach explosives to passing vehicles using magnets. (Vehicle operators largely proceeded 'buttoned-up' to avoid sniper fire.) Sometimes the fighters wore stolen Israeli uniforms and kit to sow confusion. Knowing the Israelis would come, Hamas had prepared. Weapons and ammunition were stored all over, including homes and schools.[13] Likewise for location of tunnel entrances. This permitted fighters to acquire arms and concealment at innumerable locations.

The Hamas militant presence was evidently extensive, with weapons caches and materials found in such common places as schools and hospitals. This was to be expected as Hamas and its affiliates had to avoid concentrated armouries that could be destroyed at a stroke by Israeli bombing. Reducing Hamas was a slow and painful process with losses and some friendly-fire incidents.[14] Just about anyone moving in an area being cleared (men of approximate military age) was considered a terrorist and fired upon. Three hostages that escaped their captors, and clearly unarmed, were shot dead when approaching Israeli personnel.[15] Likewise, anyone captured – bound, blindfolded, stripped to their shorts, transported to Israel for interrogation and detention – were all automatically considered terrorists. Pitched battle with IDF units was naturally avoided, employing hit-and-run tactics. Personnel sometimes surrendered when they had no escape options, but some fought to the death.

Tunnel detection, clearance, and then destruction had been very difficult for the IDF in the past, and so it became a major effort with no certainty of complete success. As in prior campaigns, destruction of tunnels from the air was minimally effective. A special Samur (Weasel) unit, specialising in tunnel warfare, undertook much of this. Destructive methods included blowing up the entrance, placing explosives in the walls to be set off, and detonating a liquid

Israeli personnel examine a tunnel entrance at left, probably considering entering and then destroying it, and a tunnel entrance inside a building is seen at right. Tunnel warfare was a fraught exercise that was performed likely hundreds of times during the Gaza war. (IDF Spokesman)

explosive poured into the tunnel. Blowing up a tunnel could bring down buildings above, either accepted or avoided. Flooding tunnels with seawater was another tactic, the pressure causing it to collapse, though taking care not to contaminate the aquifer.

The Israelis went building-by-building and burnt or blew-up any that had evidence of Hamas use, aided by the omnipresent D9 bulldozer.[16] Infantry soldiers were trained on building demolition, issued suitable explosives, and encouraged not to return them. Finding as little as Hamas scarves, a Palestinian flag, or a photograph of a martyr was rationale to destroy the building. Given that Hamas had been everywhere in the Strip, storing weapons in small numbers throughout, these criteria meant widespread destruction. In some cases this appeared wanton, following guidance to reduce the 'terrorist hive' to rubble. Given that the enemy kept filtering back into such areas, the tactic appeared to be inadequate. A division commander (brigadier general) was reprimanded for destroying Israa University in January 2024 without authorisation, though the IDF did claim the grounds had been used by Hamas. There were likely few places such a claim could not be made, and it probably was not the choice of Israa.

The D9 was a Caterpillar product modified by the Israelis with an armoured cab to protect the operator. This 'Dubi' was so tough as to seem indestructible, pushing through debris and IEDs, but was occasionally disabled by mines. Remotely controlled variants were also deployed. Its use in the demolition of Palestinian homes became controversial. The UN had advised Caterpillar that supplying these could make it complicit in human rights violations and there were civilian movements to divest from the company. The IDF sought additional D9s during the war and the USA administration held up the sale of 134 vehicles. They were delivered under the newly elected Trump administration.

The bungee-launched Skylark drones were used for artillery spotting. A new weapon was a 3kg (7lb) Spike Firefly 'Moaz' tube-launched rotorcraft drone capable of loitering, such as 'looking' into windows, before being directed by a soldier at a target to be attacked by the explosive device. Iron Sting was a 120mm mortar with the round a guided munition for accurate strikes, using GPS and a laser seeker. This was typically mounted in an M113 armoured personnel carrier (APC) or Humvee. SmartShooter was a counter-uncrewed air system (UAS, C-UAS) system with two assault rifles directed and fired by radio frequency detector and passive optics plus fire control system.

Presumably difficult Israeli leadership decisions were made to attack legitimate military targets, including single individuals, with knowledge scores of civilians would likely be killed regardless of mitigations exercised. Among the most visible of these controversial attacks was the 9 October 2023 bombing of a busy market inside the Jabaliya refugee camp targeting what Israel said was Hamas elements in a mosque within the camp. The attack killed over 60 persons. On 1 April 2024 Israeli UAVs fired on three World Food Kitchen vehicles, killing all seven workers moving food from the Israeli pier on the coast. Gross violations of rules-of-engagement were responsible, according to the IDF, and personnel were disciplined. International non-governmental organisations (NGO) delivering aid paused their work. A hostage rescue operation on 8 June 2024 in the Nuseirat refugee camp had encountered difficulties, with a firefight developing. Intense air, sea and ground fire support fell all around and entire residential blocks were shot-up. The Gaza Health Ministry summed 276 people killed and 698 injured, some likely military. Israel said it was aware of fewer than 100 casualties, but it had not stayed to count bodies.

On 10 September 2024 an area of the al-Mawasi refugee camp, filled with displaced persons in a makeshift encampment, was bombed. This had been identified by the IDF as a humanitarian safe zone it was urging residents to move to. The attack, executed without evacuation warnings, killed 19 to 40 and wounded 60 individuals. Israel said it was targeting senior Hamas personnel and a command-and-control centre. There seemed to be an endless number of these senior personnel and command-and-control centres, the latter perhaps being nothing more than someone with a cellphone peering out a window.

Whilst the IASF played a large role, most operations were not in direct support of ground operations, though hitting some targets identified by those personnel. In some instances strikes were within 200m (650ft) of friendlies, though it was also stated that fighter-bombers were delivering ordnance on targets within a couple dozen yards of friendlies.[17] Airdrop of water to troops on 10 and 11 December 2024 by 103 Squadron C-130s was likely indicative of hazards associated with overland transport. The Air Force seemed to have become an airborne demolition service, but this was sometimes exaggerated. The press would comment on daily 'bombing' and 'missiles' and 'strikes' when there were also naval gunfire and missiles, ground forces rockets and artillery, tank fire, infantry demolition charges, plus Hamas fire falling in civilian areas. (It had been estimated as many as 10 percent of rockets misfired and and/or fell short.[18])

Regardless, attacks that caused civilian suffering were a mix of legitimate hits on Hamas targets surrounded by civilians and their property, and a dismaying number of errors. The UN and many nations pressed for restraint and called for ceasefires. The USA administration of President Joe Biden suggested it would withhold 500lb and 2,000lb bombs that it felt were excessive for urban warfare when 250lb small diameter bombs (SDB) were available. The 1,000lb and 2,000lb bombs with PGM (Precision-Guided Munition) kits were particularly useful in penetrating to tunnels or largely destroying a building. Although delivery of 2,000lb bombs were deferred, a tremendous quantity of other munitions was replenished during the war. In the first 14 months the USA supplied $13.6 billion in munitions in almost 400 individual sales, though some on existing contracts. The US Congress also approved $14.5 billion in emergency aid to Israel.[19] When the new administration of Donald Trump took office in January 2025 it immediately authorised nearly $4 billion in emergency sales of munitions and any remaining hold on delivery of 2,000lb bombs was lifted. A $7.6 billion deal was negotiated to refill the Air Force's arsenal with particularly PGM bomb kits and AGM-114 Hellfire missiles. When the Trump administration placed a hold on all USA foreign aid to allow a 90-day review, Israel and Egypt were exempt.

The American administration's proposals for ceasefires were 'slow-rolled' by the Israeli government who wanted to 'finish the job' and because of internal politics.[20] In March 2024 the USA warned of consequences if Israel invaded Rafah where a million displaced persons had taken refuge amongst what Israel assessed as four Hamas battalions. It would support precision raids but not a large-scale offensive. Israel proceeded anyway via a gradual ramp-up that did not appear to be a concerted operation yet, over time, amounted to the same thing and with considerable civilian casualties. This showed the limits of American influence over Israeli defence actions and that support for Israel was becoming a political liability in an election year. There were large demonstrations against the war worldwide and exasperation that, had any nation but Israel prosecuted a war of such severity, USA aid would have been suspended and sanctions imposed.

President Joe Biden of the USA and Prime Minister Netanyahu of Israel met on 18 October 2023 following the Hamas attack. The two leaders had a sometimes tense relationship, but the USA provided generous aid to Israel during the war as approved by the President who stated he was a Zionist. (Public Domain)

A 105 Squadron F-16D is equipped with a Mk.84 2,000lb bomb with JDAM kit that, even as a PGM, was criticised as excessively destructive for urban combat. (Israel Air and Space Force)

3

EXPANDING WAR

On 7 October Hamas called for a jihad against Israel (call to arms to fight against enemies of Islam), all armed factions to join the fighting, and for uprisings in the West Bank and by Israeli Arabs. The war did bring attacks from other quarters as a 'support front'. Fire originated from Syria and Lebanon that was answered in the usual manner. The IASF struck threats in those nations as it had done in the past, particularly Iranian elements in Syria supporting Hezbollah operations. In the following year some 220 air and shelling attacks were recorded in which 300 individuals were killed. The Houthi Rebels in Yemen fired dozens of missiles and 'suicide' or 'kamikaze' drones (One-Way Attack UAV, OWA) at Israel over many months.[1] Almost all were intercepted by air defences. Apart from the alert ground-based air defences, the IASF also flew standing patrols and some intercepts were beyond Israel's borders. OWAs were also shot down by warships and aircraft of sympathetic nations including American, British and French assets in the region.

The Houthis also engaged commercial vessels passing their shores if, in their view, their nation of origin or destination in any way supported Israel. This brought USA and UK airstrikes on Houthi military infrastructure beginning on 13 January 2024, but all was restored over time by the Iranians and the irritant persisted.

Militants of the Islamic Resistance in Iraq, an Iranian-backed Shia group, fired rockets and OWAs towards Israel beginning in November 2023. The similar Popular Mobilization Forces, nominally part of the Iraqi army, also participated. They claimed to have targeted Mediterranean Sea traffic to Israel and the port of Haifa, in coordination with the Houthi, although any specific action was not evident. On 1 April 2024 one of their OWAs hit an Israeli Navy (IN) building in Eilat, close to impacting a warship at anchor. The Iraqis tried again the 8th but the drone was downed by the Sa'ar 6 corvette's C-Dome system, the marine version of Iron Dome and its first combat test. Their drone attacks resumed on 3 October 2024 with a strike on an IDF base on the Golan Heights, killing two soldiers. This effort continued at about five projectiles per day. There were rumours of Israeli strikes on the Popular Mobilization Forces in Iraq.

Israel's response to these attacks were predictable as it was beset from all sides. Netanyahu and his government went further and vowed that anyone who attacks Israel or 'harbours terrorists' would feel retribution. Netanyahu had worked for a decade to ensure that that IDF and the government was prepared to support these goals. His administration committed the IDF to persistent and extensive military actions far and wide to a scale never before experienced. 'Gloves were off' and it became clear the PM was seeking to fundamentally alter the Middle East order vis-à-vis Israel via extensive military action that was supported materially by the USA. The actions would be carried out even if it meant bringing international outrage and short-term sanctions.

ISRAEL-HEZBOLLAH EXCHANGES

Hezbollah in southern Lebanon, with assistance from Iran, began a low-level campaign of occasional shelling, rocketing, drone strikes and infiltration of northern Israel from 8 October 2023. Initially the Israeli government planned for a large response on this front, it appearing the organisation intended a 'war of attrition' via persistent

The Greek-registered oil tanker *Sounion* burns in the Red Sea on 14 September 2024 following attack by Houthi rebels, causing an oil spill. (European Union's Operation Aspides)

small-scale attacks. The initial IDF attacks were planned for the night of the 11th, and aircraft were in the air, but the operation was called off.[2] Netanyahu, in coordination with Biden, had decided against the course of action. Israel chose to hold there and focus on Gaza.

By January Hezbollah had fired some 2,000 projectiles across the Lebanese border and 30 from Syria. The IASF responded through March with some 1,000 airstrikes, some far north of the frontier. The cascade of rockets forced the evacuation of some 62,000 citizens that stretched over more than a year. Some 94,000 Lebanese civilians fled north. There were significant combat events every week, and thousands of smaller ones. Lebanese Army personnel and assets were also occasionally hit by IDF fire. By summer 2024, with some 400 Hezbollah fighters and 150 Lebanese civilians killed, the conflict was reaching a point where another war in Lebanon appeared imminent. Hezbollah had by then become the largest and best armed non-state military force in the world. Its more than 150,000 rockets, missiles and drones included systems that could reach any part of Israel. It had some 30,000–50,000 fighters, though perhaps half were of low quality.

This aspect of the war swung to and fro in level of violence, and Israel took the opportunity now and then to eliminate particularly threatening infrastructure, equipment and individuals, both in Lebanon and Syria. These brought the usual southbound rocket barrage and armed drone incursions in return. The OWAs hit IDF installations in the north of the country with reasonable precision. The IASF 'targeted killings' eliminated many Hezbollah leaders by various means. On 2 January 2024 Israeli bombs hit a neighbourhood in Beirut, killing a senior Hezbollah political figure. The group responded on the 6th with rocket strikes that the IDF stated caused significant damage to a 'strategic air base near Mount Meron', believed to mean the radar installation on the mountain.

On 14 May Hezbollah guerrillas hit a SkyStar aerostat in northern Galilee with antitank missiles. The balloon broke free and drifted over Lebanon before descending and being destroyed. On the 15th Hezbollah damaged a missile early warning aerostat in lower Galilee, 30km (20mi) from the border. Northern Command headquarters and a sensor tower beside the border were also targeted. The group was showing they could degrade the aerial threat detection array.

On 27 July 2024 some 30 rockets from Lebanon fell on a Druze village on the Golan Heights and killed 12 young people playing football whilst injuring 29.[3] Although Hezbollah denied responsibility and Lebanon condemned the act, Israel immediately vowed to respond. Airstrikes followed in the early morning darkness of the 28th with drone hits on an automobile. A bigger response on the 30th included an attack in Beirut said to have killed a top Hezbollah commander responsible for the Golan rocketing. Israel appears to have intentionally left it at that and, although Hezbollah vowed revenge, no strong reaction was forthcoming – likely hoping for a Gaza ceasefire as rationale not to strike. Yet, Hezbollah posted several videos allegedly from a UAV that had overflown Haifa and other communities, plus Ramat David Air Base (AB), unmolested. This supported warnings that the group could wreak significant havoc in Israel if prompted, with a barrage of rockets capable of reaching as far south as Tel Aviv and overwhelming air defences.

Beginning in the early hours of 25 August Israel launched a sizable series of air attacks on Hezbollah targets in southern Lebanon, with more than 100 aircraft, to pre-empt what they said was an imminent attack. Hezbollah responded with some 200 rockets and scores of drones which Israel insisted were countered with little damage inflicted. These targeted objectives only in Upper Galilee and the Golan Heights. Later in the day both sides said they had no intention of further action, and the region took a breath.

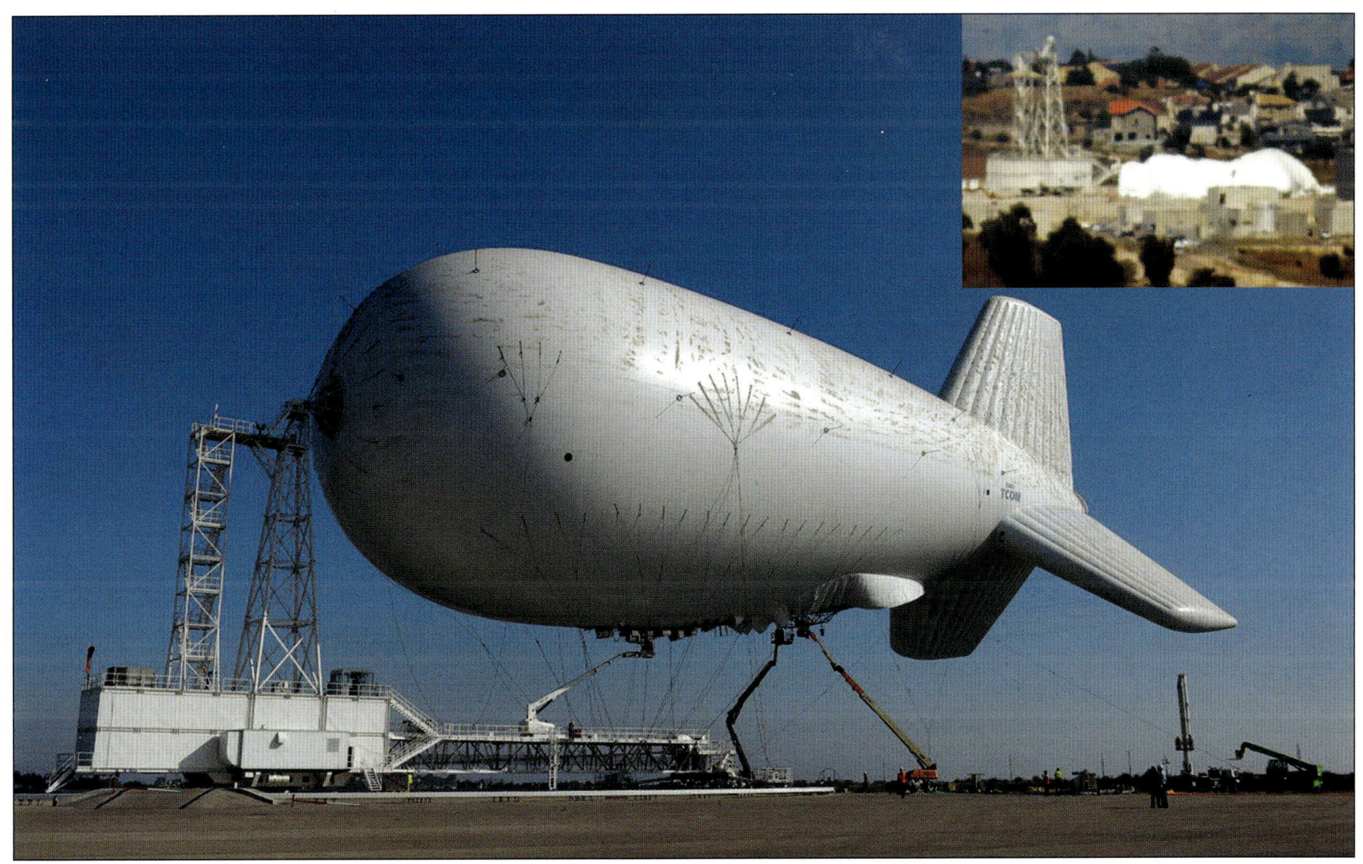

A TCOM Sky Dew high altitude aerostat is seen on 3 November 2021, probably during testing in the USA. The radar package on the bottom of the envelope has yet to be installed. The IASF subsequently employed two of these systems, one in the north and one in the south of the country. Inset is the state of the northern balloon after being damaged by a Hezbollah drone on 15 May 2024. (IDF Spokesman and Yaakev Hazmar)

EXCHANGES WITH IRAN

Iran was a concern to Israel beyond its support for Hezbollah and the Houthis. The IASF bombed the Damascus and Aleppo airports four times in October 2023 to prevent Iranian commercial aircraft bringing fighters to the area. Other strikes throughout Syria sought to inhibit shipments of arms to Hezbollah and to forestall Iranian actions. These led to the deaths of 10 senior Quds Force officers between 2 December 2023 and 2 February 2024. On 1 April 2024 the Iranian consulate building in Damascus, beside the embassy, was bombed in what was widely accepted to be an Israeli airstrike employing two Rampage missiles. Of the 10 people killed were six senior members of Quds Force with one a general officer in charge of covert operations. Also dying were Palestinian military leaders during what was believed to have been an operations planning meeting in the building that Israel claimed was actually a military headquarters.

Iran immediately blamed Israel, who did not claim responsibility (though widely accepted as 'who else?'), and vowed revenge. On many occasions the IDF used a period of intense combat to also take out worrying threats not immediately in the combat area so that any outrage would be somewhat muted by ongoing media clamour. Strikes in Lebanon and Syria during prior short bombing campaigns in Gaza had been common such events.

The uncertain nature of the expected Iranian response compelled Israeli civil defence measures to protect citizenry. To help confound the guidance of missiles and UAVs the IDF implemented periods of GPS jamming across the country. Allied nations also prepared to assist in defending Israel, some resources deployed into the region. These include American destroyers equipped with ABM systems (SM-3 Standard missiles), a Terminal High Altitude Area Defense (THAAD) battery sent to Israel, and fighter jets.

Hezbollah personnel pose beside mobile multiple-rocket launchers during an exercise. (Public Domain, Tasnim News Agency)

An example of IASF precision strike capability is illustrated in this photograph of the Iranian consulate building in Damascus, beside the embassy, moments after being bombed on 1 April 2024. The building has collapsed, but surrounding structures remain intact. (Rajanews)

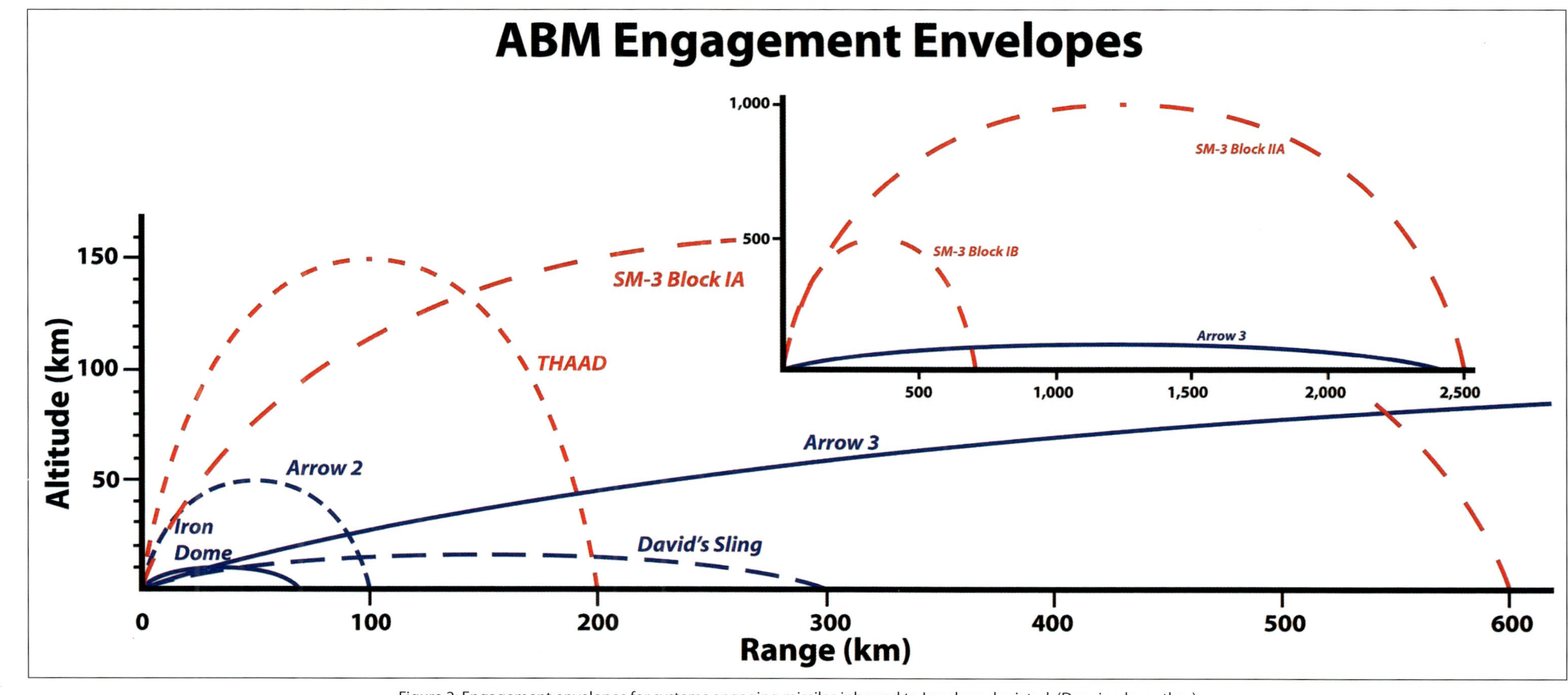

Figure 2: Engagement envelopes for systems engaging missiles inbound to Israel are depicted. (Drawing by author)

Haj Qasem
Range: 1,300km
Propellant: solid
Warhead: 500kg

Khaibar Shekan
Range: 1,300km
Propellant: solid
Warhead: 500kg
Sub-variants: Khaibar Shekan 1, Khaibar Shekan 2, Fattah 1

Emad Family
Range: 1,750km
Propellant: liquid
Warhead: 970kg
Sub-variants: Emad, Etemad

Shahab-3/Qadr/Qiam Family
Range: 1,350-1,950km
Propellant: liquid
Warhead: 700-1,000kg
Sub-variants: Shahab-3, Qadr-101/110, Qadr S, Qadr H, Qadr F, Qiam (no fins)

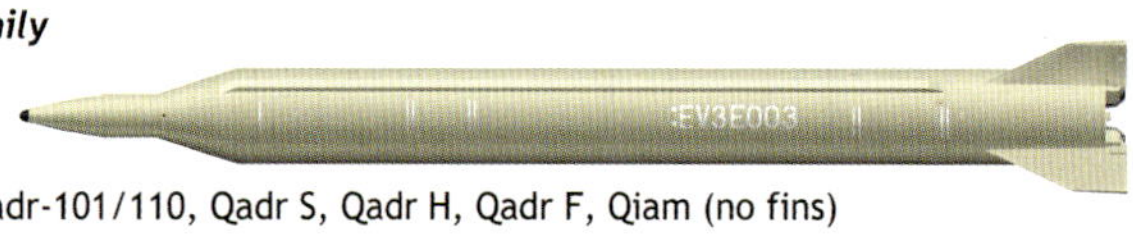

Sejil Family
Range: 2,000-2,500km

Propellant: solid
Warhead: 500-1,500kg
Sub-variants: Sejil-1, Sejil-2

Iran began employing ballistic missiles during the Iran-Iraq War of the 1980s to compensate for its meagre air force much hamstrung by sanctions and internal purges. These were initially Soviet short-range Scud-Bs that were reverse-engineered and manufactured as Shahab-1 and -2 rockets. A modified variant was the Qiam-1. Eager to move beyond these liquid-fuel systems to rockets with solid fuel motors, the Sejil emerged in the late 1990s to be followed by Zelzal, the Fattah series, and Zolfaghar. Iran then sought medium-range ballistic missiles (MRBM, 1,000–3,000km). This began with introduction of the Shahab-3, the first system with sufficient range to target Israel. Other liquid-fuelled systems followed, the Qadr series of similar design and range. The Emad was an improved Shahab-3 with 2,000km range and improved accuracy. Solid-fuelled MRBMs included the Haj Qasem and improved Qasem Basir, the Khaibar Shekan, Etemad, and Sejil-2. The Fattah series were reputed to be hypersonic, this and Khaibar Shekan warheads probably penetrating Israeli defences more frequently than others. (Artwork by Tom Cooper)

The penultimate Iranian IRBM was the Khorramshahr of 2,000km range that could deploy multiple warheads. By 2025 Iran had built a considerable industrial capacity to manufacture these missiles and fielded thousands as its principal deterrent force. Firing these at Israel, and the IASF efforts to destroy them in flight, became a unique aspect of the war and possibly a harbinger of things to come. (Artwork by Tom Cooper)

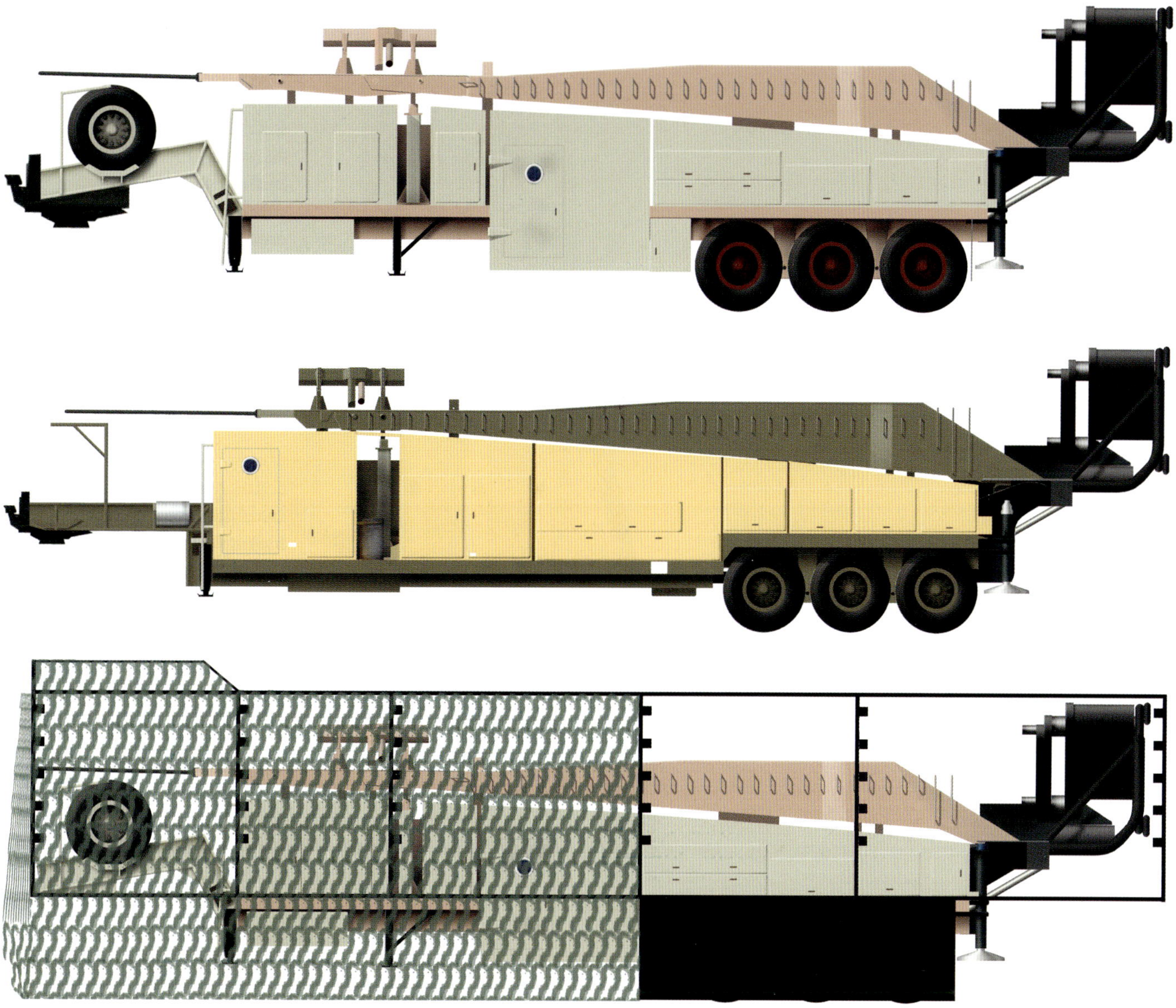

The most common means for the IRGCASF to employ its medium-range ballistic missiles was via a towed TEL with one rocket per vehicle. Once on site the tractor normally decoupled and moved away. The TEL was stabilised with jacks and the rocket raised for firing. Over the prior 15 years five generations of TELs were observed, all based on the chassis of the commercial 13.60m tilt-trailers, with a fire-control cabin and other support equipment. The heaviest had the reinforced arm to raise the Khorramshahr missile. Thanks to simple metal framing, they are easily concealed as commercial trucks, dozens of thousands of which were underway on Iran's motorways. Most conservative estimates are that over 300 had been manufactured by 2025. Shown at top is a second generation (Gen02) TEL, centre a Gen05, and bottom a Gen02 with camouflage addition to reduce potential for detection from the air. The Islamic Republic spent lavishly on such systems and Israel felt a considerable weight of these MRBMs in June 2025. (Artwork by David Bocquelet)

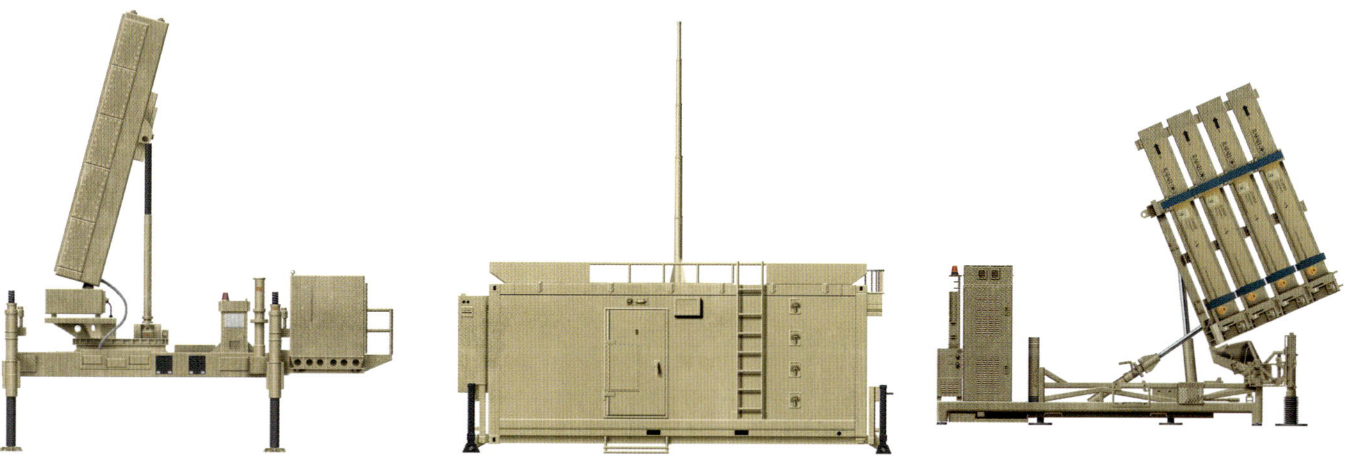

Israel's Iron Dome (Kippat Barzel) system employed an optically guided missile to engage radar-tracked projectiles. The road-mobile battery consisted of detection and tracking radar (left), the battle management and weapon control trailer (centre), and three to four missile firing units (right). The system discriminated targets on a trajectory for a populated area and engaged only those. Each firing unit had 20 Tamir missiles with an effective engagement range of 70km (44mi). (Artwork by David Bocquelet)

David's Sling filled the middle tier of the Israeli ground-based air defence array. Range was advertised as 300km (190mi), or approximately three times that of Iron Dome. The two-stage Stunner hit-to-kill interceptor missile was tube-launched from a trailer with 12 rounds, and several launch units comprise the battery. The system was designed to intercept anything from UAVs to ballistic missiles. Not shown is the radar and battle management & control unit. (Artwork by David Bocquelet)

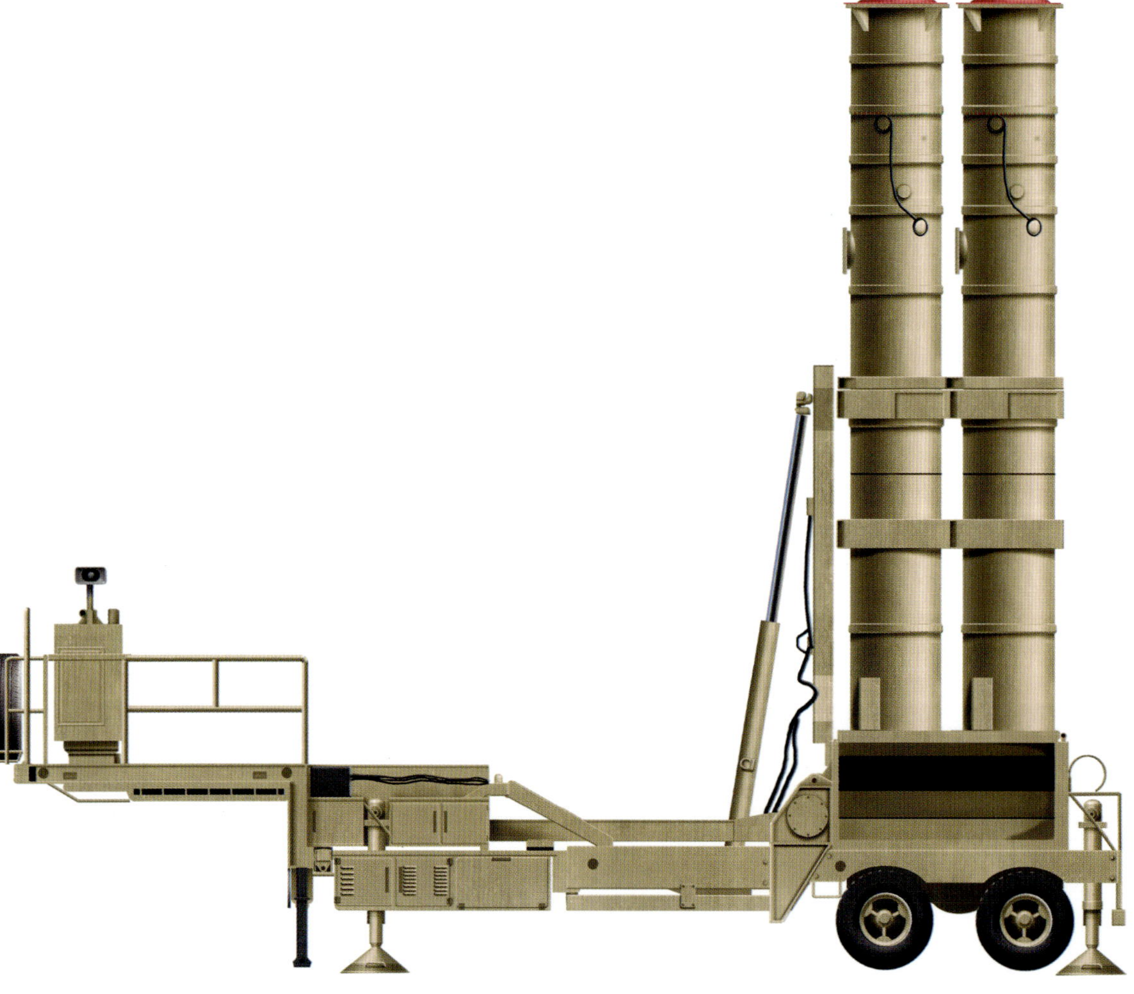

The Arrow (Hetz) anti-ballistic missile launch unit had six containers for interceptors, and there were typically four to eight units per battery. Fresh containers could be installed within an hour and 50 to 100 rounds were originally expected per battery. The system was road-transportable, but the elements needed to be erected on a prepared site. Two batteries were deployed by the time of the war. (Artwork by David Bocquelet)

The Iranian strike came on the night of 13/14 April when the Islamic government fired 120 ballistic missiles, 30 Paveh cruise missiles and 170 loitering munitions (Shahed-136 OWA) at Israel, according to the IDF Spokesman. Forces in Yemen, Iraq and Lebanon also fired rockets and drones at Israel during the attack for around 350 individual inbound projectiles. The launch of each type was timed such that all arrived approximately simultaneously. The scale of the event, with the most drones ever employed in a single attack in history to that time (soon eclipsed), was meant to overwhelm defences. The targets were the IDF installation on Mount Hermon, the Dimona nuclear site, Tel Aviv, plus Nevatim and Ramon ABs in the Negev where F-35Is and F-16Is were based that may have flown the Damascus strike. American, British, French, Jordanian and Israeli defence systems shot down 99 percent of the threats, save for those that malfunctioned and crashed prematurely. The USA claimed its forces destroyed six ballistic missiles and 80 drones near the Persian Gulf and over Jordan and Iraq. Several of the IASF intercepts were over Syria and drew Syrian air defence fire, and some over Jordan. (Jordan was reported to have opened its airspace to Israeli and American warplanes, and USA units were operating on Jordanian soil.[4])

Israel's multilayered air defence systems performed well in their most challenging workout yet. Initially the IDF reported that nine missiles reached their target area and a child was injured by debris. However, perhaps 32 projectiles struck Nevatim with only superficial damage to buildings, an unused runway and a C-130.[5] At Ramon four missiles struck with no remarkable damage inflicted. ABM defences did not extend to these bases.

Given that the Iranian attack was largely blunted, the international community urged Israel not to respond. However, leadership immediately stated it needed to retaliate to re-establish deterrence. This blow fell on 19 April when a flight of F-15Ds and/

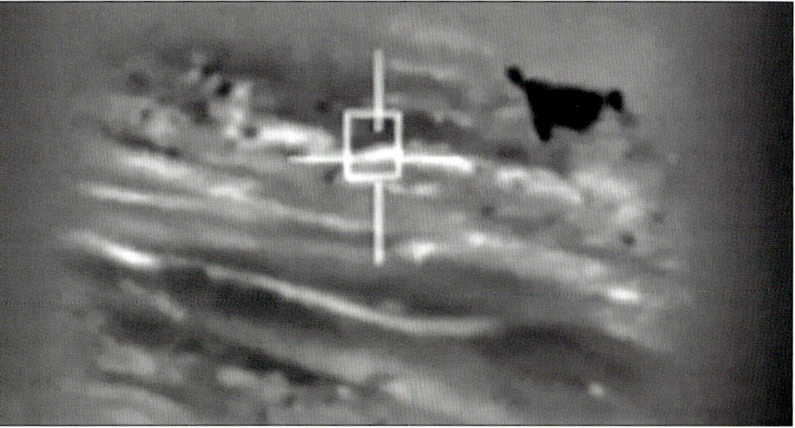

An Iranian Shahed-136 inbound to an Israeli target is seen in a head-up display video frame-grab during an intercept. At around 200kg (440lb) weight and 2.5m (8.2ft) length, and flying at a maximum 100kts, the uncrewed vehicle was a challenge to intercept. (IDF)

An F-15I stands ready on the night of 13/14 April 2024 to intercept missiles and drones inbound from Iran during the Israel-Hamas War. The aircraft is armed with AIM-120 and Python air-to-air missiles (AAM). (IDF Spokesman)

The propeller-driven Shahed-136 was a relatively simple OWA with sufficient range to fly (slowly) from Iran to Israel. The Iranians provided these to clients such as Hezbollah and Yemen. Hundreds were shot down but a few got through to torment Israel. (Artwork by Anderson Subtil)

or Is, and F-16Is (possibly 107 Squadron), fired what amounted to air-launched ballistic missiles at two targets inside Iran. The number of aircraft and rounds remained unclear at date of writing. The IS02 Rocks weapon, in likely its combat debut, was derived from the 1,900kg (4,200lb) Blue Sparrow ballistic missile simulator used in development of the Arrow system. As designed, the Rafael product had a large booster section for a lofted flight profile and a separating warhead acting as a re-entry vehicle. Rocks initially employed inertial/GPS guidance before resorting to EO for terrain scene matching or anti-radiation terminal guidance. Blast fragmentation and penetration warheads were options. The aircraft likely had centreline and inboard wing external tanks, the Rocks on one outboard station with a counterbalancing store on the opposite wing. Speculation was that the strike force overflew Jordan and Iraq. Preceding bombing of Syrian radar sites may have been to 'blind' defences to the flight. Rock booster sections were recovered east of Baghdad, suggesting a range of 700km (435mi) for the missiles. Launch aircraft were well outside the range of Iranian air defences. The radar of an S-300PMU-2 SAM system at Babaei AB, in Isfahan, was destroyed and possibly inert rounds from the F-16s were used to observe the Iranian ability to track and target the missiles. All this, with one target near a nuclear site, demonstrated the potential for the IASF to hit critical targets in any comprehensive future attack. Initially the Iranians said the nighttime attack had consisted of Israeli quadcopters – so unlikely that this was seen as justification for the ineffectual antiaircraft fire air defence forces threw up.

Iran chose not to react to the strike, easing concern of a major escalation. However, the operation demonstrated that a large match-up of these adversaries might be in Israel's favour.

On 31 July the Hamas political leader, Ismail Haniyeh, was killed by a bomb within a residence in Tehran. This also placed in jeopardy fragile ceasefire negotiations (one party murdering the other's negotiator) and was immediately blamed on Israel who was evidently not desirous of a ceasefire. (It was five months before Israel acknowledged it had committed the act.) Iran vowed revenge for this and the 30 July strike in Beirut that killed a top Hezbollah commander. Preparation included deploying Quds Force assets to Lebanon in anticipation of an expanded campaign against Israel. Commercial flights into Beirut and Al-Shayrat AB in Homs, Syria, delivering personnel and weapons, were observed by Israel. Within hours of the arms arriving, the Homs base was struck by 109 Squadron F-16Ds. Israel's September assault on Hezbollah (see later) was more incentive. Still, weeks went by with no Iranian action whilst Israel made ready and allies shuffled assets to help defend Israeli airspace. The Iranians appeared willing to let Hezbollah take the initiative, who said the tense uncertainty was part of the 'punishment.' Iran may have been hoping for a Gaza ceasefire as justification not to strike.

Some 180–200 missiles flew on the night of 1 October targeting Mossad headquarters in Jerusalem as well as Tel Nof and Nevatim ABs. Most of the projectiles were intercepted by American warships and British aircraft in the Gulf, and by IDF air defences. Perhaps 20 reached the ground. At Nevatim there was damage to buildings and a roadway, but no aircraft or personnel suffered. (Nevatim was still not covered by ABM.) Likewise, Tel Nof escaped significant damage. Civilian buildings and people (two killed) took the brunt of warheads reaching the ground or fragments raining down. The MoD was intentionally cagey about such enemy combat results, with

Under the wing of this F-16I, in a retouched photo, the Rocks flight test round shows the separable warhead at the forward end of a large booster. At the forward tip of the round is a fairing where an EO seeker could be placed. (Rafael)

reports continuing to change for months. With failures and those rockets intercepted by allied forces, the number penetrating Israeli airspace still overwhelmed available defences – most probably Iran's intention.

When the UN Secretary-General, Antonio Guterres, failed to unequivocally condemn the Iranian attack the Israeli government declared him *persona non grata*, barring him from the country. In the last quarter of 2024 Israeli authorities arrested over 30 citizens (mostly Jewish) accused of spying for Iran to include passing photographs of military sites which had assisted Iran in its targeting. Never had so many Israelis been detained for such crimes. Another arrest was made on 25 September, an Israeli-American accused of sharing information on public figures and sending images of locales. To that point there had been 25 cases investigated and 46 arrests made.

Israel immediately stated its intent to retaliate strongly. This raised tension inside Iran and residents began to relocate from Tehran. The government and nuclear site computer networks were subjected to relentless cyber-attacks. There was also evidence from leaked US defence documents of Israeli reconnaissance UAV operations over Iran. More than a week of planning and training, including consultation with USA leadership, came in preparation for the operation. In mid-October the USA deployed a second THAAD battery (of its total seven) along with its 100 uniformed personnel, positioned at Nevatim, to allow defences to respond more effectively to another strike. Military aircraft of friendly nations were also moved to the region.

The Israeli strikes came on the night of 25/26 October, Operation Days of Repentance, the USA stating that it did not participate. At least two waves of perhaps a total 150 attackers hit 20 military targets in three provinces. These encompassed missile production and air defences to include two more S-300PMU-2 radar units in Tehran. (The Americas and others had urged Israel to avoid hitting nuclear and oil industry sites.) These reduced the long-term threat to Israel and eased risks for airspace penetration in the event of further strikes. Iran tracked aircraft over Iraq and some penetrated Iranian airspace. Iran vowed a firm response which failed to materialise.

ISRAEL-YEMEN EXCHANGES

Of approximately 200 missiles and drones fired from Yemen, one got through on 19 July 2024 owing to human error. The OWA struck in the heart of Tel Aviv with minimal damage but killing one person and injuring 10. Israel responded the next day with fighter-bomber strikes on Houthi sites at the Hodeidah sea port on the Red Sea, Yemen, particularly hitting oil storage tanks and a power station that resulted in enormous fires. Operation Outstretched Arm, at 1,800km (1,120mi) range and flying nearly the entire length of the Red Sea, was one of the longest in the service's history. The mission was flown by F-35Is and some models of F-15, and with Boeing 707 tanker support. The undeterred Houthi then fired a missile on the 21st, though intercepted.

The 707 tanker fleet supported long-range IASF strike missions with operations in Yemen and Iran. Here 120 Squadron's aircraft 260 refuels a pair of F-35Is on their way to strike Iran on 18 June 2025. (IASF)

Three more Houthi ballistic missiles were fired at Tel Aviv during mid-September. Although all were intercepted, one of the rockets had targeted Netanyahu at Ben-Gurion on his return from addressing the UNGA. Israel hit back in the early morning hours of 30 September, striking Hodeidah Port and power plants in Ras Issa. A 1,900km (1,200mi) flight of the F-35Is to the target and back, was the Air Force's farthest combat mission since the 1985 operation over Tunis. The strike was repeated in the early hours of 19 December following additional missiles and drones fired by the Houthi. Israeli warplanes hit port and power generation targets near Sanaa. This was noted as employing Rampage and Popeye standoff missiles. The Popeye was then a very old weapon, not mentioned for more than a decade. Its use suggests the IASF was digging deep into its armoury to meet the high and sustained operations tempo. The rebels responded on the night of 20–21 December with a missile that managed to penetrate defences and fall in Jaffa, injuring 16 people. (In such attacks there were also commonly injuries to individuals scrambling for shelter and from panic attacks.)

Another inbound missile was intercepted on 24 December. The Israelis responded on the 26th with strikes with 25 aircraft in Sanaa that included the IAP and locations near Hodeidah that included power generation facilities. The airport suffered damage to the runway, tower and departure lounge. Yemen reported four persons killed and a dozen others wounded. Another strike occurred on 10 January.

The USA and UK began a concerted campaign against the Houthis on 15 March 2025 in an effort to dissuade them from attacking Red Sea traffic. Despite this the rebels resumed firing ballistic missiles at central Israel (intercepted) when the IDF resumed operations in the Gaza Strip on 18 March 2025 (see later). To that point the Houthi had launched 40 ballistic missiles and dozens of winged projectiles. They continued firing without success until 4 May 2025 when a missile impacted within the Ben-Gurion perimeter. This,

they claimed, was hypersonic and there was suspicion it also used a manoeuvrable warhead, both representing the latest Iranian ballistic missile technology and permitting them to evade several intercept attempts by Arrow. However, Israel stated that the system failed to intercept because of a 'technical issue.' The IASF replied on the night of 5 May with a 20-aircraft strike that included F-15Is, evidently coordinated with the Americans to deconflict. They hit a cement plant in Bajil, east of Hodeidah and the port itself. They returned the next day to bomb sites around the IAP, reportedly halting all operations and heavily damaged or destroyed three Yemenia Airways Airbus airliners.

Hours later, on 6 May, the USA announced it had reached agreement with the Houthis to cease attacks on vessels off its coast. This evidently did not include agreeing to suspend attacking Israel. The Houthis demonstrated this on the 9th with a missile attack that was intercepted by Israeli defences. On the 11th Israel issued a warning for civilians to evacuate three Yemeni ports, presumably in anticipation for an IASF attack that never materialised. Instead, another operation against Sanaa IAP was executed on 28 May after two Houthi missiles were intercepted the day prior. In the four strikes (presumably individual passes by one or more aircraft) the runway was hit again, the control tower demolished, and the last Yemenia aircraft destroyed. The airport had been operating for just a week following repairs of damage suffered on 5 May. Missiles continued to fly in small numbers during and after the June 2025 Iran-Israel War (see later). This eventually brought yet another IASF raid on the night of 6/7 July 2025. This hit ports and a power plant near the coast plus a cargo ship on which the defenders had placed a surveillance radar. The rebels also resumed attacks on vessels with any association to Israel. On 20 July 2025 the Eilat port suspended operations given the steep drop in revenue due to shipping avoiding the transit past Yemen. The business could not pay its municipal taxes and the government declined to loan sufficient funds.

An F-15D from 106 Squadron is in the final preparation for launch from Tel Nof AB on 19 December 2024 for a long-range strike in Yemen. The aircraft is armed with an AGM-142 Popeye missile under the starboard wing balanced by a fuel tank under the port wing. A targeting pod hangs on the fuselage centreline and an electronic-countermeasures pod under the port conformal fuel tank. (IDF Spokesman)

A US Navy F-35C aboard an aircraft carrier on 27 April 2024 is prepared for another mission against the Houthi Rebels in Yemen. (USA DoD)

The IN struck on 17 August hitting a Sanaa power station with missiles in response to drones launched a few days prior. An inbound Houthi rocket on the 22nd deployed multiple warheads. The Air Force responded on the 24th with more than 10 fighter-bombers hitting a military site with the presidential palace, two power stations, and a fuel storage locale. The farthest target was some 2,000km (1,240mi) from Israel. On the 28th the IASF returned to strike at least 10 sites in Sanaa evidently targeting members of the Houthi government. They managed to kill the Prime Minister, Ahmed Ghaleb al-Rahawi, during a meeting of senior personnel.

Although advertised as an 'unprecedented knockout blow' by Defense Minister Israel Katz, on 1 September the Houthi fired a ballistic missile at an Israeli oil tanker (Liberia-flagged). On 7 September a drone from Yemen struck the arrival hall of the Ramon Airport, causing modest damage and minor injuries to two individuals. There were no warning sirens set off at the airport. Though the drone had been detected it was not classified as hostile owing to human error. Other drones had been intercepted that day. Another Israeli airstrike on 10 September hit government compounds in Sanaa and elsewhere.

On 24 September a Houthi drone hit Eilat, wounding 22 individuals. An Iron Dome fault had prevented an interception. (A week before the same scenario had played out, but without casualties.) Israel responded the next day with the largest raid yet, the 19th of the conflict. Twenty fighter-bombers dropped 65 pieces of ordnance on seven military targets in and around Sanaa. Also participating were tankers and intelligence aircraft. Five headquarters and two arms depots were struck, killing, Katz claimed, dozens of personnel. The Houthis said at least eight were killed and more than 140 injured. Within hours Yemen then fired a ballistic missile at Israel that was intercepted.

Israeli airstrikes at Sanaa IAP on 28 May 2024 included destroying the control tower and the last of four Yemenia Airlines aircraft. (Ansar Media)

One of Israel's Sa'ar 6 corvettes lies at anchor at Eilat. It lacks identification markings and does not fly an ensign. It may have participated in an attack in Yemen on 17 August 2025. (IDF Spokesman)

That was around the 90th missile to have been sent north since March 2025 along with 41 drones (of a total about 150). The 9 October ceasefire in Gaza (Chapter 8) ended the exchanges that were appearing pointless.

PRESSING ON IN GAZA

Five months into the war, through March 2024, it appeared to be winding down. The IDF had hit 29,000 targets and Hamas resistance was fading. In that time the enemy launched 9,000 rockets. However, combat carried on for more than a year and after Netanyahu had promised the Rafah offensive was the worst of the fighting. The war may have wrought more death and destruction, mostly from the air, than any other in history in so short a time and in so confined a space. By April this was in excess of 70,000 tons of bombs. By summer as many as 4,000 targets had been hit in many thousands of sorties. The ability of fighter-bombers to remain over the area for extended periods given close proximity to their bases allowed them to respond quickly to time-sensitive targets located by UAVs and ground personnel – a matter of minutes. The IASF was openly mentioning 'drone strikes'; that is ordnance delivered by UAVs, a capability not previously admitted. Attack helicopters often tracked and engaged targets from across the border given the range of its missiles and the narrow width of the Strip. Even quadcopters were depositing grenades, other explosives, and shooting firearms.[6]

It was noted that 45 percent of ordnance employed by the Air Force were not PGMs. The IASF Deputy Commander explained that aircraft bombing systems were suitably accurate and that those weapons were principally employed on area targets where PGMs were not necessary. News also leaked that an AI program, The Gospel, was being used to help select targets, as well as another called Lavender. The service confirmed this but refuted claims that the output was not being closely examined before associated strike orders were issued. It also stated that the program gave measures of potential collateral damage and civilian casualties to aid in decisions to go ahead or alter the plan.

By a year into the Israel-Hamas War the potential for Israel achieving its goals appeared bleak, and the military said as much. Hamas fought on despite losing half its forces along with more than half the targeted senior leadership killed. In late summer a third of the enemy battalions remained effective whilst some previously destroyed were reconstituting. Areas previously pacified had to be re-entered once or twice more. Some 90 percent of the rocket stores were also claimed eliminated. Rockets still occasionally flew across the border, usually when it was important for Hamas to make clear they were still active. In this effort the IDF was laying waste to large segments of the Strip, displacing approximately 90 percent of the residents (most more than once), and killing tens of thousands of people, much to the horror of world viewers. Initial understanding of the need to react to the 7 October attack had dissipated and criticism was levelled at Israel for its excesses.

A week-long ceasefire beginning on 24 November 2023 saw 105 hostages released for 240 Palestinian prisoners. This particularly allowed Hamas to rid themselves of the most burdensome captives such as children, elderly people and those requiring medical care. This also had them appearing compassionate. The parties could not agree on terms for extending the truce and so fighting resumed on 1 December, the opponents determined to carry on. Four other hostages were released unilaterally by Hamas, and a few others freed in rescue operations, but around 80 remained captive. Some died whilst being held. Others were inadvertently killed in IDF actions and intentionally killed by their captors during rescue attempts. Rescue operations usually also resulted in scores of civilians becoming

An Israeli Apache gunship launches a Hellfire missile, such fire particularly assisting ground forces calling for air support. (IASF)

casualties. Some of the hostages remarked that the most terrifying moments during their captivity was enduring IASF bombing.

Coming to believe some of the deceased hostages had been buried in Gaza cemeteries, the IDF dug in 16 graveyards seeking these corpses. They reportedly also took corpses from morgues for examination. The desecration yielded nothing. There was also evidence the IDF used cemeteries as military posts and vehicle pathways. None of this played well in world media. That the militants had used cemeteries as rocket launch points is very likely.

Once again, in April 2024 after six months of fighting, it appeared the IDF had done all it could in Gaza. It estimated it had killed 12,000 enemy and wounded thousands more, or more than half the pre-war strength. By mid-May this had become approximately 14,000 dead. (The rounded numbers are indicative of the uncertainty in generating such figures.) The number of targets being engaged had dropped precipitously. Only one brigade remained in the enclave and most of the reservists had been released. However, on 5 May Hamas fired a rocket into Israel and there was fear it was seeking an attritional war. The Rafah offensive began the next day and the Army was busy again. With so few forces left, much of the Hamas battalions were able to slip away and continued to control most of Gaza. There was no end in sight.

Several proposals to increase aid deliveries all met with Israeli rejection. The aid crisis could have been resolved by Israel opening all crossings and permitting the usual number of trucks to enter, but it said it could not do this owing to ongoing combat operations. Members of Netanyahu's Cabinet and many in the public did not want *any* assistance going in, preferring collective punishment and starving the occupants into submission. So, the PM sought middle ground and insisted (unpersuasively) it was adequate.

Deliveries always fell desperately short of need. Instead of pressuring Israel to change policy, in March 2024 the USA proposed bringing aid in by sea from approved sources. Israel did construct an earthen pier for ships to offload cargo. To further facilitate this, the US Army brought across the ocean a floating dock and causeway where aid could be unloaded and then taken ashore on trucks. The effort required 1,000 personnel. Installation was opposite the Netzarim Corridor. Operation began in May, the cargo coming from Cyprus where it was inspected. The pier could accommodate 150 trucks a day, so not a full solution. It was damaged several times in rough seas and in July the project was concluded at a cost of $320 million and an American service member killed. During the 20 days of operation it had supported delivery of 8,800 metric tonnes.

Netanyahu announced on 23 June 2024 that the most intense period of the war was coming to an end, and forces were poised to take on Hezbollah in the north if required. That possibility and another exchange with Iran risked bringing the conflict closer to the regional war that all still feared could emerge.

The American floating dock and causeway is seen in place beside a Gaza beach on 16 May 2024. The pier near top of the image was the one the IDF built as a temporary measure. (Public Domain)

An Israeli M-109 fires into Gaza as these guns did there and into Lebanon on a frequent basis with tens of thousands of rounds. (IDF)

In early October renewed fighting in the northern Strip was underway when the first anniversary of the war was marked with Hamas rockets fired into Israel. More flew east to mark 2025 new year. Talk in the government of ever-more severe measures to bring Gaza and Hamas to heel did not initially gain traction. This included laying siege to the northern districts in an effort to starve-out Hamas personnel – along with everyone else. One minister called in November 2023 for Israel to drop a nuclear bomb on the Strip, but his comment saw him temporarily suspended from his duties by the PM – a rare rebuke by Netanyahu for inflammatory speech from members of his government.[7] There were also calls to annex the Strip, found new settlements, and declare the northern portion a closed military zone. These proposals were at least initially rejected.

The surge of fighting greatly impaired humanitarian relief deliveries and the UN warned of starvation of noncombatants being imminent. On 16 October 2024 the USA cautioned Israel that a suspension of military assistance, consistent with its laws, would follow if Israel did not permit a minimum number of relief trucks to enter the area within 30 days. After 30 days the USA assessed Israel was doing enough.

Haniyeh had been replaced as Hamas leader by Yahya Sinwar, who was perceived as more of a hardliner and whom Israel believed to have been a key architect of the 7 October 2023 attack. The IDF succeeded in killing Sinwar on 18 October 2024 and this was hailed as a potential 'off-ramp' to declare victory and accept a ceasefire. However, Netanyahu immediately insisted that the mission was incomplete, and Hamas stated no hostages would be released until Israel withdrew from the Strip and released Palestinian prisoners. At that time no negotiations had occurred for about a month. When they did resume in Qatar, a nation which served as mediator and hosted the meetings, Doha soon concluded the parties were not engaging constructively and withdrew. That the Israeli government was not doing everything possible to obtain quick release of the hostages was deeply disturbing to many of the citizenry. It undermined a long-standing expectation fundamental in the nation's consciousness.

The Hamas leader Yahya Sinwar is seen pre-war and just before his death on 16 October 2024. The smaller image is from a UAV video, the injured man in a damaged Gaza building. (IDF and Public Domain)

4

PIVOT NORTH

Israel had anticipated since the start of the war that it might have to undertake a large-scale operation against Hezbollah. Through April 2024 there had been 3,100 individual attacks emanating from Lebanon, and Hezbollah had begun shooting down IASF drones with SAMs. The IDF began to conduct training during spring 2024. The 810th Mountain Brigade was formed to suitably protect the Hermon outpost and Mount Dov (a.k.a. Shebaa Farms). The latter, on the Golan border, was Hezbollah's *casus belli* for confronting Israel. Israel insisted it was a disputed boundary between Lebanon and Syria (occupied Golan Heights) whilst Hezbollah said it was the last bit of Lebanese territory occupied by Israel.

The IDF initiated a significant reorientation in mid-September 2024 as ground forces began redeploying from Gaza to the northern frontier and reserve brigades were called-up in preparation for a potential ground offensive. With intelligence indicating Hezbollah was preparing a major campaign, Israel took out a senior commander with an airstrike in Beirut on 20 September. Days prior, on the 17th, there were hundreds of blasts from booby-trapped pagers purchased by Hezbollah to circumvent IDF monitoring of digital communications via cellphones. This was followed the next day by similar blasts from hundreds of walkie-talkies. Israel eventually took responsibility for these acts, having bobby-trapped the devices before delivery. The explosions injured thousands of individuals whilst killing but a handful. Many of those injured were innocents caught in the blast and so Israel was criticised for the indiscriminate act many saw as dastardly whilst Israel proudly talked of its cleverness.

ANOTHER LEBANON INVASION

Hezbollah was reeling from these blows when the IASF executed some 300 airstrikes by approximately 100 warplanes on 21 September and a similar number on the 22nd. These were said to have hit rocket launch sites that had been prepared for the imminent campaign. Hezbollah responded with approximately 100 projectiles falling near Haifa with minor damage and casualties. The group also attempted to target defence contractor Rafael's offices and Ramat David AB. The exchanges continued over the next week. Although claiming to be moving to a 'battle without limitations', on 25 September Hezbollah fired a single ballistic missile towards Tel Aviv – its first such attack on the major population centre. This, they said, targeted Mossad headquarters but was, likely as anticipated, intercepted. It was presumably meant to send a message of capabilities and, at least unspoken, restraint in hopes of staving off a war that would seriously undermine their organisation. However, Israel kept up the campaign with 700 killed (mostly civilians) including targeted strikes on senior Hezbollah leadership. As many as 100,000 civilians fled for safety in the north and Syria, and 200,000 more temporarily relocating from Beirut and surrounding areas.

Eight F-15Is struck underground Hezbollah headquarters sites in the early morning hours of 27 September, destroying or seriously damaging six buildings in a Beirut suburb. The Hezbollah tunnel complex across Lebanon rivalled that within Gaza in extent and sophistication. These were definite IDF targets. The attack killed Hezbollah founder and leader, Hassan Nasrallah, and other

This dramatic image was said to show a Hezbollah drone destroyed by an Israeli aircraft, likely by an air-to-air missile, in August 2024. (IDF Spokesman)

commanders as another grave setback to the organisation.[1] It was reported to have possibly been performed using a new deep-penetrating guided bomb recently delivered by the USA to reach the underground bunker. The 2,265kg (5,000lb) GBU-72 was likely dropped by an F-15I (eight participating). Other reports were that 2,000lb Joint Direct Attack Munitions (JDAM) were employed. The attack caused tremendous collateral damage. On the 28th Hezbollah fired rockets that fell in the West Bank environs of Jerusalem with little result.

Over the year of confrontation with Hezbollah, IDF special operation teams had conducted some 70 missions inside Lebanon to reconnoitre some 700 enemy positions and attacking some assets evidently intended to support infiltration into Israel. One that the IDF spoke about occurred on 8 September 2024 targeting an Iranian underground missile production complex at Masyaf, Syria. The deeply buried facility was believed to be nearing delivery of missiles with up to 300km (190mi) range. It was assaulted by 120 IASF Shaldag (Unit 5101) special operators supported by Unit 669 Aeromedical Evacuation Unit, airlifted by four Yas'urs helicopters flying up the Mediterranean coastline. This required aerial refuelling given that the target was in excess of 250km (150mi) from Israel, beyond Lebanon's northern border. Simultaneously, the IASF conducted airstrikes elsewhere in the country to distract

Lebanese are seen commemorating Hezbollah leader Hassan Nasrallah. (Tasman News Agency)

defences in addition to also hitting personnel at the targeted site. The team then eliminated remaining defenders before penetrating the complex. During approximately 2.5 hours the operators were on the ground they demolished the site and then withdrew without casualties.

On 30 September 2024 special operators paved the way for 36th Division to begin on 1 October what was described as a limited ground offensive. The goal was stated as creating conditions permitting evacuees from northern Galilee to return home. Lebanese residents of 30 villages south of the Awali River were

The Israeli KC-130H tankers had a vital role in aerial refuelling the assault helicopter fleet fitted with aerial refuelling probes – CH-53s and some UH-60s. This KC-130H 545 is refuelling a pair of 118 Squadron Sea Stallions. (Nir Ben-Yosef collection)

The Merkava tank was designed and built in Israel since the 1980s with crew survivability a key parameter. The latest variant, the Mk IV, features the Trophy Active Protection System to defeat anti-armour weapons such as guided missiles and RPGs. The smooth-bore 120mm main gun is supplemented with .50cal and 7.62mm machine guns plus 40mm grenade launchers. There was no tank-on-tank combat during the 2023–2025 war, so the Merkava provided flat-trajectory fire and its main threats were mines and anti-tank missiles fired by enemy ground personnel. (Artwork by David Bocquelet)

The Namer continued a long line of Israeli APCs based on tank chassis, in this case the Merkava IV. The .50cal machine gun could be controlled remotely from within the vehicle and a variety of other weapons were installed. As with its tank brother, the Namer was equipped with an active protection system. It could accommodate a dozen personnel, including a crew of three, with passage through a rear hatch. (Artwork by David Bocquelet)

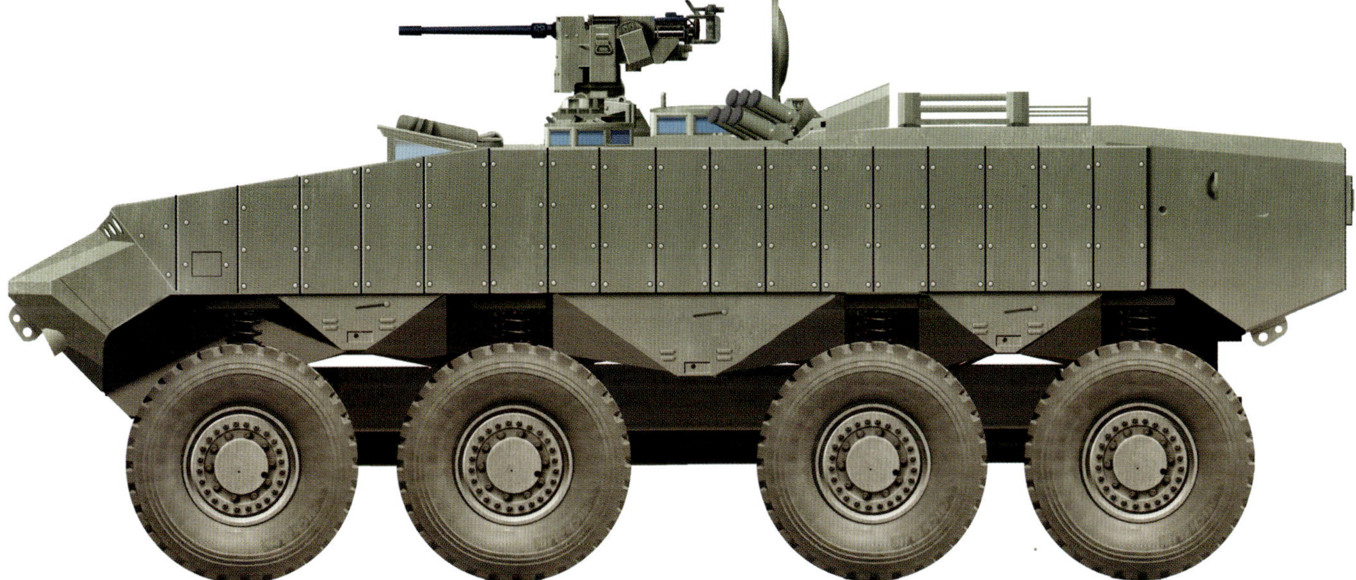

The Eitan APC was a wheeled vehicle with overall lighter weight than tracked APCs. The lower 'footprint' avoided the problem of broken tracks experienced more often in urban combat and not tearing-up surfaces as much. An active protection system, non-explosive reactive armour and other features increased protection for the dozen occupants. The Eitan was stilll new in 2023–2025 and so not available in large numbers. (Artwork by David Bocquelet)

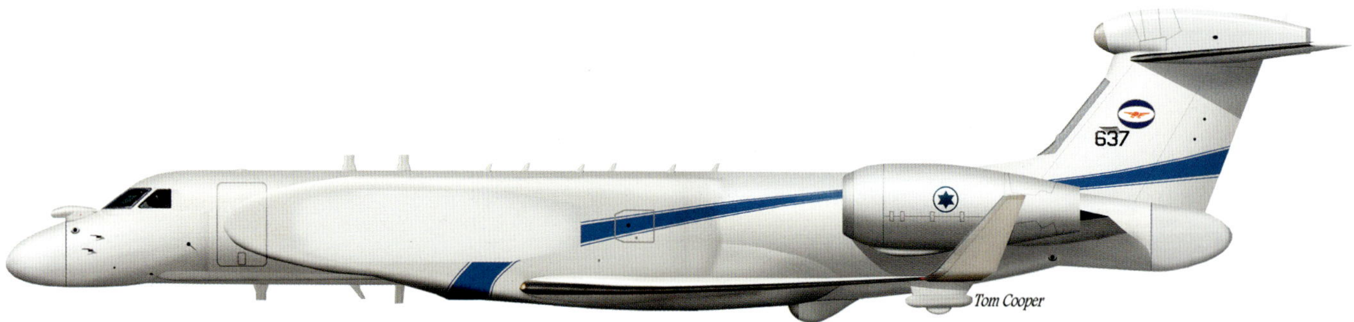

The modernization of the IASF's electronic warfare (EW) capabilities took a large step forward in the mid-2000s with acquisition of Gulfstream G-550s modified for the role. Named 'Eitam', the two aircraft principally provided airborne early warning services and so operated near active fronts, such as Iran, during combat. A third aircraft was an Oron configuration (shown) with more EW content. Aircraft 637 shows the minimal colour and markings and bears the 122 Squadron badge. (Artwork by Tom Cooper)

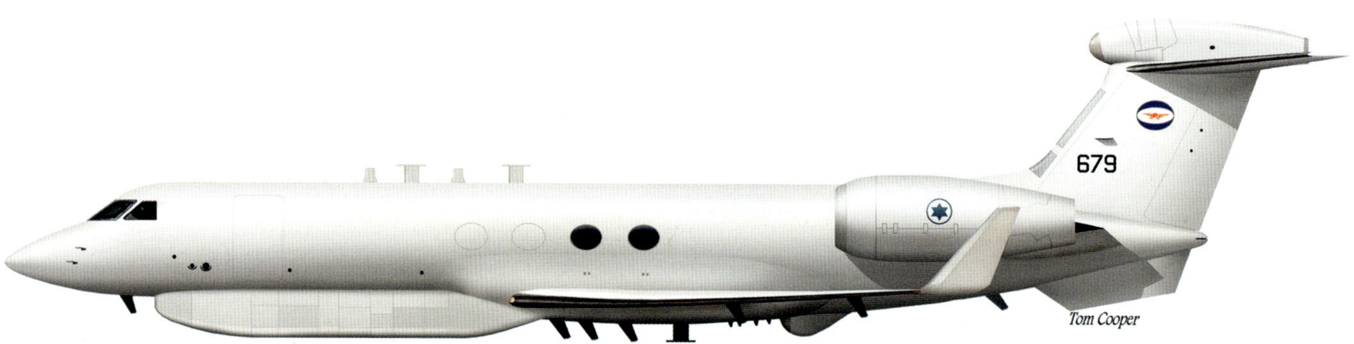

Dedicated airborne EW came via the Shavit signal intelligence (SIGINT) platforms based on the Gulfstream G-550 that offered extended endurance. These were also operated close to combat areas and had minimal markings for low-profile deployments beyond the borders. Ground-based EW resources and packages added to aircraft such as UAVs, helicopters and transports were also available. (Artwork by Tom Cooper)

Beechcraft Super King Air B200 number 622, from 100 Squadron, with tip tanks, is shown in an observation and communications support configuration in which it was operated over areas of combat or monitoring threats. This required numerous additional antennas for radio relay or flying command post missions. It has also been fitted with an electro-optical turret on its belly to monitor surface activity over land or sea. The Beechcraft could respond more quickly than UAVs, the onboard operator providing verbal input as well as image downlink. (Artwork by Tom Cooper)

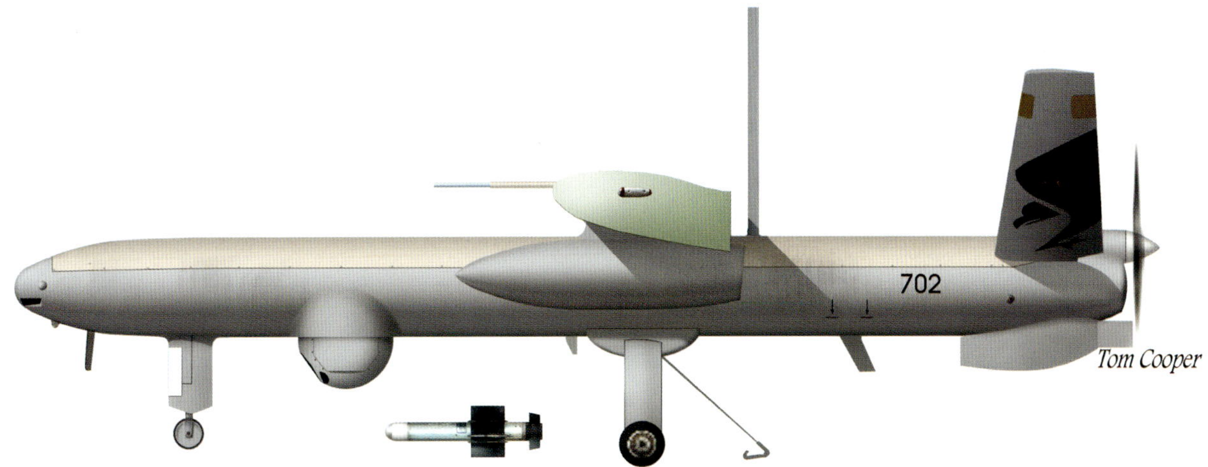

The Hermes 450S was a significant step up from the mini-RPVs to a semiautonomous UAV. Introduced in 2003, it continued flying into 2025. Revisions were seen as differences in bottom sensor domes from the mid-2000s. The Hermes 450S was recovered by arrestment wire and often had the tall antenna above the mid-fuselage. Aircraft 702 displays the tail markings of 166 Squadron based at Palmachim AB. It carries a pod under each wing first observed in May 2021 over the Gaza Strip. The Hermes 450s were also known to be optionally armed with a small missile called Mikholit (shown) for antipersonnel and soft target engagement. (Artwork by Tom Cooper)

The Hermes 900 Medium-Altitude/Long-Endurance UAV was introduced in 2016 and it was endlessly busy over Gaza and then elsewhere in 2023–2025. This UAV had a 318kg (700lb) payload and satellite communications (SATCOM) for very long-range operations. It possessed underwing carriage options and multiple, rapidly interchangeable sensor packages, and was regularly armed (note pod beneath wing). The aircraft depicted was shot down over Iran in June 2025. (Artwork by Tom Cooper)

Photo-reconnaissance was always important to the Israelis, and antiaircraft threats drove the adoption of drones. With the need for persistent observation for counter-terror operations, Israel became a world leader in such UAVs. The pinnacle of this evolution appeared in 2010 with the Heron TP, named Eitan by the IASF. It offered exceptionally long range and high altitude operation. This IAI Heron TP from 210 Squadron, has the EO turret rotated for takeoff and landing. (Artwork by Tom Cooper)

By the mid-2000s the Israeli attack helicopter fleet had come to rely entirely on AH-64 Apaches that were progressively upgraded, the ultimate being the AH-64D Apache Longbow. After much budgetary angst, a mix of new and remanufactured aircraft allowed the capability to be acquired. Aircraft 726 of 113 Squadron is shown ready for an extended duration combat mission with Hellfire missiles on the launch rails and external fuel tanks. Noteworthy is the SATCOM antenna dome above the stub wings, the IR jammer atop the helicopter, and the protruding self-defence antennas on the nose. (Artwork by Luca Canossa)

The Black Hawk became the standard troop helicopter in the air force in 2002. This Sikorsky UH-60L (a.k.a. S-70A) from 123 Squadron is finished in desert camouflage. It has the common IDF/AF yellow helicopter chevron plus the owl (Yanshuf) tail marking. Aircraft 587 is equipped with many of the Israeli self-defence systems added to its rotorcraft including all-around sensors and flare/chaff dispensers. (Artwork by Luca Canossa)

Since the 1970s Israeli S-65 and CH-53 heavy-lift rotorcraft have been painted in overall brown (FS30099). The aft fuselage yellow chevrons assist identification by ground forces to avoid fratricide incidents. Rotorcraft 048 is seen here with 118 Squadron markings. It has the stencil for the Yas'ur 2025 upgrade, subdued national markings, an aerial refuelling probe, the SATCOM antenna dome atop the aft fuselage, flare/chaff dispensers (more under the sponsons), and the full suite of self-defence sensors/antennas around the helicopter. (Artwork by Luca Canossa)

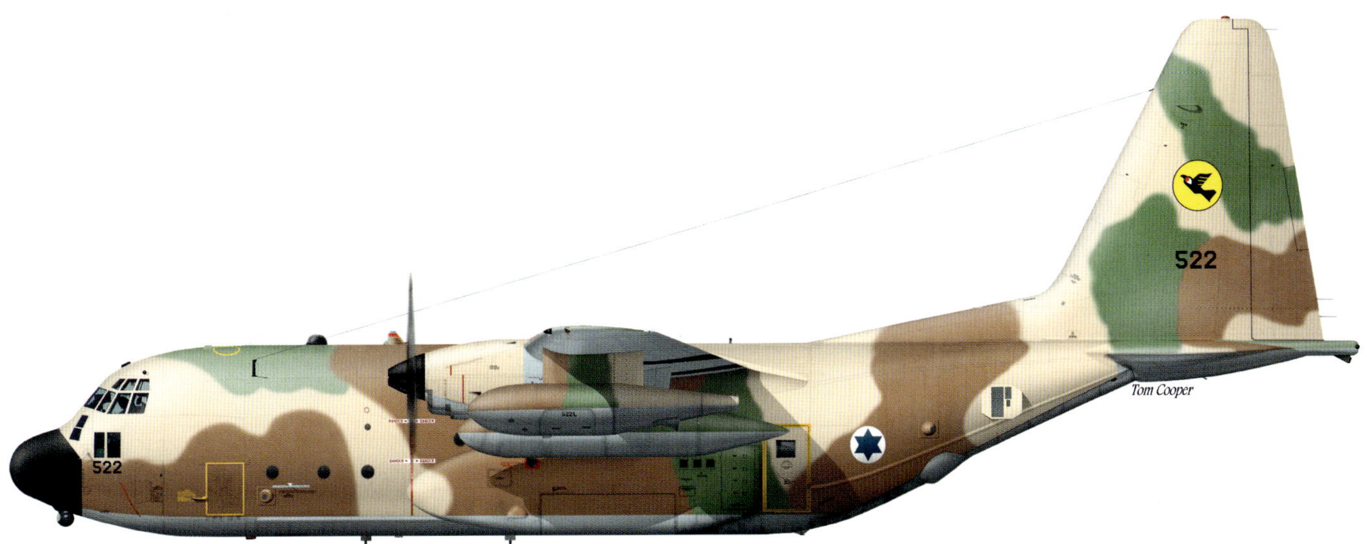

The IASF fleet of Hercules transports included five KC-130H tankers for refuelling assault helicopters fitted with aerial refuelling probes – CH-53s and some UH-60s. Before the war it was believed not all of the aircraft were operational, but this was likely corrected in short order. At least one long-range special operation required refuelling of the Yas'ur (CH-53) helicopters. Aircraft 522 bears the tail badge for 131 Squadron and has an electro-optical ball turret under the nose supporting low-light and low-altitude operations. (Artwork by Tom Cooper)

At the time of the war the IASF operated six tanker conversions of Boeing 707 airliners. These machines could refuel the Air Force's fighter-bombers given its aft end boom. Not all of the aging aircraft may have been operational at the time of the war, but this was surely rapidly made right. Aircraft 275 shows the typical finish for the Israeli 'KC-707s' throughout its long service life. The aircraft has a SATCOM antenna on the top centreline supporting long-range communications. (Artwork by Tom Cooper)

This 120 Squadron machine illustrates the meagre markings and a grey paint scheme adopted late in the 'KC-707' service. The jets were aged by 2023 and likely only conducted no more than two missions per day. However, these duties were vital given the many long-range missions with heavily loaded fighter-bombers. There were not enough Israeli AR assets for every long-range mission, so they were used prudently and likely supplemented with refuelling from USAF tankers. The extensive 'antenna farm' on aircraft 264 suggests additional roles such as airborne command and control (C^2). (Artwork by Tom Cooper)

Although the IASF has enjoyed air superiority over the most frequently targeted countries for decades, it does not take chances with possible encounters involving enemy fighters seeking to knock down Israeli attackers and surveillance platforms. Consequently, most missions have fighters equipped for air-to-air combat close by to respond as necessary. Fighters were also very busy knocking down attack UAVs inbound in the hundreds from multiple quarters. This F-15D (nose name 'Explosive Hand') of 133 Squadron at Tel Nof is configured for air-to-air with AIM-120Ds and Python 5s under the wing, all the latest air-to-air missiles. On the right-hand conformal fuel tank (CFT), forward station, is an older AIM-7R. The aircraft has also been upgraded as evident by the SATCOM antenna dome behind the rear cockpit. (Artwork by Tom Cooper)

The IASF F-15s date back to the 1970s, though most of the oldest airframes had been retired. The remaining F-15A/B/C/Ds were subjected to repeated upgrades to keep them relevant on current air war 'battlefields.' This F-15C (nose name 'Eitan') of 106 Squadron, based at Tel Nof AB, has CFTs in the wing 'arm pits' where a jammer pod and AIM-120D AMRAAM (Advanced Medium Range Air-to-Air Missile) is carried. The nose of an AIM-7R is visible on the opposite side forward mount, mixing old and new weapons on the jet. Wing pylon mounts a GBU-31 JDAM GPS-guided 'smart bomb' and Python 5 missile. The kill marking on the nose is for the 1985 Tunis mission employing GBU-15s. (Artwork by Tom Cooper)

With air-to-ground the order-of-the-day, air superiority fighters like the F-15 were most frequently seen with bomb and missiles suitable for the mission, often Israeli-developed ordnance. This F-15A (nose name 'Firecracker') carries a Spice 2000 (2,000lb bomb with precision-guided munition [PGM] kit) but also a jammer pod, Python and AIM-120C-7 missiles (upgraded As), and a centreline tank for extended mission range/endurance. Under-wing tanks could also be loaded. The Spice free-fall bomb had GPS guidance as well as an electro-optical seeker for man-in-the-loop directed end-game targeting. A Spice 1000 (1,000lb bomb) is also seen at front and, inset rear, a Spice 500 that also has deployable wings for extended range via glide. The aircraft has a Syrian kill roundel on the nose, earned in 1980. (Artwork by Tom Cooper)

The 2023–2025 war was an opportunity for the Israelis to introduce its new air-launched ballistic missiles in especially striking targets in Iran, a distant and vast country. The Rocks weapon is seen under the wing of this F-15D, but was carried by F-16s as well. It was probably around 1,900kg (4,000lb) and likely 700km (435mi) range. Without the option to carry wing external tanks such missions likely had minimal air-to-air missiles and required airborne refuelling. However, 706 of 106 Squadron is armed with AIM-120A and AIM-7R on CFTs. (Artwork by Tom Cooper)

Whilst UAVs provide a good bit of the reconnaissance capability, high-speed and rapid-response might be required via a fighter-bomber. This F-15D carries a centreline LOROP (Long Range Oblique Photography) camera pod called Ophir. Camera ships were operated by 133 Squadron. It is still loaded for any air-to-air encounters with Python 5 and AIM-120C-7. Aircraft 450 also bears the kill marking for the Tunis raid. (Artwork by Tom Cooper)

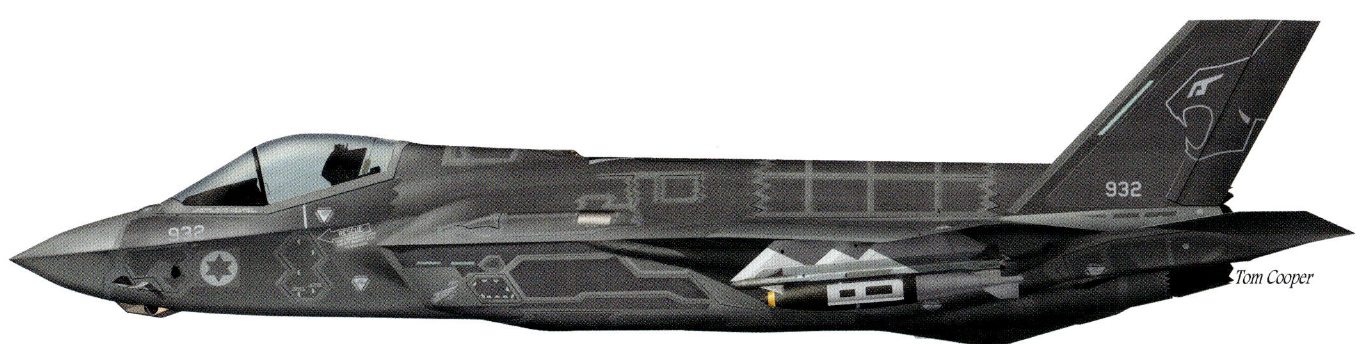

Three IASF units operated the stealth F-35I airplanes (conventional variant) from Nevatim. The low-observable characteristics may have been useful for some missions, but electronic warfare probably weighed more heavily in penetrating defended airspace. Consequently, flights with external stores (GBU-32s and AIM-9Xs shown) to increase strike potency were employed, a capability Israel matured during the war. (Artwork by Tom Cooper)

This Boeing F-15I, coded 205, is from 69 Squadron based at Hatzerim AB. It carries the full LANTIRN (Low Altitude Navigation and Targeting Infrared for Night) equipment suite and is fitted with a SATCOM antenna. The CFTs were always carried and, with no other external tanks and a heavy weapons load, this aircraft likely did not go far beyond the Israeli borders without aerial refuelling. It is shown armed with six 2,000lb GBU-31s fitted with JDAM (Joint Direct Attack Munition) kit, but the BLU-109 bomb possessing hardened case for penetrator performance ('bunker busting'). (Artwork by Tom Cooper)

The F-15I was procured especially for long-range, heavy weight, ground attack missions. Aircraft 246 carries a total 16 GBU-39 Small Diameter Bombs (SDB) on adapters. The GPS-guided bombs had pop-out wings for extended range. The relatively light weapon, with 250lb bomb, was well-suited for urban combat in that it reduced collateral damage and casualties. However, the primary motivation of carrying SDBs was hitting multiple targets with as many weapons on each jet as practical. The aircraft also has an AIM-120C. Most fighter-bombers had at least two AAM for contingencies. (Artwork by Tom Cooper)

Another new (introduced in early 2025) and relatively light weapon was the 350kg (770lb) Ice Breaker. This was powered and with wings for 300km (185mi) range, autonomously or manually guided. It could fly a low profile flight and, with low-observable qualities, reduced the potential for shoot-down. Aircraft 267 carries one on the middle CFT adapter and another is shown separately. The jet also has LANTIRN pods plus Python 5 missiles outboard, AMRAAM inboard, above the external tanks. A Spice 500 weapon is also shown. Light bombs like Ice Breaker and Spice 500 permitted more to be carried on a jet. (Artwork by Tom Cooper)

Every IASF fighter-bomber that could be put into the air was flown relentlessly over the two-year war. Aircrew, too. This old F-16C of 101 Squadron is prepared to deliver Spice 1000 bombs at long range given the three external tanks, yet it still carries IR-guided missiles. Indicative of high operations tempo and high weapons expenditure was the installation of old AIM-9Ms on F-16 wingtips: heavier Python 4s were usually carried on outboard underwing pylons as shown. (Artwork by Tom Cooper)

This F-16I, aircraft 874, is configured with SDBs on the dispenser/adapter. The 107 operated from Hatzerim AB. (Artwork by Tom Cooper)

The Delilah stand-off, optically-guided missile, required the centreline datalink pod. Aircraft 844 of 201 Squadron also has a Litening pod off the intake, a lesser LANTIRN-like system. The jet has a UAV kill marking from 2012, scored with a Python 5. Delilahs were deployed in large numbers to strike targets in Syria, but also against Hezbollah in Lebanon and the Houthi rebels in Yemen. (Artwork by Tom Cooper)

This Israel Air and Space Force F-16I of 119 Squadron is characteristic of the type, produced specifically for long-range missions with heavy ordnance and PGMs. It is armed with two Spice 500 precision-strike bombs and carries external tanks for a long-range strike mission such as executed over Iran and Yemen in June 2025. It also has AIM-120C-7 radar-guided missiles mounted at the wingtips, though the potential for air-to-air engagements on 2025 missions were very low. (Artwork by Tom Cooper)

Equipped similarly to its mate, 854 carries a Spice 1000 as well as a centreline tank. This was a typical configuration for long-range stand-off strike missions such as over Syria not requiring tanker support. 201 flew from Ramon AB. (Artwork by Tom Cooper)

This jet carries rocket-boosted Rampage stand-off missiles, Python 5s and AIM-120Cs. Large numbers of Rampage missiles were deployed to strike targets in Syria, early on, and then in Yemen and Iran. Aircraft 882 is shown as photographed while taking-off for a mission to hit Houthi targets in early 2025. (Artwork by Tom Cooper)

A 107 Squadron F-16I carries the large Air LORA air-launched ballistic missile, wingtip AMRAAM, the high-capacity Israeli wing external tanks, and a centreline tank, for an exceptionally heavy takeoff weight. The majority of missions with such loadings saw the F-16Is releasing Air LORAs at targets in Iran from high above the area between Ramadi and western Baghdad. (Artwork by Tom Cooper)

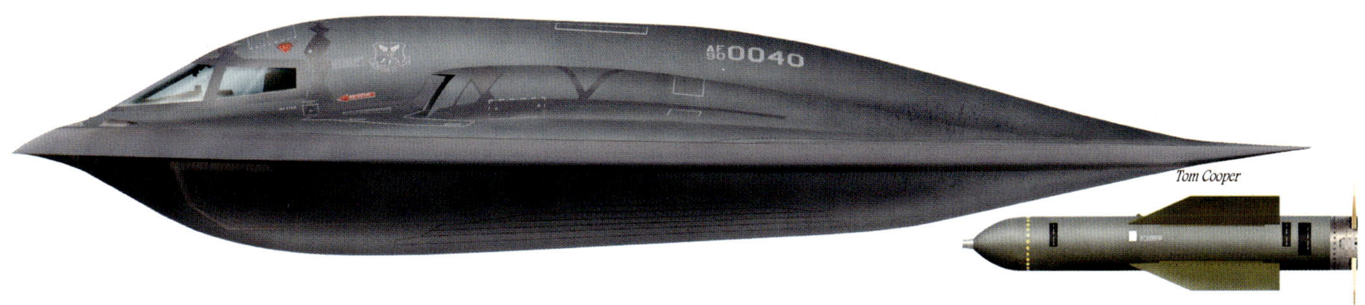

The American B-2A stealth bomber was employed for such missions as precision strikes on high-value targets. This was demonstrated on 22 June 2025 with the bombing of Iranian nuclear facilities. Each of the seven aircraft dropped two 30,000lb Massive Ordnance Penetrator (MOP) GBU-57 bombs (shown) after having flown from Missouri, the 509th Bomb Wing, and then returned. Israel had gone to war against Iran knowing it could not destroy the nuclear facilities, and so was soon asking the USA to act. Even then, the American weapons could not penetrate to the deepest Iranian targets. (Artwork by Tom Cooper)

Aerial refuelling of airborne assets was vital to extend range and endurance of combat aircraft. The USAF deployed dozens of KC-135 and newer KC-46A tankers (latter shown) into the region to support operations. There are strong indications these American aircraft also refuelled Israeli jets on long-range combat missions, particularly to Iran. Training for such refuelling had been performed many times in the past and within months of the war. (Artwork by Tom Cooper)

There is evidence some of the Israeli UAVs lost over Iran were shot down by Islamic Republic of Iran Air Force (IRIAF) interceptors, evidently only F-4E Phantom IIs (upgraded to Dowran II standard). Some boosted and glide weapons were also shot down. The very old aircraft carried equally old Fatter (Iranian upgraded AIM-9J-1 Sidewinder) and AIM-7E-2 Sparrow missiles, though possibly reconditioned in-country. (Artwork by Tom Cooper)

Iran was one customer for the superb Russian S-300 air defence system. (Russia was reluctant to deliver the system once ordered, for international diplomatic reasons, and was compelled only after losing an associated court case.) One of the towed transporter erector-launcher (TEL, 5P85TE2) with four missile canisters and MAZ tractor, is shown for Iran's medium-range S300PMU. Associated equipment is a mobile command and control centre and a radar unit. The Israelis made such equipment primary targets when they first began attacking Iran. The IASF claimed to have destroyed all three of Iran's very costly S-300s. (Artwork by David Bocquelet)

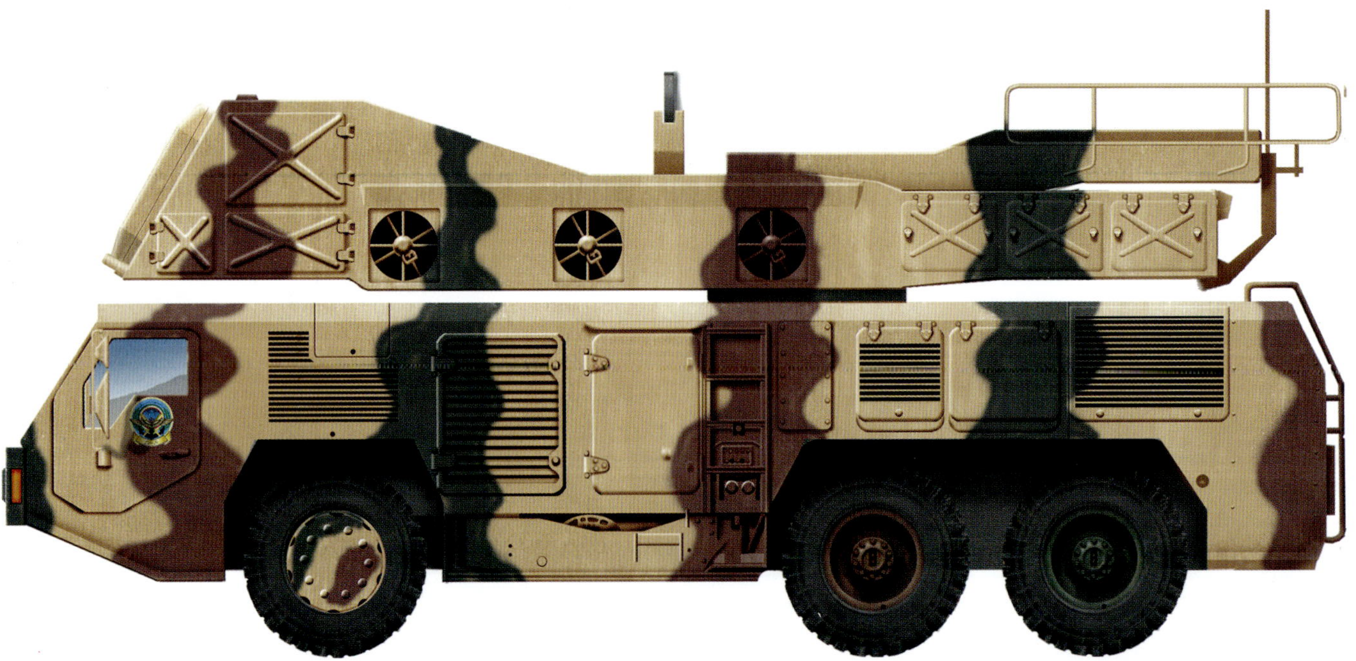

The 3rd Khordad was a medium-range air defence system developed and manufactured in Iran, with the assistance of China, which the Israelis and Americans had to deal with. It was based on the Soviet/Russian Buk system. Shown is the transporter erector-launcher and radar (TELAR) vehicle for three Taer-2B interceptors at 1,000kg (2,200lb) with a range of 90–105km (55–65mi) or Taer-3 at 1,400kg (3,090lb) and 100+km (62+mi). There were other radar and TEL units. The system was operated by the Islamic Revolutionary Guard Corps Aerospace Forces (IRGCASF) and is reputed to have shot down an American MQ-4C drone over the Strait of Hormuz. As this unit was mobile, targeting was more difficult. The IASF did well with EW jamming but worked to destroy as much of such equipment as able with disputed results. (Artwork by David Bocquelet)

A newer Iranian air defence system was the long-range Talash (or Talaash) based initially on the Soviet/Russian Kub. The mobile Hafez 3D is the fire-control PESA (passive electronically scanned array) radar for the Talash SAM (surface-to-air missile) system. The Talash was developed on the basis of Iranian experience with MIM-23B I-HAWK and RIM-66 Standard. Maximum target acquisition range was 300km (185mi) and there were two such units per battery. Unsurprisingly, and although developed in cooperation with the People's Republic of China, its Sayyad-2 and Sayyad-3 missiles have an aerodynamic configuration derived from that of the RIM-66. This and other systems provided a layered defence that required considerable effort to overpower. (Artwork by David Bocquelet)

The Talash fires four Sayyad-2 or -3 interceptors from each TEL, on 6x6 truck chassis, such as shown. There were three TELs per battery. Engagement range, depending on model of interceptor missile, was advertised as 90–104km (55–65mi). The Iranians claimed the system had an anti-ballistic missile (ABM) capability. By 2025 the Talash was augmented by service entry of the similar Khordad-15. (Artwork by David Bocquelet)

Iran's Bavar 373 SAM system employed TELs such as the one shown to complicate targeting of this element. The locally developed system (with Chinese assistance) was claimed to be competitive with the Russian S-300 system, at least in its long range (approximately 200km/125mi, though during an October 2022 test its Sayyad-4 interceptor demonstrated 347km/216mi). The TEL has containers for four Sayyad-4 missiles and there were six TELs per battery mounted on the Zoljanah 10x10 truck. The system was the longest-range Air Defence Force (IRIADF) surface-to-air missile and two batteries were operational in June 2025. How much trouble the Bavar 373 caused the Israelis during the 12 days of air combat over Iran is unclear, but they did not bring down any inhabited aircraft. The two Bavar 373 battalions were a significant threat and were targeted by the IASF, but claims of success were unsubstantiated. (Artwork by David Bocquelet)

The map depicts the nations and territories engaged by Israel during the 2023–2025 war. Most were visited by Israeli combat aircraft and replied with rockets and drones. Israeli ground forces were active in the Gaza Strip, West Bank, southern Lebanon and southern Syria. Special operations forces conducted pinpoint raids beyond those areas. (Map by George Anderson)

advised to leave. On 2 October bombs fell on central Beirut for the first time since 2006 and more followed in the coming weeks. As the IDF and Hezbollah engaged in significant combat, on the 3rd Israel was talking of sending in another division, suggesting an expansion of the operation. On the 4th a key border crossing between Lebanon and Syria was bombed to slow the flow of armaments to the enemy. Rockets continued to fly southward whilst Iran vowed to bring all regional resistance forces to bear on their enemy.

On 6 October Hezbollah rounds landed in Haifa. On the 7th, the first anniversary of the war in Gaza, Hezbollah fired 240 rockets into Israel and the IDF responded with even heavier bombing of Beirut's largely-Shia southern suburb, targeting enemy buildings and tunnels. The reserve 146th Division began operating north of the border on the 8th and another reserve brigade committed on the 18th. Hezbollah's most successful attack occurred on the 13th when an OWA got through defences and hit a Golani Brigade training base approximately halfway between the border and Tel Aviv. Four soldiers were killed and some 60 injured. On the 19th a drone targeting the PM's residence in Caesarea struck the home, though Netanyahu and his family were not present. This result was days before being announced, reflecting an Israeli policy to avoid acknowledging enemy successes for both tactical and political reasons.

Talk of a 21-day ceasefire, seeking to avert an all-out regional war, gained no traction with Israeli leadership who felt the IDF was gravely degrading the northern threat. Yet, Hezbollah struggled to respond as its leadership had been decimated and Israeli intelligence agencies appeared to have penetrated the organisation to a disturbing extent. Further bombing in Beirut and in the Beka'a Valley targeted armouries and infrastructure to keep the organisation reeling. Some 320 rockets were fired on 12–13 October, continuing to place at risk towns and military installations. Two weeks of Israeli bombing had displaced upwards of a million people. Sometimes evacuation warnings were issued, sometimes not. Approximately 1,300 people were killed, a toll surpassing that of the 34-day 2006 war and

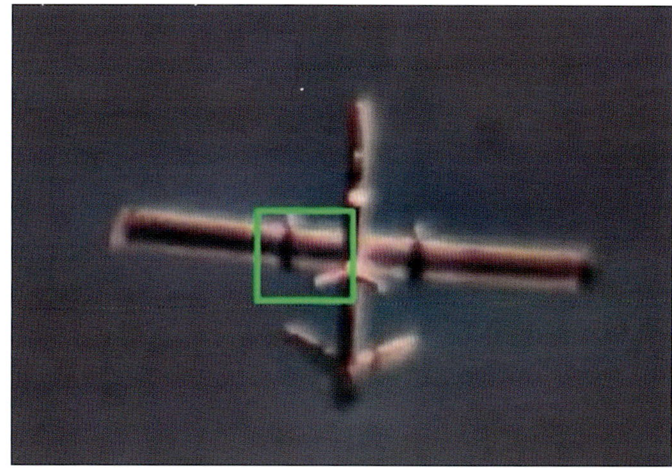

Allegedly an image of an IASF Hermes 450 over Lebanon taken by Hezbollah personnel on the ground, the targeting box is likely superimposed for dramatic effect. (Hezbollah)

suggesting that fewer restraints were being observed to reduce civilian casualties.

The Israeli operation in southern Lebanon had injured several United Nations Interim Force in Lebanon (UNIFIL) personnel, and the organisation protested. On 13 October Israel advised the UN to withdraw the mission altogether. On 2 November a commando raid captured a senior Hezbollah individual at Batroun, some 50km (30mi) north of Beirut. By November the IDF staff was signalling that it had done all it believed it could in the north, yet operations continued principally for political reasons. On 13 November the MoD announced another expansion of the ground campaign and that any ceasefire must see Hezbollah disarm and move all assets north of the Litani River. Rockets continued to fly south and civilian casualties in Lebanon exceeded 2,600 killed and 12,000 injured.

By late November the Israeli ground campaign in Lebanon had exceeded its 'limited' scope and advanced to the Litani River. A 60-day ceasefire was declared on the 27th during which the terms of the 2006 ceasefire were to be implemented. This required Israel

Israeli combat personnel and a Namer APC advance into Lebanon during Israeli ground offensive in the country during 2025. The vehicle mounts a CARPET rocket projector on the rear, used to clear minefields. (IDF)

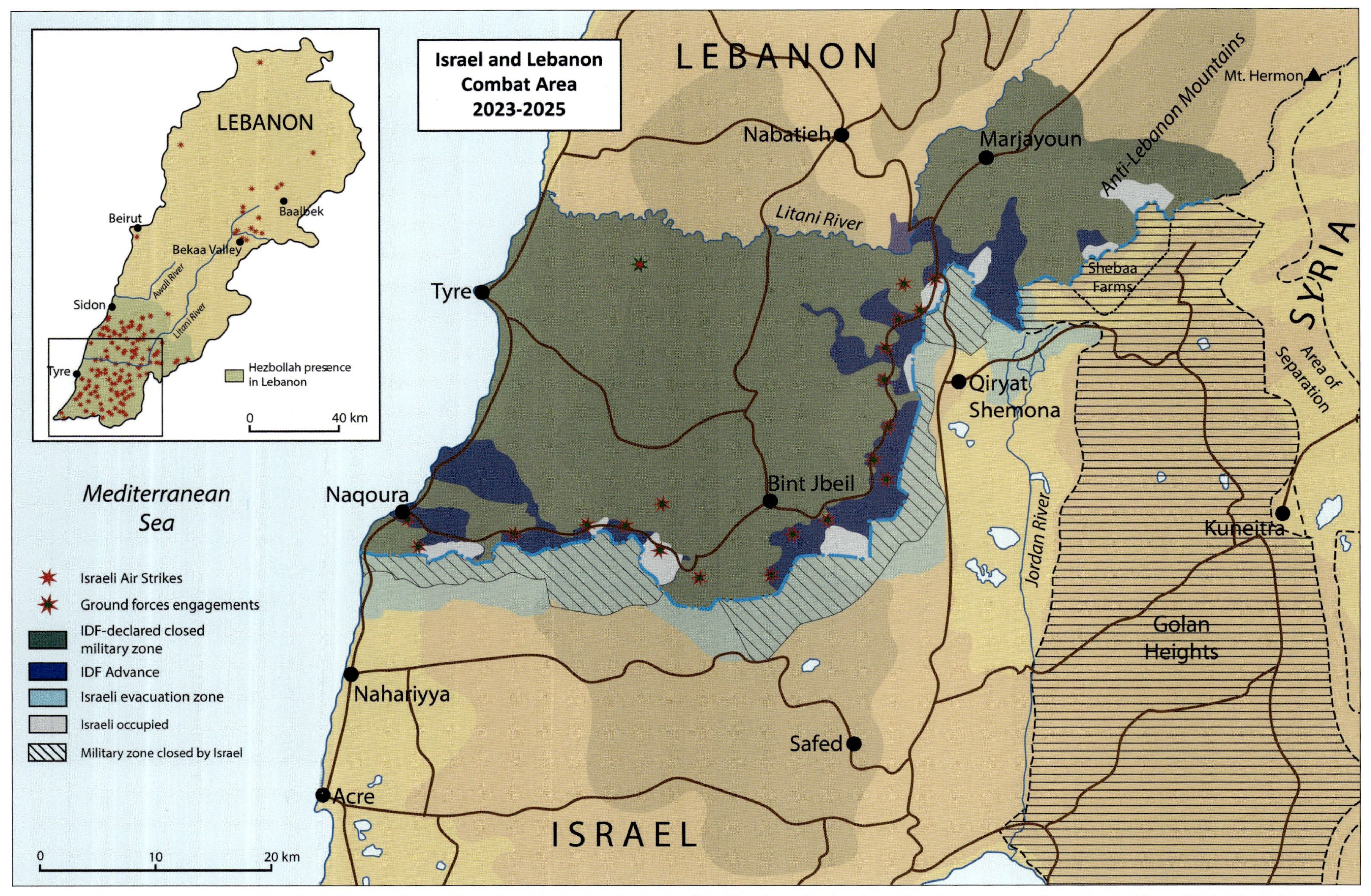

It is notable that Israeli penetrations of the Hezbollah operating area in southern Lebanon were localised and significantly smaller than that achieved in prior decades by similar-sized forces. This is either indicative of exceptional caution or the severity of the battles. (Map by George Anderson)

to withdraw its forces from the country, Hezbollah to evacuate to north of the Awali, and the Lebanese Army to move into the area to, with assistance from UNIFIL, enforce terms of the ceasefire. In the final hours before the ceasefire began the IASF conducted a final torrent of strikes near Beirut city centre. Within a day the IASF was bombing Hezbollah elements in the exclusion zone and, days later, Hezbollah fired rockets across the frontier. However, the situation soon stabilised.

Lebanon counted 4,047 persons killed and 16,638 injured, mostly via IASF action. The IDF counted 300 Hezbollah fighters killed and more than 7,000 wounded, plus 557 individuals in Syria of whom approximately 70 were civilians. During the long northern front combat 60 IDF personnel were killed, 31 inside Israel, and 46 civilians also fatally injured. Some 5,000 rockets and missiles had passed across the border, mostly southbound, during the 14 months of hostilities. By the end of October 2024 Lebanese officials had counted more than 11,000 individual airstrikes.

The Lebanese government struggled to acquire the resources to assume full control of the south and sought assistance. On 5 September the Army offered a plan for peacefully disarming Hezbollah by the end of the year, or start the disarmament by then. The IDF failed to leave southern Lebanon by the 26 January 2025 deadline, saying that the Lebanese military deployment into the south, and Hezbollah withdrawal, was going too slowly. It expressed a need to remain in the area for an additional 30 days. Israel said Hezbollah elements were still active south of the Litani and the IDF engaged targets on occasion. It set down in two buffer zones and five locations. Its sappers blew-up homes and other buildings in the area claimed to be part of Hezbollah infrastructure, though this extended at times to virtually razing entire villages. On 18 February Israel stated that it needed to retain outposts for another month.

Residents of northern Galilee were hesitant to return home, and the IDF prevented Lebanese residents returning to theirs. Militants fired rockets into Galilee after the January–March 2025 ceasefire in Gaza was breached (see later). This brought a flurry of airstrikes on 22 March. The IDF continued to engage Hezbollah assets and individuals throughout the country and inside Beirut on occasion, usually via bombing. The UNIFIL counted dozens of ceasefire violations, most committed by Israel. The peacekeepers themselves were fired on several times by the IDF. By the end of November the UN had counted scores of attacks (1,600 by another count, nearly daily) that had left 300 dead, 127 noncombatants. That month the IDF had killed Hezbollah's Chief-of-Staff Haytham Ali Tabatabai. And on it went into 2026. The Lebanese Army stated on 8 January 2026 that it had completed the first phase of the disarmament having taken operational control in the south of the Litani and was continuing to collect arms that had been 'confined.' Israel emphasised that the disarmament was barely evident and Hezbollah was working to build back up.

By the end of May 2025 the IDF still occupied five sites across the Blue Line to monitor the situation and stated that it would likely be an indefinite stay. Netanyahu appeared to be leaning towards a phased pullout if progress was being made on the ceasefire terms but was working against what appeared to him to be an effort by Hezbollah to regroup. Lebanon protested angrily that Israel's almost-daily bombing was limiting its ability to re-establish sovereignty in the area and for the Army to continue disarming Hezbollah. It warned that Hezbollah could insist it still had a role to play in pushing the enemy over the border. The government pointed out Israel had many means to monitor the area without being onsite. In early February 2026 the IASF began spraying an unknown chemical from aircraft over southern Lebanon and southern Syria. It warned

UNIFIL to cease patrolling in those areas but, other than saying it was non-toxic, did not reveal the nature of the chemical that spread onto towns and agriculture. Some of the ceasefire violations were seen by Lebanon as pressure to recognise Israel or join the Abraham Accords. Whilst there were direct negotiations between the states, Lebanon considered the attacks aggressive blackmail.

On 28 August 2025 the UN Security Council agreed to disband the UNIFIL peacekeeping mission in southern Lebanon, there since 1978, within 16 months. It then numbered 10,800 personnel. That southern Lebanon would become peaceful appeared doubtful. It was all quite fraught in that, given Shiite support for Hezbollah and resistance to disarmament, the country could slide into another period of civil strife.

CHANGES ON THE SYRIAN FRONT

The IASF was not finished with Syria, returning to Damascus on 2 October 2024 to hit a residential building that saw three killed and three wounded. However, monumental changes were in the offing. During late November Syrian rebel forces abruptly launched a large-scale offensive after years of near-dormancy. This was chiefly made possible by the ongoing Middle East war, taking advantage of a government battered by Israeli actions, a greatly diminished Hezbollah, Iran focused on striking Israel, and Russian preoccupation with its resource-draining war in Ukraine. In 11 days the rebels seized major cities. On 8 December the Syrian Army collapsed, and President Bashar al-Assad had fled the country.

Israel, concerned that these forces might continue rolling south, occupied the UN zone, separating the occupied Golan Heights and the rest of Syria, as a precautionary measure. During late summer 2024 Israel had begun earthmoving to create a miles-long berm within the zone, in violation of the 1974 disengagement-of-forces agreement. This may have been in anticipation of renewed fighting in Syria. With the many disparate armed groups in the country, the conflict in Syria was unlikely to end quickly whilst a new government was being formed. That the change in government would greatly undermine Iranian influence was seen as a win in Israel. The Russian mission was also likely to withdraw.

There was a fair chance the new government in Syria would be jihadist and fundamentalist Islamic, which Israelis took as an article of faith would threaten their security. Consequently, it moved to eliminate weapons Syrian forces might bring to bear against Israel. The first attacks occurred on 9 December with the IASF hitting Syria's chemical weapons assets. On the 9th and 10th some 350 aircraft sorties and 130 strikes worked to eliminate tactical resources – the IDF later summarised these as 500 strikes. Targeted were warplanes, drones, air base assets, ballistic missiles, air defences to include 90 percent of SAMs, tanks, and manufacturing sites to include bombing in Damascus and other major cities. On the 9th, the IN and IASF sank the remnants of the small Syrian Navy, some 15 vessels at anchor in Latakia and Al-Bayda, whilst also targeting anti-ship missile storage. More attacks followed through the 17th.

Israeli ground forces crossed the frontier to destroy depots, structures and firing positions south of Damascus. There were soon nine reported IDF outposts in the new buffer zone. They also occupied the upper peak of the Mount Hermon summit and settled in for an indefinite stay.

The interim Islamic government declared its benevolence towards Israel whilst struggling with ethnic violence that claimed hundreds of lives. Israel immediately labelled it an 'extremist Islamic regime' that was sure to threaten Israel sooner or later. It did not initially undertake any diplomatic approach to the new

A 133 Squadron F-15A (393) prepares to taxi from its shelter carrying JDAM bombs, Python and old Sparrow missiles, and a jamming pod. It is participating in strikes on Syrian targets after the overthrow of the Assad government. Below are two of the Syrian Navy's vessels being targeted whilst tied up in port. (IDF Spokesman)

A pair of Syrian Gazelle helicopters lie destroyed after an attack by the IASF on Mazzeh Airport on 11 December 2024. (Public Domain)

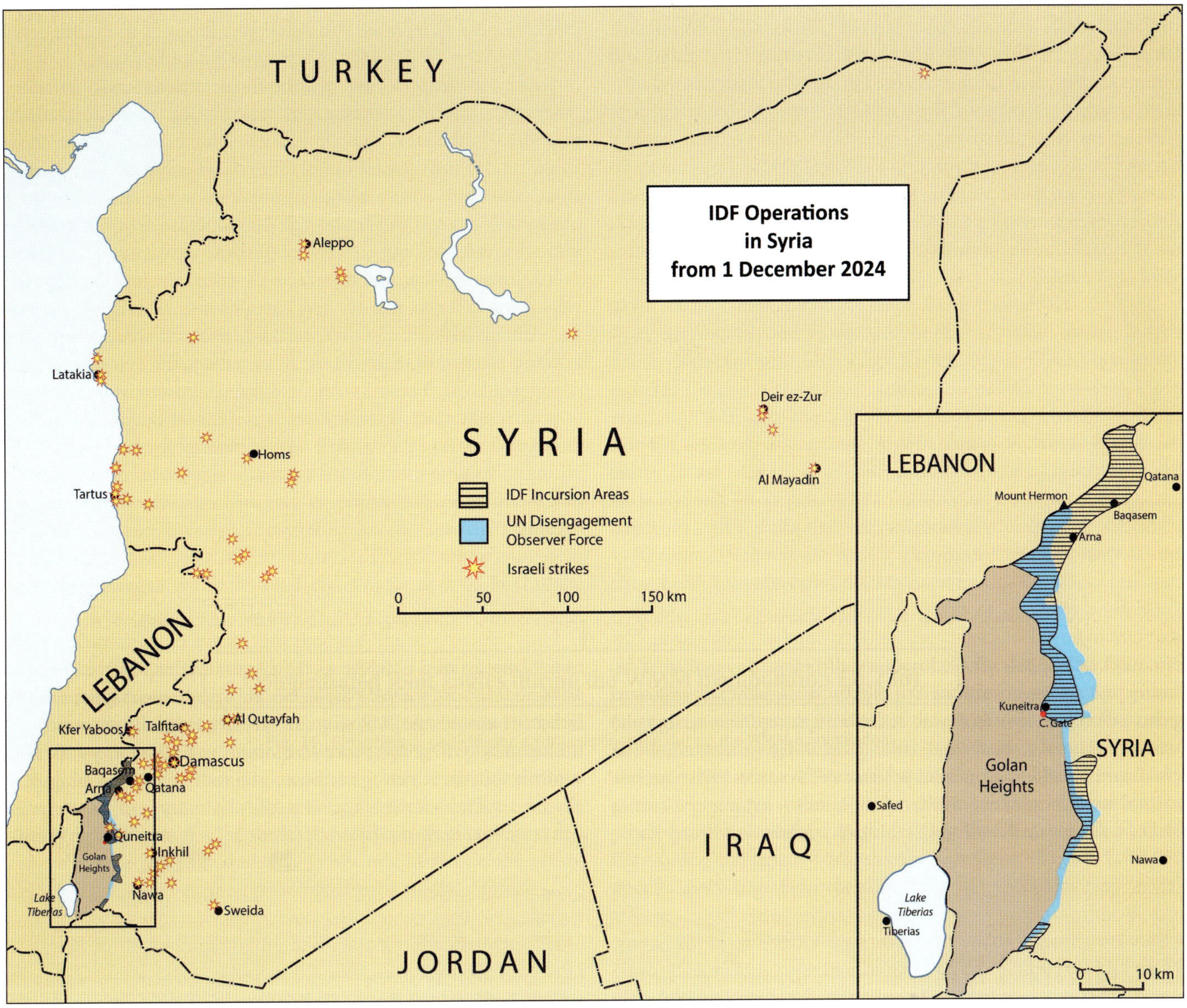

Israeli strikes and incursions into Syria beginning in December 2024 are depicted. (Map by George Anderson)

In IDF armoured brigade replenishes ammunition in preparation for operations inside Syria. (IDF)

government but instead acted to prepare for the worst eventuality. On 10 March 2025 the IASF was back to hit radar installations and command centres in southern Syria. On the 13th it attacked Islamic Jihad targets in Damascus. The stated intent was to prevent the new government from deploying forces in the south of their country facing its only external threat and persistent tormentor. This was a vast area of southern Syria that encompassed the Daraa, Qunietra and Suwayda provinces. Although identified by Israel as a DMZ, the IDF deployed significant forces into the area, several kilometres across the border.

Through December 2025 Syria counted some 1,000 IASF airstrikes and 400 incursions. As these undermined the new government's efforts at internal unification, the ultimate Israeli goal appeared to be keeping Syria a fractured state, with internal strife, that could not threaten Israel. Yet, others sought to engage the new government constructively. Türkiye worked for a defence pact that could include deploying combat aircraft to two air bases in the centre of the country.[2] Saudi Arabia also strove towards good relations, hoping to displace Iranian influence. The Americans announced on 13 May that they would conditionally waive long-standing sanctions, subject to six-month reviews, and work towards normalised relations to give Syria 'breathing room' to stabilise. The UN lifted similar sanctions on 6 November. The new Syrian President, Ahmed al-Sharaa, announced in early May 2025 that his nation was in indirect talks with Israel to halt attacks and return to terms of the 1974 disengagement agreement. Seeing the way the 'wind was blowing', word emerged on 16 May that Israel was holding direct talks in Azerbaijan with Syrian representatives. During late

June 2025 it was reported the states were engaged in negotiations, with American mediation, to reach some accommodation.

Israel intended to hold the newly occupied Syrian territory indefinitely, though claiming this was in part to protect ethnic minorities in the area. The IDF declared a buffer zone around these Druze and Kurd communities. They were courted as potential allies, seeking to ensure against unrest spilling over into the Druze community on the Golan Heights. The outreach was not received with wide welcome, but on 30 April the IASF struck a militant group near Damascus accused of attacks on the Druze. By July the sectarian violence across the country saw significant combat between pro-government Bedouin and Druze factions, with other Muslim groups heading to join. With hundreds of casualties, the situation greatly concerned Druze families living in Israel. Hundreds of these people went to assist their brethren whilst dozens of Syrian Druze fled to Israel for safety. More IASF strikes were conducted on 15 July, hitting government forces attempting to intervene in the violence that Israel said was intending to attack Druze. The next day Israel bombed the MoD building and other targets in Damascus, warning that more would come if the army did not steer clear of the Druze. It was looking to many that Israel just could not help itself and that bombs were its only means of diplomacy.

On 18 July Syria said it would pull its forces from the area and Israel agreed to cease its attacks inside the country whilst urging the warring factions to desist. Israel also delivered relief supplies to the Druze. However, the IDF still conducted occasional strikes inside the country. On 2 December Netanyahu called for a vast Israeli-controlled DMZ buffer in southern Syria stretching to Damascus.

5

GRINDING ON

The war in Gaza became the longest sustained campaign in Israel's history. There appeared no viable plan for the post-war governance of Gaza and the national unity Cabinet dissolved on 17 June 2024 over this issue. Israel had expressed vague intentions of a government without the PA or Hamas, and certainly not an Israeli military administration, possibly with whatever government introduced in 'bubbles' as areas were cleared. However, this would eventually require Hamas to be completely eliminated in a process that was becoming protracted. The Israeli opposition, backed by families of hostages, began a campaign calling for an end to the war. This saw weekly or more frequent mass protests of tens of thousands. Gallant repeatedly asked for a 'day after' plan and definition of what Netanyahu's 'total victory' literally meant. At one point he called the phrase gibberish, it being clear the PM was playing to public sentiment and not informing the MoD on conduct of the war. Netanyahu called Gallant anti-Israeli and replaced him on 5 November with Foreign Minister Israel Katz. This drew vehement criticism, Katz being more extreme. On the same day a close ally and former aide to the PM was arrested for allegedly leaking classified documents, seeking to undermine negotiations with Hamas. Far-right elements of the government coalition threatened to bring down the government if the war was ended before Hamas was destroyed and all the targeted leadership killed. Some made calls for ethnic cleansing and territorial expansionism with no repercussions from the PM, party or Knesset.[1]

DIPLOMATIC FRONT

One of Netanyahu's motives to continue the war was his wish to remain Prime Minister. During the course of the war Netanyahu's popularity rose and fell and so the potential for him winning re-election and forming another government was by no means certain. The war repeatedly delayed his corruption trial. Hence, it appeared perpetuating the war ensured his political survival. Hamas was by then fighting for its existence with even Arab states and organisations calling for them to disarm and surrender authority. Their principal goal was to survive, and the hostages helped ensure that. Consequently, neither side felt compelled to make significant compromises to bring an end to the war.

The USA, Egypt and especially Qatar served as mediators for ceasefire negotiations, the sides refusing to sit together. The stated Israeli conditions for ending the war was Hamas disarming and the Strip demilitarised whilst Israel retained military control, all hostages released, and stand-up of civil governance not including Hamas or the PA. Hamas wanted an end to the war and for Israel to withdraw entirely before releasing hostages. Both appeared to draw out the negotiations when it suited political currents. In two instances Israel killed members of the Hamas negotiating team via airstrikes (as detailed elsewhere). The message was that Israel did not want an end to the war and negotiations were just a stalling tactic to placate those calling for progress.

The release of hostages held by Hamas were joyous events in Israel and elsewhere, well covered in the international press. Release of Palestinian detainees was less so. (IDF Spokesman)

There had been many proposals for a ceasefire. On 29 July 2024 the Arab League, the EU, and 17 other countries called for Hamas to disarm and relinquish power. Hamas and Israel did arrive at a mediated ceasefire on 15 January 2025 that took effect on the 19th. Bombing continued to the last hours and Houthis fired more rockets. Under the agreement Hamas was to deliver a list of the individuals to be released. When this did not occur on time, owing to what they said was a technical glitch, Israel immediately resumed bombing until the list was delivered three hours late. The Israeli government had approved the ceasefire, though one minister resigned, calling it capitulation. Some other ministers fully expected the war to resume after the first 42-day period expired and threatened to bring down Netanyahu's coalition if this failed to occur.

In its first period the ceasefire saw 33 hostages released whilst Israel let go nearly 2,000 Palestinian detainees. The IDF was to begin a phased withdrawal from urban centres but continued to occupy a strip inside the border fence and the Philadelphi Corridor, occupied by the IDF in defiance of those terms in order to control the Rafah Crossing. There was tension between Egyptian and Israeli troops in the area and a firing incident in which an Egyptian soldier was killed. Israel sought to cancel the Philadelphi accord but Egypt refused.

The pause in fighting permitted some reflection in Israel. Whilst the war continued Netanyahu would not permit a thorough review of the security lapses instrumental in success of Hamas's attack. Many concluded this was to protect himself from fallout as he continued deflecting blame. The IDF chief-of-general-staff, Lieutenant General Herzi Halevi, announced on 20 January 2025 he would resign on 6 March over the military's failures. Military Intelligence (A'man) director, Major General Aharon Heliva had resigned in April 2024 over his organisation's shortcomings. The IDF delivered its report by 30 January documenting a probe into those errors and Shin Bet's (Security Agency) report emerged on 5 March. The latter pointed to actions and policies of the right-wing government that had exacerbated internal tensions and projected an appearance of weakness, statements that infuriated Netanyahu. There was plenty of finger-pointing, especially at the political echelon.

The Americans assessed that Hamas had recruited nearly as many or more new fighters as those it had lost in the past 16 months of combat. Israel admitted it had not destroyed Hamas, only reduced it from a 'terror army' to a 'guerrilla army.'

Both sides accused the other of ceasefire violations. Dozens of Palestinians were killed in IDF actions that also held up aid that expanded suffering within the Strip. Jordan flew relief supplies in helicopters via an 'air bridge' across Israel, supplementing ground transport that some Israelis obstructed. The opponents occasionally paused prisoner/hostage releases. Mediators successfully worked to resolve disputes whilst talks on later phases of the ceasefire made little headway.

Details of the second and third phase of the ceasefire, remaining to be hammered out, were expected to see the last hostage released and Israeli withdrawal from the Strip with a declared end to the war. However, Israel intentionally slow-rolled those negotiations and sent low-level individuals signalling meagre interest. Netanyahu preferred that Phase A continue indefinitely rather than withdraw entirely and accept the war ending uncertainly, with the potential his government would fall. The IDF said it would continue operating in the Philadelphi Corridor. Israel eased the blockade in January, but only 56 percent of the usual flow of humanitarian assistance was permitted in. To coerce Hama's conciliation, the IDF halted the entry of all aid trucks into the enclave on 2 March 2025 and cut remaining electrical and water supply from Israel. It appeared Israel had entered the truce with intent of undermining it and not fully complying with terms.

Although Israel stated that suspension of aid was because it was being stolen by Hamas, making resumption of deliveries conditional on accepting Israeli terms to extend the ceasefire told a different story. International aid groups operating there and the US Agency for International Development review concluded that theft was minimal. Israel made no demands to better control aid distribution.

An IDF Merkava IV and Namer APC occupy the Rafah Crossing, in the Philadelphi Corridor, on 7 May 2024 to the consternation of Egypt, though not because the vehicles crushed the garden. (IDF Spokesman)

Given the high population density, paucity of land, and the arid conditions, the Gaza Strip had relied on UN aid for many decades. As the occupying power, Israel was required by law to ensure such aid reached the populace.

One factor in delaying negotiations for the second phase of the ceasefire was Netanyahu's travel to Washington to speak with the newly elected Donald Trump. Even before being sworn into office, Trump had weighed into the imbroglio. During the 2024 campaign for the presidency Trump declared that Hamas would not dare to have attacked if he was in the White House and that he would end the war on his first day in office. On several occasions he would growl stern declarations whilst squinting at the camera saying that if Hamas did not immediately release all hostages unconditionally or accept a ceasefire proposal without seeking adjustments 'very bad things' would happen. Hamas and the Palestinians dismissed such threats given there was nothing the Americans could do that Israel was not already doing. Trump, famously narcissistic, had an inflated opinion of his strengths as a leader and how Hamas saw American intimidations.

Trump held the view Israel was historically the victim in most or all circumstances and deserved all assistance from the USA. He considered Bibi Netanyahu one of the world's most gift national leaders. Trump also needed the Evangelical Christian vote; a group that strongly backed Israel.[2] During his first term the President ordered the USA embassy relocated to Jerusalem, undermining decades of policy seeking to avoid alienating Arab sensibilities. (At

Israeli Prime Minister Benjamin Netanyahu, left, confers with USA President Donald Trump, right, in the Oval Office on 29 September 2025. (Public Domain)

that time only two other nations had their embassies in Jerusalem.) He also had the USA formally recognise Israel's annexation of the Golan Heights. The USA cut off funds to Palestinians, ceased funding UNRWA, and had the PLO mission in Washington removed. Trump and Netanyahu, together, ensured there would be no movement towards a two-state solution whilst they remained in office, and likely facilitate more settlement activity.

During the meeting with Netanyahu on 4 February President Trump announced the USA would 'take over' and rebuild the Gaza Strip into a 'Riviera.' He had been pressing Arab nations to accept most or all of the inhabitants in a population transfer. Seeking to 'clear out' the territory, the inhabitants were unlikely to be permitted to return. He later walked-back this statement given resistance from Arab states to take the expelled individuals and the outcry at the implied ethnic cleansing. Later still, he said the intent was to create a 'freedom zone.' All this showed some lack of understanding of the conflict. Most could see that any rebuilding under this scheme would likely benefit Israelis. Trump threatened to withhold financial assistance funds if Egypt and Jordan failed to take expelled persons, but nothing came of this. Israeli efforts to find countries willing to take such people, with compensation, also came to nothing.

Arab nations expressed strong opposition to Trump's proclamation as unethical if not unlawful. This was re-emphasised during an Arab League summit on 28 February 2025. Hamas agreed to turn over governance duties to an international body but refused to disarm without a comprehensive peace settlement in place. On 4 March Egypt offered an Arab plan to rebuild the Strip over five years with the inhabitants *in situ*. Arab states promised $53 billion for the effort. Elections for a new Palestinian government would occur soon after this process began. Trump rejected all this in favour of his own notion for which little solid planning was being undertaken.[3] Egypt tried again, stating its willingness to host a conference addressing reconstruction once a ceasefire went into effect. Trump insisted that the area was uninhabitable given the rubble and unexploded ordnance. This ignored the fact that millions of people were living amongst all this and had during all previous Israeli onslaughts and subsequence rebuilding.

Trump's hardline stance in favour of Netanyahu's far-right agenda went so far as moving to expel from the USA any foreign nationals who had advocated anti-Israeli or pro-Palestinian (by extension anti-Semitic according to some) views. Organisations that condoned such free speech were intimidated into changing policies permitting this. The UK banned the group Palestine Action because some members had undertaken vandalism of military resources. This only saw its protest grow and the number of arrests expand into the hundreds at each illegal rally as people protested what appeared to be a misuse of anti-terror legislation.[4]

WEST BANK VIOLENCE

Racial tensions in Israel and the territories were palpable in the months following 7 October 2023. Some Jews looked at their Arab neighbours with hatred and Israeli Arabs 'ducked their heads.' In the West Bank militant settlers found an opportunity to harass Palestinians in venting their anger, take their property, and induce flight. They were confident the Netanyahu government would look the other way, and the authorities would little restrain them. Militant settlers were clearly emboldened by Netanyahu's rhetoric and that of some of his ministers. One of the guiding principles of the Likud was that 'The Jewish people have an exclusive and indisputable right to all parts of the Land of Israel.' They sought to hasten realisation of the Greater Israel these officials spoke of and undisputed Israeli sovereignty over the 'sacred land of our ancestors.'[5] At the same time the new right-wing USA administration lifted sanctions against certain settlers and groups that had been accused of such violence. It nominated as ambassadors to Israel and the UN individuals who agreed Israel had a Biblical right to annex the West Bank, West Bank settlements were not illegal, there were no such people as Palestinians, and there was legally no such place as the West Bank or East Jerusalem.[6]

There were West Bank Palestinian protests against the occupation and general strikes in sympathy with Gaza defenders during the early months of the war. The PA clamped down on anything that might lead to violence. The IDF responded as usual, to include detaining people solely because they might cause trouble and to serve as 'bargaining chips' for prisoner exchanges. By 23 October 800 persons had been detained, 500 said to have affiliation with the Hamas party. By mid-November it was 1,800. A tremendous increase in militant settler and IDF repression saw property seizures and damage, plus injury and death of Palestinians, mount to new heights. The military isolated local towns and villages with hundreds of checkpoints, roadblocks and locked gates controlling movement and, in some cases essentially besieging communities via denied utilities.

West Bank settler youths hurl rocks at Palestinians whilst a soldier looks on. (Public Domain)

Settler violence amounted to more than 1,270 incidents over a year. The same pace was experienced beyond, with more than 100 per month. Dozens of instances of land illegally seized from Palestinian farmers and shepherds were experienced, threats and beatings driving the lawful owners away. Farm animals were killed, crops were damaged or destroyed, pickers attacked, and owners prevented from working their land. Foreigners who sought to insert themselves between the Israelis and Palestinians to discourage the depredations were similarly assaulted and murdered, and deported. This intimidation and violence succeeded in driving 1,000 residents from their homes, abandoning six communities. There were instances of settler extremists assaulting Israeli security forces when they attempted to intervene. They generally acted with impunity, contrary to law. (Israelis living in the West Bank were subject to civil law but the Arab residents to military law.) Although senior government leadership articulated a policy of intolerance to unlawful settler actions, in some cases the soldiers and police stood by and did nothing or contributed. In the age of cellphone video and online posts the behaviour was all-the-more evident. When complaints were lodged the military said the incidents would be investigated, but seldom was there any outcome. (Israeli organisations that had historically monitored such activities and filed complaints had long before given up.)

Palestinian violence as incitement or in response was considerably mild by comparison. The PA's forceful policing actions to suppress militant activities only fuelled internal strife. Yet, the IDF was concerned with Hamas and PIJ members beginning a major terror campaign – 'Gazafication'. Israel recorded 1,245 security incidents in the past year, 255 considered significant and 10 pre-empted, costing 24 Israeli lives. Perhaps 15 militant 'brigades' had formed in major population centres to confront occupation forces. On 28 August

2024 a series of IDF counterterror raids and airstrikes were carried out as the largest action in years – Operation Summer Camps. The military classified the West Bank a combat zone. More IDF activities followed over the coming months, including numerous raids and airstrikes in the northern part of the territory during November. By that time some 500 Palestinians had been killed and 6,000 wounded.

Israel stepped up operations in the West Bank on 21 January 2025 with Operation Iron Wall. This began with an assault on Jenin to include infantry, armour and airstrikes that left widespread damage. Refugee camps in Tulkarem and Nar Shams were also assaulted and residents dislocated. Jenin and Tulkarem Brigades irregulars were especially targeted. The PA police contributed to some aspects of the operation. All this was likely, in part, to placate the far-right ministers who insisted that the military campaign against threats to the State continue, despite the ceasefire in Gaza at the time, or they might bring down the government. By the end of February observers counted 38 airstrikes in the West Bank and tanks were operating there for the first time in 20 years. Operations included demolishing homes and apartment blocks under military authority that displaced 39,843 persons who were told they could not return. The destruction included more than 850 buildings the IDF said was to simplify access. (Human Rights Watch subsequently assessed this as a war crime and crime against humanity.) The Army would declare areas closed military zones and expel the residents, though Israeli settlers could stay. To many observers this appeared to be a planned effort to claim more land for settlements in the name of combating terrorism. The government announced that the military could be expected to remain in some refugee camps over the coming year.

From the beginning of 2024 the IDF and civilian terrorists were responsible for the death of 690 Palestinians in the territory by the

Israeli troops advance in Jenin, in the West Bank, during January 2025's Operation Iron Wall seeking to suppress terrorist activity. (Public Domain)

end of September 2025, with 667 of these by government forces (470 by direct fire and 199 by airstrikes) and 12 by settlers. Through 5 December there had been 227 deaths during 2025 with 1,680 settler attacks, and normality throughout the territory was disrupted. This was the highest toll since records by outside agencies began to be kept in 2008. On the Israeli side were 39 civilians, perhaps half settlers, and around 20 soldiers killed. The Army stated that terrorism had decreased by 70 percent. Settler attacks in that period summed to 2,660.

The ICJ rendered an opinion on 19 July 2024 that the occupation was illegal and in violation of conventions prohibiting racial segregation and apartheid. Illegal practices included confiscating land, building settlements, depriving residents of natural resources, and denying them self-determination. It also stated trade or investment with Israeli businesses having any role in the occupied territories was to be avoided. (Subsequently, the 45-million member European Trade Union Confederation said it would adhere to this direction.) Such judgements had been rendered by other bodies previously. This was followed on 18 September by a vote of the UNGA that overwhelmingly called for Israel to end the occupation within 12 months. On 16 July 2024 the Knesset voted by a wide margin in favour of a resolution opposing a Palestinian state west of the Jordan River. Not only did Israel fail to comply with the UN resolution, but on 23 July 2025 the Knesset passed a nonbinding resolution calling for the government to extend sovereignty over all settlements in the West Bank, what it called an 'inseparable part of the Land of Israel.' A similar bill was passed on 22 October. The change in the American administration in January 2025, with a strongly pro-Israeli President, was seen by many right-leaning Israelis as an opportunity to annex the territory in the event of substantial movement towards a Palestinian state.

At the end of May 2025 Israel announced the largest expansion of settlements in 30 years, seizing more land. Construction of over 28,000 new housing units were approved that year. Minister Smotrich championed an old plan to build 3,401 units in area E1 Settlements, extending from East Jerusalem, that would effectively isolate Arab East Jerusalem, displace hundreds of residents, and cut the West Bank in two by severing the last land link between Judea and Samaria available to Palestinians. Smotrich's stated intent was to make a Palestinian state impossible for practical purposes. This had previously attracted so much opposition from foreign states that Israel had deferred the plan. Now they felt Israel had nothing to lose and, for Netanyahu and his party, everything to gain. With the plan quickly approved, eviction notices were sent and demolition begun to make room for road construction. In early December Israel announced plans for 17 new settlements and extension of services to 40 others. Three military bases would be moved into Palestinian areas in the northern West Bank vacated under the Oslo Accords. Israel also announced intentions to double its population on the Golan Heights.

Israel's long destructive combat in Gaza, with tens of thousands of deaths, the anti-Palestinian actions in the West Bank, and Netanyahu's vocal support for a 'Greater Israel', was worrying for neighbouring states. Past practices of expelling Palestinians across the border and the growing expansionist rhetoric aroused fear of violent confrontation. Jordan decided in August 2025 to reintroduce conscription, beginning in February 2026, after having eliminated it in 1992. On 23 September 2025 Israel temporarily closed the Allenby Crossing, the only official crossing point between the West Bank and Jordan, and imposed other movement restrictions. It offered no rationale for these actions.

The IDF operations in the West Bank throughout 2025, with armour and airstrikes for the first time in decades, were expected to extend into 2026. Tamping down Palestinian terrorism and enforcing the occupation went hand-in-hand during such actions. (IDF)

Israeli ground forces advanced through a devastated neighbourhood in the Gaza Strip. Vast swaths of the Strip were reduced to ruin in this manner, bringing widespread discredit to Israel. (IDF Spokesman, Amit Agronov)

After the Gaza ceasefire took hold in October 2025 (see later) settler violence ticked up again to the highest rate ever recorded – 264 incidents in less than a month. This was particularly aimed at disrupting the olive harvest. The goal appeared to be igniting a third Intifadah that would justify a greatly expanded military crackdown, expulsions and possibly annexation. By that time the government was beginning to look at reining in the extremist settlers from perpetrating what General Halevi had called a pogrom. However, Defense Minister Katz had announced in 2024 that Israel would no longer use administrative detention (as applied to Palestinian) to hold settlers. Since Palestinian prisoners accused of violent acts were being released in exchange for hostages held by Hamas, the government decided it was unreasonable to continue holding Israelis detained for violent acts against Arab civilians in the West Bank. They, too, were released. When two Jenin suspects were killed whilst surrendering on 27 November 2025, Katz praised the suspicious action. 'Terrorists must die!'

RENEWED GAZA OFFENSIVE

By mid-March 2025 Hamas had agreed to release one hostage and return four corpses whilst negotiations continued. However, in the early hours of 18 March Israel abruptly declared the truce terminated and resumed bombing the Gaza Strip. Ground operations restarted the following day in the central and southern sectors, including retaking control of the Netzarim Corridor. Factors in Israel's decision to resume hostilities were extensive American military efforts in recent days to crush the Houthi and Trump's vocal support for raining destruction on Hamas – and by extension the Strip and all its inhabitants. The American administration had rushed through authorisation for $3.8 billion in emergency assistance that included tremendous quantities of munitions.

Hamas fired three rockets towards Tel Aviv on 20 March, all intercepted or falling in open areas. Three more followed on 5 April. The support front actors also resumed their attacks. Millions of leaflets dropped in the Gaza Strip sought to direct the movement of people that were restricted from using vehicles or to pass through the north-south divide.

With aid and services having been cut, by the second week of the offensive famine began to take hold. On 25 April the UN stated that it had no more food to distribute. In May malnutrition was becoming acute, with some of the most vulnerable perishing. Fresh water was scarce. Observers called it a war without limits and the USA, which normally applied pressure for Israel to ease human suffering during war, blamed Hamas. Observers speculated that Israel sought to make life so unbearable residents would line up to leave.

The IDF effectively occupied 77 percent of the territory given its range of firepower and control of movement. Plans were in work

Israeli forces once more gather at the Gaza border for a fresh ground offensive into the enclave during May 2025, Operation Gideon's Chariots. After 19 months of combat, with brigades and divisions repeatedly committed and moved, reservists were growing weary of call-ups. (IDF)

for a greatly expanded operation, with five divisions and 50,000 personnel, to permanently occupy large segments of the territory and engage in a protracted counterinsurgency operation that could consume at least a year according to one official. In early May 2025 tens of thousands of reservists were being called-up in preparation for this surge that was approved by the Cabinet on the 4th, described as a 'conquest' for indefinite occupation. The renewed offensive began on 16 May with the stated goal of isolating portions of the Strip to facilitate Hamas's destruction and freeing of hostages. As before, the operation was presaged with a flurry of airstrikes that killed hundreds of noncombatants. On the 18th the IDF announced it had executed 670 airstrikes on Hamas targets in the past week. That there were so many targets remaining after 19 months of combat, in which the IDF claimed to have eliminated 'tens of thousands of terrorists,'[7] spoke volumes for what seemed an endless if not futile war.

An Israeli proposal for another 40-day ceasefire covering release of 11 hostages was rejected by Hamas. Weeks later Israel expressed willingness to discuss a permanent ceasefire with Hamas disarming. Hamas was unmoved but did release an Israeli-American soldier hostage on 12 May as a sign of goodwill to the USA. The next day the IASF assassinated the new Hamas leader, Mohammed Sinwar, by bombing a Khan Yunis hospital where it said an underground command post was located. The bombing killed 26. This may also have been designed to endanger the latest round of negotiations in Qatar. Hamas fired three rockets into Israel on 26 May. There had been more calls from the Israeli far-right to redouble the punishment the IDF was delivering.[8] Some in the government advocated for reintroducing Israeli Gaza settlements.

An indication of these aspirations was introduction of another border-to-coast road in April–May 2025; the Morag Corridor, between Khan Yunis and Rafah. The name derived from an Israeli settlement in the area vacated 20 years before. Dividing the Strip into three segments via these Israeli-controlled roads appeared to be preparation for a prolonged occupation that could see 75 percent of the Strip held within two months. There was also the Mefalsim Corridor north of Gaza and the Kissufim

Corridor north of Khan Yunis for a total five zones. Each of these required clearing of buildings and cultivated fields whilst also bisecting established roads.

Israel expanded the border security perimeter to approximately 1.0km (0.6mi) by demolishing thousands of buildings and taking over farmland. By April 2025 this effort had consumed some 135km^2 (52mi^2) or 17 percent of the Strip. Seventy-one percent of Gaza was rendered no-go areas by the IDF. More evacuation orders and declarations of 'dangerous combat zones' encompassing most of the northern and eastern regions. By June 2025 these encompassed nearly 80 percent of the Strip. Defense Minister Katz made clear the evacuated areas would be considered free-fire zones, anyone remaining considered combatants and fired on without warning. Supposed safe areas were limited to a strip astride the southern coastline. Crowding the destitute population into a smaller and smaller area was seen as a measure to encourage emigration, though these people had nowhere to go and no means of getting anywhere. Declared safe zones were attacked when the IDF identified a target, many times without warning, and so hundreds were killed in such areas.

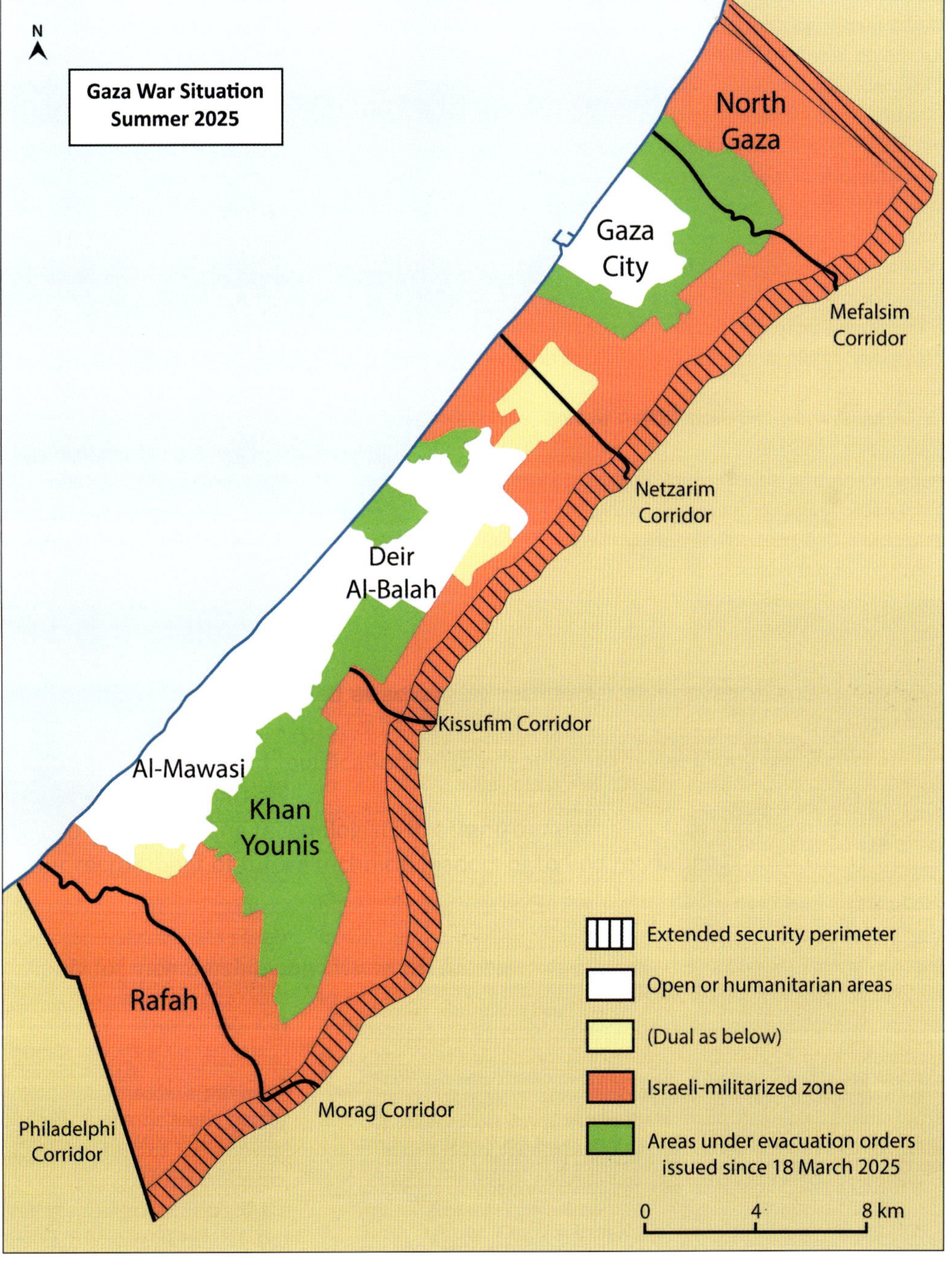

The map illustrates the basic combat situation in the Gaza Strip battlespace by summer 2025. (Map by George Anderson)

On 6 June it was revealed that Israel was arming rival militias and criminal clans to confront Hamas as another means to hasten the organisation's demise. Among these was Popular Forces organised by Yasser Abu Shabab, previously imprisoned by Hamas for drug trafficking and said to number several hundred fighters that busied themselves protecting aid vehicles. The government program was promptly denounced as unwise given that these organisations were weak and their weapons would likely be turned on Israel eventually. Netanyahu had approved the program without consulting his Cabinet.

Israeli attacks on and searches of hospitals attracted particular attention. These sought purported Hamas command posts below hospitals, but tunnel entrances and arms caches were also found. Personnel were detained as terrorist accomplices but not charged. Substantial damage to the facilities were commonly sustained. Most hospitals were forced to close for this reason and also lack of fuel and supplies, causing a near collapse of the health care system.

Some operations to kill or capture individuals were accompanied by considerable collateral damage and casualties. In some cases Israel insisted the individuals being targeted had participated in the 7 October 2023 attack. Israel made this claim in many suspicious incidents. It is doubtful this was true in all cases, but it had the effect of silencing critics. That identification could be made under combat circumstances, with enough confidence to justify certain collateral effects, was unconvincing. Numerous 'tragic mistakes' saw innocent civilians killed, these mounting throughout the war. The 'fog of war', soldiers desperate to protect themselves and their comrades, and aggressive tactics were largely to blame. These and accusations of intentionally targeting noncombatants and non-military targets would bring an IDF response that an inquiry would be opened with a thorough and professional investigation. Seldom were results, if any, made public before the next incident displaced the prior one in the media's attention.

Observers also assessed that Israel was intentionally targeting journalists, especially those with a strong following and who posted negative reports of Israeli military and occupation activities. Of the Arabic-language media journalists operating in the territories, more than 200 were killed during the war, becoming the deadliest conflict for journalists. Some were intentionally targeted when the IDF concluded they had some association with terrorist cells. Organisations including Amnesty International found that Israel was seeking to silence reporting from popular journalists. Some media organisations ceased informing the IDF of their staff's locations fearing they would be targeted.

More and more former military and civilian Israeli defence officials openly criticised the conduct of the war. In April 2025 hundreds of Air Force reservists signed a letter, published in major Israeli newspapers, calling for negotiating release of hostages even if that meant ending the war. They observed that the war served mainly political and personal motivations and was unnecessarily leading to military and civilian casualties. Although the reservists did not refuse to serve, the IASF commander and CGS had them all dismissed.[9] Soon the military signatories of similar letters numbered in the thousands. A reservist organisation encouraged soldiers to refuse call-ups. Netanyahu was unswayed.

Polls in that period showed up to 70 percent of the Israeli public agreed all should be done to bring the hostages home and the war ended as soon as possible whilst 21 percent felt the war should continue. By July 2025 even within Netanyahu's Likud party the majority preferred an end to the war. A Hebrew University survey found that 40 percent of the soldiers asked said they lacked motivation or were only slightly motivated whilst 13 percent said they were motivated. Suicides were way up and eligible personnel sought retirement despite the ongoing war.

One reservist stated he had been called-up four times in 22 months and served over 300 days in combat zones. This may not have been typical but exemplified the problem. Once deployed into the combat zone the soldiers were committed until the unit pulled out. Once that happened it was a short trip home, but the process became increasingly frustrating. Although there was a rotation of about two weeks, this was inconsistent, and the members became more irate. The IDF was struggling with a personnel shortage and great strain on those serving, and sought avenues for recruitment. It seemed every combat unit spent some time in the nightmarish Gaza cauldron (even Navy frogmen), and noncombat units found some role. A growing number of reservists stopped responding to the 'recruitment' by their unit. Even those suffering post-traumatic stress disorder were being pressed back into service.

By July 2025 the IDF was suffering a 7,500-person shortfall.[10] Israel decided to reach out to individuals in large Jewish communities abroad seeking approximately 700 persons per year willing to serve.[11] Israel also sought to attract 30,000 asylum seekers in Africa to immigrate to Israel where they would serve in the military with a promise of settlement in the occupied territories.

Air Force personnel prepare an F-16 for a mission with a JDAM bomb installed. (IASF)

On 25 June 2024 the Israeli Supreme Court ruled that exempting young ultra-Orthodox men (Haredi) in religious studies (Yeshiva students) from conscription, which had been the de facto practice since founding of the state, was illegal. Their community was about 14 percent of the population. The IDF began immediately drafting these individuals whilst the ultra-Orthodox community staged noisy protests. On 21 November the MoD issued arrest warrants for 1,126 of these men who refused to respond to their draft notices, of which 3,000 had been sent out. Another 7,000 notices were pending. However, the Haredim continued to resist service and the government, needing support of religious parties, was attempting to push through legislation exempting them.

AID FLOTILLAS

As deprivation in the Gaza Strip became more and more evident to world viewers, some people chose to take assertive measures to deliver aid by sea. Such attempts had been made since the blockade was first introduced in 2008, in one instance with violence and deaths when the ship was boarded. This caused a years-long rift with Türkiyc. These were more visible efforts to defy the blockade than to deliver meaningful quantities of aid. The IDF opposed them by actively discouraging their progress and then seizing the vessels. The ships would be taken to Ashdod where the aid was removed, with promise it would be distributed, many of the activists flown out on commercial flights, and the ships released. All this was played out several times, very much in the public view.

Each time Israel actively opposed aid delivery by sea it repeated that the blockade was legal. As the overall blockade of the Gaza Strip impeded delivery of humanitarian aid, courts had repeatedly found it to be in violation of humanitarian law. Further, interfering with freedom of navigation in international waters was unlawful – the intercepts all occurring outside the Gaza legal limit. Such might be permissible if enforcing a legal blockade. Placing the civilian crew of such vessels at risk during a seizure is also unlawful. Israel also stated that the vessels and crew were approaching a war zone and so was acting for their safety, though the only party with means of endangering the vessels was Israel.

On 2 May 2025 a crew aboard an activist aid ship en route to Gaza said they were twice attacked by a drone in international waters off Malta and nearly sunk. Israel was the suspected attacker, but made no comment. An IASF C-130 was tracked flying into the area and patrolling for hours at low altitude prior to and after the attack. Another aid ship approaching Gaza waters in June was shadowed by drones the entire journey. It was seized in international waters on the 9th. The vessel was surrounded by quadcopters that sprayed a physically annoying white substance onto the craft whilst communications were jammed. Another such vessel was boarded on 27 June after being circled by Heron drones.

A flotilla of aid boats was en route during early September 2025, this exceptionally large with more than 40 vessels and over 500 personnel. One of these was attacked in a Tunisian port by a drone hovering overhead that dropped an incendiary device. Other ships were en route to Gaza when, on 23 September, they reported 14 incidents between Tunis and Crete in which drones had dropped explosives and unidentified objects on and near the craft, plus communications jamming. Israel warned significant measures would be taken if the flotilla approached further. Four vessels reported being damaged, and one had an unexploded device on its deck. Personnel feared for their safety. The next day Spain and Italy said that they would send national ships to assist but would not enter the Israeli exclusion zone. The intercepts began on 1 October, the flotilla saying it detected 20 unidentified vessels 3nm ahead. Water cannon were used to discourage ship progress and one was rammed. Arrested were 437 activists. More intercepts occurred on 8 October.

The intercepts drew the usual international outcry. Colombia cancelled a free trade agreement with Israel and the Israeli diplomatic delegation departed.

An Israeli service member was captured on video boarding a flotilla boat. Inset is a drone dropping explosive or incendiary devices on a boat. (Freedom Flotilla Coalition and Public Domain)

LOGGERHEADS WITH THE WORLD

Within months of the war's beginning, the world witnessing the extent of Israel's furious campaign, international support for its actions steadily waned, replaced with revulsion. Whereas previously people had said whatever 'beef' Hamas had with Israel did not justify the excesses of 7 October, this now became what happened on 7 October did not justify Israel's excesses in Gaza. The government's message of 'if you're not with us, you're against us' was offensively simplistic to many outside the country who saw rights and wrongs on both sides. Netanyahu was steadfast at insisting Hamas must be destroyed, at whatever cost, to prevent another 7 October. The government and Israel's supporters insisted the IDF was the most moral armed force in the world (without stating criterion or how the comparison was made) and its restraint was actually slowing the progress of the war and placing its soldiers at additional risk. (Former CGS General Halevi remarked in September 2025 that the MoD lawyers had never restricted his actions or orders during the time he oversaw the war, though many had accused them of hampering the Army's progress towards victory.) Governments and organisations sought to end the perceived Israeli impunity from accountability evident in the past by bringing cases before international legal bodies.

International condemnation of actions by the State of Israel were too readily equated with an anti-Israeli bias and even anti-Semitism, the latter claim as ugly as the racism itself. There was a definite rise in anti-Semitic acts during the war, but the accusations went beyond this. Some insisted that support for a Palestinian state was anti-Semitic because it would – so claimed – result in the destruction of Israel, the declared Jewish state. Protests of Israel allegedly committing genocide was likewise assessed as anti-Semitic, as was almost anything perceived as anti-Israeli, despite these being acts by a secular government of a multi-ethnic country. Opposing Israeli policies were labelled anti-Israeli, implying a desire to see the nation substantially diminished if not eradicated. The name-calling

was generally a way to 'change the subject' or shame speakers into silence. If it were not this then labelling opponents as terrorists and puppets of Hamas was also common, especially by Trump and his supporters when responding to those protesting associated White House policies. Hamas came to be a boogieman for criticism within the USA of Trump administration actions and unwaveringly firm supporter of almost all Israeli actions. Officials accused protesters and others expressing disagreement as leftist, extremists, terrorists and Hamas dupes. It muddled clear and dispassionate discussions about the war.

Protests around the world included those on American university campuses. In some cases these shut down operations for many days or weeks as administrators tried to mediate a path between recognising freedom of speech, academic freedom, and obstruction. Those on the right of the political spectrum in the USA denounced this as leftist radicalism and indications of American educational institutions being awash with anti-Semitism and radical liberal ideology. After a time, the universities began to take firm steps to clear the protesters to include expelling students and police action. When Donald Trump returned to office, he began a campaign intimidating universities to seek deep changes, seeing them as hotbeds of anti-Semitism and the Radical Left. He also worked to deport foreign students who had participated in the protests and others critical of Israeli actions.

Regarding humanitarian aid, Israel insisted it was complying with international law and was permitting sufficient deliveries into the Strip. That Hamas stole or redirected substantial aid, contributing to a manufactured food crisis to discredit Israel, was refuted by the NGOs on the scene and outside agencies conducting reviews. Initially declining to use the word 'starvation', Israel continued to insist implausibly that none was occurring and indications of such was a Hamas ploy. The message later changed to no starvation owing to Israeli actions or inactions but only those of Hamas who was not

The vast majority of the 2.2 million Gazans were displaced multiple times during the two-year war, travelling the ruins of their community and facing privation. (Public Domain)

surrendering entirely and immediately to Israeli demands. The UN and some 100 aid agencies operating there emphatically disagreed and even Trump observed there was 'real starvation.' The humanitarian crisis, appearing only bound to grow, brought international pressure in various forms intending to alter Israel's behaviour.

Many nations imposed sanctions. It could not be business as usual given Israel's excesses. Twenty-five nations sent a message of appeal on 21 July 2025 to stop the 'drip' of aid and resume full supply without delay to arrest mass famine that was setting in. The UK, France and Canada threatened to impose sanctions if the offensive was not suspended and humanitarian aid allowed to flow immediately. Twenty or more countries followed suit. Spain recommended the European Union suspend its cooperation agreement with Israel and embargo arms shipments. It also said it would consider suspending a long-standing free trade agreement with Israel and place other bilateral support on hold. On 2 September 2024 the UK restricted supplies of military equipment to Israel supporting combat aircraft and ground attack that 'might be used in serious violations of international humanitarian law.' France did likewise in October. Britain subsequently froze trade negotiations. Slovenia was the first EU member to outright ban commerce of military hardware, this on 1 August 2025. In September Spain annulled hundreds of millions of dollars of weapons contracts with Israeli manufacturers. Germany also expressed concern with the Gaza situation, urging Israeli restraint and allowing aid to move. Germany had usually been in lockstep with Israeli policies since its founding or, at a minimum, did not make public statements denigrating such. Under the new circumstances this approach was seen as not in Germany's self-interest. On 8 August 2025, with the Israeli decision to further expand the war (see later), Germany suspended all military sales for which the equipment could potentially be employed in Gaza. It was then providing 33 percent of Israel's imported arms, the second largest total after the USA. In Italy, on 8 September 2025, there were mass protests and strikes for its government to join those recognising Palestine (it did not) and to halt the transit of weapons to Israel via Italian ports. Some dock workers walked off the job rather than work whilst American vessels carrying arms to Israel were docked. The action also reflected anger at Israel's obstruction of aid flotillas.

Israeli companies were banned from the 2025 Paris Airshow when they refused to remove attack weapons from their displays. They were not permitted to participate in several other arms expositions in Europe. (Half of Israel's arms exports, a significant portion of the economy, were to European customers.) Microsoft terminated cloud computing services for the IDF after it learned it was being used to surveil Palestinians. Organisations and nations began to divest from Israeli businesses. This was, incidentally, falling in line with a long-standing Palestinian program called Boycott, Divestment, Sanction that attempted to reproduce the pressure on South Africa decades before to end apartheid. Other European states called for Israel to be banned from international events like sporting competitions. Where Israelis appeared at such events others boycotted. Some nations cut off diplomatic relations and would not admit those with Israeli passports. There were moves to arrest common IDF soldiers during their travels abroad when evidence of potential complicity in war crimes was presented to local authorities. Ministers Smotrich and Ben-Gvir were sanctioned by several countries for their inflammatory anti-Palestinian rhetoric. The UK sanctioned some West Bank settlers over violence perpetrated against Palestinians.

A David's Sling Stunner interceptor is seen being launched on 26 February 2024. This medium-range system was employed against cruise missiles and some ballistic missiles. Elements not seen are radar and command-and-control facilities. The system attracted foreign customers. (IDF Spokesman)

Amongst the new weapons the IASF brought to the fight was the long-range Rampage. This 201 Squadron F-16I (869) is preparing to depart for the long roundtrip flight to Yemen on 10 January 2025 armed with two of these missiles, two wingtip AIM-120 missiles, and a full complement of drop tanks. (Public Domain)

The small fleet of F-35Is, still under delivery from the USA, played significant roles during the Gaza war to include long-range strikes in Yemen and Iran. Particularly the latter likely benefitted from the stealth qualities of the jet as well as its advanced systems. The fleet flew thousands of sorties and more than 15,000 operational hours. The 116 Squadron aircraft 905 has wingtip pylons and launchers for AIM-9X AAM. (IASF, Amit Agronov)

Evidence of alleged Israeli war crimes emerged from the Gaza Strip and elsewhere almost immediately. The humanitarian crisis in Gaza was amongst the issues raised as accusations of Israel committing genocide. This was on the lips of hundreds of millions of people worldwide by the end of 2024. The legal definition of genocide includes 'acts committed with intent to destroy, in whole or in part, a national, ethnical, racial or religious group.' The conclusions were based on the wholesale destruction and tens of thousands of deaths in the Gaza Strip accompanied by mass population displacement, the collapse of the health care and sanitation systems, and starvation from obstructing adequate supplies and NGOs. Likewise, were attacks on Palestinian educational, religious and cultural sites in the occupied territories. Seizure and clearing of land for corridors and the expanded buffer zone was undermining the residents' rights to self-determination. All made the area almost uninhabitable and was in great measure not clearly collateral to combat operations – evident to many as a systematic campaign to obliterate Palestinian life in the enclave.

At the end of October 2025 it was learned that the US State Department had logged hundreds of potential instances of possible human rights violations by the Israeli military during its campaign in Gaza.[12] On 10 June 2025 a UN commission concluded that Israel's actions constituted war crimes and crimes against humanity. Human Rights Watch and Amnesty International all concluded genocide was occurring. In July 2025 two Israeli human rights groups, B'Tselem and Physicians for Human Rights Israel, came to the same conclusion. The International Association of Genocide Scholars, more than 600 individuals worldwide, concluded in September 2025 that Israel's actions met the legal definition of genocide and constituted war crimes and crime against humanity. On 16 September 2025 an independent inquiry of the UN Human Rights Council also concluded that Israel's action in the Gaza Strip constituted genocide. It detailed four specific acts under the Convention on the Prevention and Punishment of the Crime of Genocide. It also concluded that Netanyahu, Gallant and President Isaac Herzog had incited these acts or failed to prevent them. Charges of genocide were raised at the ICJ, the case brought by South Africa. The Court found on 26 January 2024 that the accusations of inciting and commission of genocide were plausible and asked Israel to take measures preventing genocide. On 20 May the International Criminal Court (ICC) prosecutors recommended arrest warrants be issued for Netanyahu and Gallant, in addition to three Hamas leaders (two subsequently killed), for alleged war crimes. (That the Israelis and Palestinians were treated equally under the law was a source of outrage for some, seeing expressed moral equivalency as repugnant.) The Court issued the warrants on 21 November.[13] On 8 November Türkiye issued arrest warrants for Netanyahu and 36 other Israeli defence officials on charges of genocide and crimes against humanity during combat in Gaza and actions against aid flotillas. These include Katz, Ben-Gvir and Lieutenant General Eyal Zamir.

Israel insisted all these organisations were misrepresenting facts, taken in by Hamas lies, and anyone expressing such conclusions were duped mouthpieces of terrorists. It decried all the judgements and conclusions as outrageously one-sided, biased and unprecedented. (In fact, scores of national leaders had been indicted on similar charges.) On 5 June 2025 the American administration imposed personal sanctions on six of the ICC judges in response to what it assessed as politicisation and abuse of power in rulings unfavourable to Israel and the USA. (Neither Israel nor the USA were ICC members.) It

Major General Tomer Bar, Air Force commander, sits beside the CGS, Lieutenant General Herzi Halevi, for a situation assessment at the IASF headquarters in Tel Aviv on 14 April 2024 during the first Iran attack on Israel. (IASF)

then sanctioned three Palestinian human rights organisations that had sought ICC investigations of alleged genocide by Israel, claiming this was illegitimate targeting of Israel. In July 2025 The Netherlands' National Coordinator for Security and Counter-terrorism identified the Israeli government as a security threat for disseminating disinformation and undermining international justice institutions.

There were repeated cries of anti-Israeli bias over such declarations, especially from the UN. Israel dismissed the arrest warrants as an absurd PR stunt by a corrupt judiciary, amounting to anti-Semitism. Supporters asked why Hamas was not likewise being 'persecuted.' This ignored many statements by innumerable international bodies condemning Hamas behaviour. However, Hamas was not a member state of the UN and so not subject to terms of the UN charter, with review of violations, as was Israel. Hamas was also not subject to the Laws of War as are nation states, but its leadership and others could be (and were) indicted for crimes against humanity.

International efforts were also made to advance Palestinian statehood. This would make Israel's action against a nation-state and not just a campaign against stateless 'terrorists.' France announced on 24 July 2025 that it would recognise a Palestinian state in September when the UNGA reconvened. This was noteworthy in that it was a major European power adding its voice to the 145 or so other states already having recognised Palestine. The UK, Canada and Australia followed suit, but Britain made it conditional on Israel addressing the appalling conditions in Gaza, agreeing to a ceasefire and revived effort towards the two-state solution. Belgium also said its recognition was conditional on all Hamas-held hostages being released and the organisation ceased to govern Gaza. It considered targeted sanctions to pressure Israel. These nations and others also sanctioned Ministers Ben-Gvir and Smotrich.

The PA had given France commitment in mid-June 2025 to institute reforms and hold elections soon. France also insisted Hamas would have no role in Palestinian governance and must surrender its weapons. The PA had been criticised for not immediately condemning the 7 October 2023 attack but did say the attacks on civilians had harmed the Palestinian cause. On 23 April 2025 it called for Hamas to lay down its arms and release all remaining hostages, adding that retaining hostages was lending Israel justification for genocide.

A UN conference on advancing the two-state solution was held in late July 2025, with the USA and Israel boycotting. The conference made important declarative statements about ending terrorism. This New York Declaration called for an immediate ceasefire, release of all hostages and establishment of a viable Palestinian state based on the two-state solution with Hamas disarmed and ceasing to govern in Gaza. The PA agreed to hold long-delayed elections in 2026 without Hamas. On 12 September the UNGA voted to endorse the conference recommendations. Netanyahu's response was to sign an order pushing ahead with the E1 settlement plan that would split the West Bank, stating emphatically 'there will be no Palestinian state' – another life's goal for the man.

The formal recognitions came in September at a UN summit on the Palestinian statehood question, hosted by France and Saudi Arabia. France gave its recognition on the 22nd and on prior days Australia, Canada, the UK and Portugal. Coming were five more to include Belgium. Most nations offered to help reach a solution, apart from declarative statements. The American administration had been unable to convince the countries not to take this step and was one of only 10 UN member states to vote against holding the summit. The USA was the only permanent member of the Security Council who did not recognise a Palestinian state. Its no-vote could deny

Palestinian Authority President Mahmoud Abbas and visiting Russian President Vladimir Putin pass an honour guard on 2 June 2012. Abbas served for 20 years in the post and was criticised for stagnation and corruption within the PA. (Public Domain)

Palestine member status at the UN and so recognition appeared, in the short-term, to be a hollow gesture.

American and Israeli representatives did not attend the summit, the latter labelling it a charade. As expected, Israel and the Trump administration denounced all as deluded reactions to Hamas slander, illegitimate, anti-Israeli motives, and a reward for terrorism. Vituperative rhetoric notwithstanding, they insisted that a negotiated settlement between the sides was the path forward not an imposition by outside bodies. This evidently assumed the acting nations did not see that such was impossible under the present Israeli government or any over the prior decade. Outside pressure was essential. The natural question was how long after 7 October, and after how much blood and destruction, would resuming efforts at achieving a two-state solution not constitute a reward. They saw statehood was a right, not a reward.

The USA and Israel began to retaliate diplomatically, willing to sacrifice long-standing relationships. Ireland's support for Palestinian statehood and backing of South Africa in bringing of genocide charges at the World Court was cause for Israel to close its embassy in Dublin. The new USA administration terminated financial assistance to South Africa, in part, for its stance against Israel's war in Gaza. The announcement by Canada to support Palestinian statehood was cause for President Trump to impose trade tariffs that might have been held in abeyance during ongoing trade talks.

Netanyahu and his Likud party insisted a Palestinian state would be jihadist, imposed on its ancestral homeland and bent on Israel's annihilation, and so accepting it would be national suicide. After 7 October the majority of Israelis agreed with this position. Some members of the Cabinet threatened to dissolve the PA and annex the West Bank. Apart from the Americans, nearly everyone strongly advised Israel against taking such steps. The Americans not only rejected efforts to recognise a Palestinian state but also ceased recognising the PA as a foreign government. It began refusing non-immigrant visas for anyone presenting a Palestinian passport and revoked the visas of many PLO and PA officials. This last denied the diplomats' ability to attend UN meetings in New York, a move coordinated with Israel to ensure PA leadership could not attend the UNGA meetings in September 2025. It violated USA's obligations as host of the UN on its territory.

On 28 October 2024 the Knesset voted to ban UNRWA activities within Israel and territory under its control and cease cooperating with it, labelling it a terrorist organisation. This followed revelations of evidence that 12 Hamas sympathisers had been working within the organisation of 14,000 inside the Gaza Strip and assisted in the 7 October attack (later amended to participating). Seventeen nations suspended funds to UNRWA, but all except the USA reversed this when Israel failed to produce significant evidence. The UN investigation did identify nine workers who were suspected and they were dismissed. Gallant later stated that 185 personnel were military members of Hamas and 51 with the PIJ. One combatant described finding explosives and combat equipment in UNRWA buildings.[14] (In time Israel implied every entity in Gaza, including foreign, were tainted by Hamas contact and there was a conspiracy of silence about it.) Regardless, the Israeli law severely impaired UNRWA's program of assistance to Palestinian refugees, but it continued to work inside the Strip. By fall 2025 some 400 UN staffers had been killed, more than in any other conflict.

The Israeli legislation had more to do with a right-wing opinion that UNRWA was perpetuating Palestinian 'victimhood' as refugees (grown to 5.9 million) and their 'right of return', this tarnishing Israel's image as an occupier and any perceived legitimate claims to occupied territory. Israelis holding this opinion also insisted that any claim to refugee status and right of return did not extend to descendants of those who had originally fled or were forced from their homes in Palestine. This suggests they believed these 'issues' would dissolve with the death of the last of those original refugees.

The General Assembly asked the ICJ to assess whether Israel was violating the UN charter and its obligations as an occupier with the law banning UNRWA. When the Court held associated hearings beginning on 28 April 2025, Israel derided the proceedings and chose not to attend. At that time they offered that 1,462 UNRWA employees in the Strip were Hamas terrorists and more were likely to be identified. It also stated the organisation permitted teaching of hatred towards Israel in schools it supervised. On 22 October 2025 the Court rendered an opinion that, as an occupying power, Israel was obligated by law to work with the UNRWA to facilitate humanitarian aid delivery and not to use starvation as a weapon of war. It found that the Agency had not violated impartiality rules and that the residents of the Gaza Strip had been deprived of adequate aid by Israeli policies. Israel called the opinion 'shameful', the USA adding it was 'corrupt', both saying the UN body was being anti-Israeli. Israel insisted it was fully compliant with international law.

The Israeli economy took a big hit from spending on the war that exceeded $55.6 billion, the reduced workforce, decreased consumer spending, loss of business (reduced investments, import and exports), and downgraded national credit rating. During 2024 emigration rose sharply as some Israelis sought to get away from the discord. On 15 September 2025 Netanyahu admitted that Israel faced a period of isolation and economic contraction over what he insisted was 'an extreme Islamist agenda' negatively influencing nations opposing what the PM insisted were essential defence actions. Israel was risking becoming a pariah as in past decades. The defence industry would have to be built up (again) to ensure adequate self-reliance. Netanyahu's opposition disagreed, saying none of this was fated and friendly nations were only responding to Likud's extreme and flawed policies extending an unnecessarily harsh war and not part of a vast international conspiracy hoodwinking scores of national leaders. Israel appeared to suggest Hamas had perpetrated the largest and most successful campaign of misinformation in history extending to all parts of the globe and affecting governments, independent inquiries and individuals alike. Israel's information, on the other hand, was to be taken at face value as unquestionably factual and without bias.[15]

The world Jewish community was also torn by the prolonged Israeli war on its neighbours, the occupation, and especially the harsh measures in the Gaza Strip. By 2025 much of the support that had followed the 7 October 2023 attack had dissipated to be replaced with unease if not revulsion. Phrases like 'I support Israel, but do not agree with what it is doing' distanced the speakers from those who backed Israel and Netanyahu without question. A positive answer to the question 'Do you believe Israel shares some blame for the 7 October attack?' split families and friendships. A rift formed that widened as the war continued.

Netanyahu was steadfast at insisting Hamas must be eradicated and anyone who attacked Israel would feel retribution. However, he and his government went further. Opponents of Israeli policies and actions would suffer consequences. The criticisms and calls for restraint were judged by Israelis as a double-standard from people who simply did not understand their circumstances. As before, the intent was to 'circle the wagons' and weather the storm with a sense of the righteous underdog. It was 'Israel versus the world', and Israelis were convinced they would prevail. Whilst Netanyahu strongly believed that any sign of weakness in the Middle East makes one 'roadkill', he was prepared to exploit weakness in others to benefit Israel.

6

IRAN-ISRAEL WAR

Before or soon after Trump returned to office, he and Netanyahu evidently discussed further diminishing Iran's support for destabilising forces beyond its borders and to ensure it never developed nuclear weapons. The manner of any future action remained unclear, but USA intelligence agencies predicted Israel would attack Iran's nuclear facilities during 2025.

The IAEA believed there was 400kg (880lb) of uranium enriched to 60 percent, below the 90 percent required for a bomb. The final enrichment step could conceivably be performed within months. All this aroused deep suspicions that a weapons program was the goal. Netanyahu had argued for more than a decade that Iran was on the verge of building a nuclear weapon and suitable delivery system given its equally expansive ballistic missile program. The assessment that Iran was actively pursuing nuclear weapons was not universally shared by intelligence agencies around the world. Trump chose to believe the Israeli evaluation despite USA intelligence services having concluded otherwise. The Israeli agencies had an outsized reputation based on past performance and their own boasting. They were better than most but had gotten some critical assessments badly and tragically wrong. Both leaders surrounded themselves with individuals who reflected their world view and were more likely to deliver welcomed answers.

NUCLEAR IMBROGLIO

In March 2025 President Trump made clear that unless Iran made significant concessions with respect to its nuclear program within 60 days, beginning 12 April, a military option may become necessary. The USA's demands included creasing uranium enrichment verifiably (including by American inspectors), surrendering highly enriched material, and dismantling any weapons program. The Iranians considered the 'negotiations' tantamount to *diktat* and evidently 'slow-rolled' the talks. As this progressed through May the American military began to amass resources near Iran for a potential strike. Joint exercises – one such on 4 March – and contingency planning with the IDF was also underway. Given that the IASF had earlier neutralised three of Iran's four S-300 air defence systems, any aerial offensive could go a bit easier. However, other systems would still be demanding to suppress and Iranian responses, especially in striking at Israel and American assets throughout the Middle East, could be significant. The Iranians were training and improving systems in preparation. Unlike Syria, their counter-air assets were not to be taken lightly. Unconventional responses to an attack, with terrorist tactics in the USA and elsewhere, were also to be considered.

Trump gave more time at the end of May for negotiations to make progress, and some of the forward-deployed resources were pulled back. He also admitted to urging Netanyahu not to strike whilst

Minister of Defense Israel Katz and Secretary of Defense Pete Hegseth stroll down a hallway at the Pentagon on 18 July 2025. These men collaborated on joint operations against Iran in June that year. (USA DoD, Staff Sgt. Noel Diaz)

dialogue continued. In a telephone conversation between the leaders on 9 June Trump said that he counselled the Gaza war be wrapped up soon and for Netanyahu to cease threatening Iran. During his campaign for President, Donald Trump had boasted that he would end the wars in Gaza and Ukraine during his first day in office. Initially encouraging Netanyahu to pound Hamas even harder, and providing the arms to do so, ran contrary to this intention. However, five months into his term, having made no progress in Ukraine and with the Gaza war looking very bleak, Trump needed a 'win.' Netanyahu may have been concerned that any final deal between the USA and Iran would leave the latter's nuclear program fundamentally intact, as had the JCPoA, and so only further stretch out weapons development.

The IAEA issued a report on 31 May assessing that Iran was not compliant with its non-proliferation obligations – though with no evidence of a weapons program. Iran angrily retorted that it would impede further inspections and move to accelerate its enrichment program. Concern that an Israeli strike was imminent arose anew, this potentially provoking a major regional conflict. The USA began preparing its diplomatic missions in the area for possible retaliatory attacks.

On 7 June 2025 Iran disclosed that it had clandestinely stolen thousands of classified documents pertaining to Israel's nuclear facilities, approximately two weeks after Israel arrested two of its citizens for security breaches on behalf of Iran. The Islamic Republic stated the documents were sure to assist its own nuclear program and would eventually be made public. This revelation seemed to parallel an Israeli operation that had collected an archive of Iranian nuclear documents in 2018 that showed Iran had a weapons programme up to 2003.

ISRAEL PRE-EMPTS

Israel may have judged this the best time for striking Iran. Netanyahu, once again feeling his political mortality, likely assessed the window of opportunity might soon close on what he had made his life's mission to prevent a 'second Holocaust' of the Jewish people. Decades of Iranians chanting 'death to Israel', threatening ballistic missiles strikes, and arming proxies attacking Israel, had become too much.

Two top secret American intelligence documents had been leaked on 18 October 2024 that outlined Israeli resources and plans to strike Iranian nuclear facilities. This included details of a training exercise, drone strike routes, and preparation of 40 Rocks and 16 Golden Horizon air-launched ballistic missiles. The latter had not previously been

disclosed but was believed to be a variant of the system that yielded Rocks. All were located at Hatzerim AB, suggesting F-15Is and F-16Is were the principal launch platform. There was also mention of a stealth UAV designated RA-01 operating from Ramon AB. The documents also referred to Israel's nuclear strike capability. Their contents suggested both a close operations planning relationship between the two nations as well as the extent of American surveillance of Israel to gather information withheld by that country.

Trump's 60-day negotiation timeline expired on 13 June, a day after the IAEA board voted formally that Iran was non-compliant. In the early morning darkness of that day Israel launched what it called a pre-emptive strike against Iran that, it stated, had enough highly enriched uranium for nine nuclear weapons that could be constructed in a short time. The government said the operation would extend across several days or weeks. The USA denied playing any role but would assist in defence of Israel and had clearly been forewarned hours or days in advance.

The initial strike involved more than 200 fighter-bombers, in five waves, delivering some 330 individual munitions on over 100 targets throughout the country. The formations likely flew through Syrian and Iraqi airspace – Iraq announcing its airspace closed. They focused on the principal enrichment facility at Natanz and individual scientists, ballistic missile facilities, air defence assets (including air bases) plus key national military leadership and their headquarters to include the Ministry of Defence headquarters in Tehran. Israel released video of drones being launched and striking ballistic missile transporter erector-launchers (TEL) and silos, claiming these were the work of hundreds of Mossad personnel infiltrated into the country with their equipment to contribute to the campaign. It was speculated some or most of these personnel actually operated from Kurdistan or other sites outside Iran and Israel. Their targets were said to include air defence systems, and the IASF appeared to operate with near impunity from the first. Israel also stated 'ground commando units' operated inside the country during the war and executed 'deception tactics.' Iran evidently succeeded in shooting down 11 UAVs – Israel acknowledging some of these whilst Iran offered convincing evidence. Other claims to have brought down combat aircraft and captured aircrew were clear propaganda. This they said included an F-35I and the pilot being female.

At top is an image of a UAV shot down in Iran. At bottom, on the left was an image taken on 29 October 2024 in Lebanon and at right a posting on X of what was likely a cellphone video shot on 18 June 2025 in Syria, the Golan Heights. These reveal a previously unknown aircraft shape with planform intended for radar evasion (stealth). This was surely an Israeli aircraft and the altitude plus airspeed suggested a UAV, most probably the reported RA-01 operating from Raman AB. There may have been a propeller-driven version as well as one jet-powered. (Public Domain)

A flight of 106 Squadron F-16Is prepare for take-off in a long-range mission to strike targets inside Iran during a night in June 2025. They carry the 600gal outsized wing drop tanks and 300 gallon centreline tank plus AMRAAM missiles on the wingtips. The underwing stores are GBU-39 SDB standoff weapons. (IDF Spokesman)

This image of an apartment building in Tehran shows a hit on 13 June 2025 with great precision to kill a targeted individual. The impact shows witness marks from the wings of the standoff munition. Unseen is likely extensive damage inside the building that would inflict collateral casualties, though windows of adjacent apartments remain intact. However, the impact appears to have been at a floor junction that may have diminished blast intensity inside the immediate rooms. (Mizan New agency)

Israel asserted without compunction it had killed nine nuclear scientists and experts. The deliberate targeting of such noncombatants, with high potential for collateral casualties, was held forth by foreign observers as a war crime. Israel insisting these individuals were legitimate targets does not make it true.[1] Similarly, targeting military leadership whilst sleeping in their homes was certain to involve collateral casualties unlike striking them at their workplace. Israel appeared to have eliminated the military chief of the armed forces (his replacement killed days later), the chief of the IRGC, the head of the IRGC air force, and the head of the central headquarters, plus a close security aid to the Supreme Leader. The name of the overall operation, Rising Lion, would suggest Israel hoped to spark a revolt to unseat the Islamic government. Israeli rhetoric reflected the same aspiration. However, the nation was only drawn closer together under the enemy assault.

Iran's initial response involved more than 100 OWAs, most intercepted by Jordanian and Israeli defences. Some Israeli intercepts were over Syrian and Saudi Arabian territory. A second IASF wave of strikes came on the 13th and a second Iranian response with 100–150 ballistic missiles, amongst them Houthi rockets. With American assistance, most of the Iranian missiles were destroyed, but the few that got through caused modest damage and casualties. Iran's leadership warned that it reserved the right to strike at the regional bases of any country that helped defend Israel. This was a message to the USA to restrain Israel. Given Israel was armed and enabled by the USA, Iran certainly considered it complicit. However, any strikes on American assets would risk a response that would widen the war.

A further wave of Israeli attacks and Iranian missiles were exchanged early on 14 June. On the 15th the reciprocal attacks were being made in daylight. These later IASF missions were usually on the order of 50–60 aircraft. Standoff munitions were evidently the preferred weapon and Iran reported shooting down many of these. The Iranian fire brought significant destruction and loss of life in the Galilee region and in central Israel. At some point a missile fell near the Kiryah (military headquarters), in Tel Aviv, and another destroyed the military intelligence training building north of the city. Tel Nof AB was also said to have been hit. Israel responded by attacking Iran's energy sector with bombing of oil and gas facilities, and later the state-run television news studio in Tehran on the premise its broadcasts also served military, incitement and propaganda purposes. Bombing of the national police headquarters and a notorious prison in Tehran seemed only intended to undermine public order as part of hoped-for regime change. The IASF bombed an inactive heavy-water nuclear reactor on the 18th that could be used to produce plutonium but spared the one functioning reactor in the country as this would have released highly radioactive material.

Impacts by Iranian ordnance on or near security targets were off-limits to media and reports even from Israeli sources censored such that the extent of damage to such facilities were difficult to assess. The training building showed four missile impacts to obtain a hit. On the 18th Israel alluded to possibly intentionally targeting Iran's Supreme Leader, Ayatollah Ali Khamenei. A news report in the USA a few days prior alleged that Netanyahu had proposed assassinating the Supreme Leader, the Mossad having contrived a scheme. However, President Trump had nixed the idea. Netanyahu claimed the report was false. Later, Trump and Netanyahu noted whereabouts of the man were known and he could be eliminated without great effort.

Although Israel decried Iran targeting population centres – which, given the poor accuracy of the missiles, may not be true – it had itself targeted individuals and facilities inside Iranian cities to include hitting residential areas and apartment buildings. The accuracy of the ballistic missiles was hundreds of metres for the older models and tens of metres for the newer. The accuracy of Israeli aircraft-delivery munitions was presumably metres. Defense Minister Israel Katz threatened to change targeting such that 'Tehran will burn.' Apart from being an irresponsible statement from a senior government official, this would have been a difficult goal to achieve given that the city was built primarily of concrete.

This image purports to show a flight of eight F-15Is en route to Iran in daylight during the June 2025 war. The aircraft have every external fuel tank that can be mounted plus JDAM bombs, but no AAM are evident. (IDF Spokesman)

Collateral casualties from IASF strikes were significant and at least one entire apartment building was brought down. On 19 June a missile struck the main hospital complex in Beersheba which Israel insisted was intentional and crossed a line, or another line as this has been asserted several times in prior days. Iran said, credibly, it had been targeting a nearby technical park that served the IDF but later correcting this to a command and intelligence centre. (Israel had hit an Iranian hospital whilst attacking a missile base.) It subsequently warned Israelis to stay clear of military and intelligence sites. The technology park was hit a day later.

The IASF bombed Mashhad Airport in eastern Iran, targeting the Boeing 707 tanker aircraft. This was its farthest penetration and possibly the longest range combat mission ever for the service.[2] However, most targets in the far north and east of the enormous country were likely hit with very long-range standoff missiles – Rocks, Golden Horizon and Air LORA – owing to aircraft range and paucity of aerial refuelling assets. (Aircraft contrails were visible from the ground and people were posting comments and cellphone pictures on social media, allowing the extent of operations to be tracked.) The Israelis also destroyed some 50 combat aircraft at the IAP in Tehran and elsewhere, knocked-out radar and some runways, but did not attack civil aviation and its airports. Given that Iranian air power posed no threat to Israel, this targeting appeared to be general punishment and possibly a sign principal targets (obscure) had grown scarce. Some of the aircraft claimed destroyed were likely decoys as Iran had evacuated its flyable jets to far eastern fields. The Iranian Air Force did launch aircraft early in the war for attempted intercepts, likely F-4Es and F-5Es, possibly with drone shoot-downs.[3] Ground-based intercept radars were soon destroyed or jammed, making more attempts impractical. Iran also reported that Israel had launched a determined cyber war on national infrastructure, but that this had been blunted.

It seemed Iranian efforts to overwhelm Israeli defences with repeated large barrages was being somewhat successful. More missiles reached the ground – some 22 by the end of the 14th. By the fourth day Iran had fired 370 ballistic missiles and, of 30 total impacts, those in Tel Aviv and Haifa soon exceeded the number from the 1991 Gulf War. An oil refinery in Haifa and elements of the power grid had been hit. In Iran the IASF claimed to have destroyed a third of the missile launchers (120, 40 percent by the 19th), plus striking missile and drone storage in addition to production facilities. Apart from above-ground TELs there were also hardened shelters for these vehicles and bunkers from which rockets could be fired directly, their destruction more problematic. Some 70 SAM batteries were also said to have been struck. An alleged attack on a convoy of military vehicles transporting weapons suggests real-time surveillance from overhead drones. By the 19th the volume of ballistic missile barrage fire had decline significantly to 'dozens.' However, Iran insisted this was due to employing more accurate missile types, substituting 'quantity with quality.'

A Hardened Aircraft Shelter at TBF1 Mehrabad is shown with a penetration hole from an Israeli munition, probably on 14 June 2025. Given that no other damage is evident, the warhead appears to have not detonated. (Tom Cooper collection)

The size of the Air LORA weapon is evident in comparison with the F-16I carrying two during taxi, with little else, and an inserted flight test image showing a release. This air-launched ballistic missile offered considerable standoff distance and was likely used to prosecute a number of targets in Iran during June 2025. (Israel Aerospace Industries)

This image titled 'Attack on an Iranian air defence missile battery' shows an Iranian SAM missile transport/launch vehicle, with personnel nearby, targeted by an IASF aircrew. Possibly from 16 June 2025, it is a frame-grab from a video recording of a cockpit display. (IDF)

Within days the IASF claimed to have achieved air superiority over Tehran. It continued striking targets in the capital, including Quds Force headquarters, and warned residents of some districts to evacuate. Yet, Iran still said it was shooting down inbound missiles over Tehran. The death toll had reached only 24 in Israel thanks to its early warning system, the vast number of bomb shelters, alerting means, and an effective civil defence organisation. (People could download a cellphone app that would send warnings of missiles inbound to their area.) Lacking these, Iranian casualties were more than 10 times those in Israel. Iranian attacks slackened during the night of 16/17 June, but the government said on the 17th that a 'punitive operation' was coming and advised residents of Tel Aviv and Haifa to evacuate. Missiles and drones from Yemen and elsewhere added to the mix. By the 18th it seemed Iran had fired more than 400 missiles and, with those expended in 2024 plus the losses to IASF attacks inside Iran, there was speculation reload rounds would soon run short. Overnight raids on the 18th, reportedly the 11th wave, were said to include the hypersonic Fattah-I missile that also had a manoeuvring re-entry vehicle.[4] Multiple sub-munitions were also deployed by some rockets. All these certainly complicated the intercept task. Forty sites had been hit inside Israel and the West Bank to that time. On the 19th another complication arose when Iran began firing missiles with multiple warheads.

On 16 June Iranian authorities raided a three-story residential building in Tehran said to have been the assembly facility for the drones and explosives. Other 'workshops' in Esfahan, Mashhad and Shiraz were found. At least five 'Mossad agents' were executed. Something of a Mossad paranoia gripped the nation. The government

A leafy Israeli suburb lies in ruin after an impact from an Iranian ballistic missile warhead. Such damage had never before been experienced in Israel and had barely been imaginable before Israel and Iran came to blows. (Tom Cooper collection)

subsequently arrested 700 'mercenaries' said to be Israeli agents or individuals supporting its subversive activities inside the country. Weeks after the war Iran accelerated the expulsion of nearly half a million undocumented Afghan labourers and their families in the belief some may have aided Israeli operations.

AMERICA STEPS IN

Iran declined to attend a sixth round of talks with the USA and instead some in the government suggested the Republic should withdraw from the NPT altogether and close the Strait of Hormuz, choking oil/gas transit. Netanyahu said Israel had set back Iran's nuclear program 'a very, very long time', but experts disputed this given that the deeply buried facilities remained intact. Israel had gone to war knowing it could not destroy the Iranian program. On the 14th the government spoke with the USA about becoming more involved, though without specifics, and the Americans initially demurred. It was widely believed only the USAF could successfully bomb the deeply buried nuclear sites, especially that at Fordow. However, this also risked radiological release. It may have been Netanyahu's hope from the beginning that the USA could be compelled to help 'finish the job' once the IASF had destroyed the air defence array and Iranian ability to strike USA assets in the region had been diminished.

By the 17th Trump had soured on negotiations and wanted to bring the Iranian threat to an end. He seemed to be leaning towards joining the fighting but weighed the potential for sparking a wider conflict. The President called for Iran to 'unconditionally surrender' and advised the 10 million residents of Tehran to evacuate. The Department of Defense sent more than 30 aerial refuelling tankers to the region to support potential operations that could include refuelling Israeli aircraft. The IASF tanker fleet was too small to refuel the number of aircraft being sent on the Iranian missions. Yet, the strike aircraft still conducted more than 600 'contacts', though some from USAF tankers.[5] The refuellings may have been employed to respond to emergencies, reach the farthest targets, and extend loiter

time to aid fighters searching for TELs whose mobility challenged targeting. Word emerged of an F-15I that could not feed from a wing tank and faced an emergency landing in an intervening country. A tanker finally reached it and permitted the aircraft's mission to be completed.

On 19 June President Trump announced his intent to allow up to two weeks for diplomacy to run its course. This brought cries of dismay from Israelis who foresaw potentially two more weeks under Iranian bombardment. To that day Israel claimed to have destroyed two-thirds of the ballistic missile launchers, but evidence suggests some were decoys. With approximately 500 missiles having been fired, this suggested Iran still had up to 1,000 medium-range missiles remaining. At a rate of about 10 percent penetrating the defensive shield, up to 100 more successful impacts inside Israel with an equal number of fatalities could be anticipated before exhausting the supply or the 14-day window. Even American contribution to reducing the nuclear facilities would not necessarily ensure an end to the war.

The first instance of diplomacy were talks with Iran by three European nations, hosted by France, exploring alternatives. Iran again stated it would insist on continuing to enrich uranium, and so the basic American/Israeli demand remained unmet. Trump's two-week pause was, however, a ruse. In the early hours of 22 June (local time) seven B-2A bombers dropped sixteen 13,600kg (30,000lb) GBU-57 Massive Ordnance Penetrator bombs on Fordow and Natanz. Simultaneously, more than 24 Tomahawk cruise missiles, fired from a submarine in the Arabian Sea, impacted Isfahan. Although ingress and egress were along much the same path as the IASF missions, the USAF conducted air defences suppression strikes before the B-2s arrived.

The Iranians retaliated on 23 June with ballistic missiles targeting the American Al Udeid AB in Qatar. All but one projectile was intercepted, the lone warhead falling in an open area. Iran also continued to trade blows with Israel and significant damage was being suffered by both combatants. On the 22nd Israel counted a total 525 missiles and 1,000 drones having been fired at it.

An IDF-released image purports to show a strike beside an Iranian ballistic missile TEL. The missile is visible in the boxy structure (casting a shadow to right), yet to be erected. However, the lack of secondary explosions suggests this may have been a decoy. (IDF)

A B-2A (infrared image) of the 509th Bomb Wing at Whiteman Air Force Base, Missouri, is being prepared on 21 June 2025 for the 18-hour mission to Iran and back. It carried two of the GBU-57 Massive Ordnance Penetrator bombs (wings not yet attached in image). (USAF)

On the 23rd Israel signalled that within days it would have achieved all its objectives. There was reason to believe it was running short of ABM interceptors and the percentage of Iranian missiles penetrating the shield was increasing, though possibly owing to more capable warhead systems being employed. That evening, in Washington, Trump announced a ceasefire mediated by Qatar. Iran was to cease attacks within six hours and then Israel six hours after that. A final wave of Iranian missile launches saw one hit a residential building in Beersheba and kill four individuals. As was its wont, Israel unleashed a final round of bombing in Iran into the 24th – the 12th day of the war – that brought an angry rebuff from Trump. The last targets included another nuclear scientist. Israel then said it intercepted two missiles fired beyond the ceasefire limits and responded with more strikes in Iran. A phone call from Trump elicited a promise from Netanyahu to desist. Aircraft already inbound to targets were reportedly recalled.

The IASF stated it had hit 900 targets inside Iran, including 200 missile launchers (claimed to be half the total). Targeted killings included 11 nuclear scientists and 30 high-level defence officials. The final Iranian casualties were 657 fatalities and more than 2,500 injured whilst Israel summarised 29 deaths and hundreds wounded. It also reported having performed thousands of UAV flight hours and struck 500 targets from armed UAVs. Israel said its ABM systems (including THAAD) had been 86 percent effective against Iranian ballistic missiles, suggesting approximately 70 had reached the ground and 36 hitting populated areas. Against Iranian drones it claimed 99 percent success rate.[6] The damage in Israel was estimated at $1.8 billion and included about 25 buildings that needed to be razed and rebuilt. Tens of thousands of claims for government compensation were submitted.

The validity of Iranian casualty figures has been questioned, these potentially inflated to place Israel in bad light. There are,

This 25 May 2023 test firing of a Khorramshahr-4 medium-range ballistic missile shows the simple and inexpensive TEL the Iranians built. Derived from the North Korean Hwasong-10, the missile had a 2,000km (1,240mi) range with a 1,500kg (3,300lb) warhead. (Iranian Defence Ministry)

however, no independent sources for such numbers and they do not appear beyond reasonable. An impartial author will also question the very low Israeli figures given government censorship potentially concealing military casualties from disclosure. Iran fired 40 percent more missiles than in earlier barrages that were acknowledged to have hit military targets, and more got through defences in June 2025. That they failed to target such military assets, air bases continually generating and recovering sorties, and cause associated casualties, is not credible. There is substantial evidence that Nevatim was hit multiple times. However, the bases likely had the best defences and the satellite images of impact craters at bases independent researchers were able to obtain for the April and October 2024 strikes posted none for the June 2025 barrages. Far-right ministers wanted Shin Bet to control coverage of damage to even public property as it generated 'bad press.' This reflected a willingness in the wider government to withhold damage and casualty numbers. There is evidence of diligent work to 'scrub' from the Internet particularly images of damage in Israel from enemy action and other material generally portraying Israel unfavourably. Israel seems to have induced online media companies to also remove such material.

GAINS?

Soon after the B-2 strikes President Trump claimed the three facilities were 'obliterated' and later that the entire nuclear program was 'totally obliterated.' Netanyahu declared that Israel had achieved all its goals. However, subsequent assessment and intelligence collection concluded that the nuclear targets were not destroyed. (The Isfahan facility had underground chambers so deep that even the GBU-57 could not reach them and no attempt was made. There was also reason to believe there were undeclared nuclear sites.) The Iranian program may have only been set back months or a few years, and the existing quantity of highly enriched uranium remained

unaccounted for. The program remained fundamentally intact, ballistic missile manufacturing could be reconstituted, regional proxy war capabilities rekindled, dead personnel replaced, and the will to undertake these steps only redoubled as the theocracy survived. These conclusions did not fit the political 'spin' and so politicians downplayed such reports as inconclusive, politically motivated, and denigrating the efforts of the 'brave men and women of the armed forces.' In January 2026 Trump began threatening Iran again to reach a nuclear deal, thus implicitly acknowledging the programme remained extant and considered a threat.

Near-term Israeli achievements likely just delayed the threat but established some level of deterrence and won political accolades at home. It was speculated that, should Iran choose to continue its enrichment program, Israel might need to work over the long-term to continually impede such efforts through various means to include future bombing that could also require continual degradation of restored air defences. On 27 June Defense Minister Katz revealed that he had instructed the IDF to formulate an 'enforcement plan' to include 'maintaining Israel's air superiority, preventing nuclear and missile development, and responding to Iranian support for terrorist activity.' This, some feared, could induce Iran to pursue a nuclear weapon, even if it had not been on that path previously, for its own deterrence. By the end of December Jerusalem and Washington were grousing over Iran's efforts to ramp-up ballistic missile production. Israel threatened bombing to degrade the effort.

On 2 July Iran declared it would no longer cooperate with the IAEA, in violation of the NPT, but did not repudiate that treaty. Yet, agreement to resume cooperation was reached on 11 September. On 27 September the UN re-imposed sanctions on Iran for failure to show sufficient NPT compliance. Shipments of arms to its proxies in the region also resumed in an effort to reassert Iranian influence.

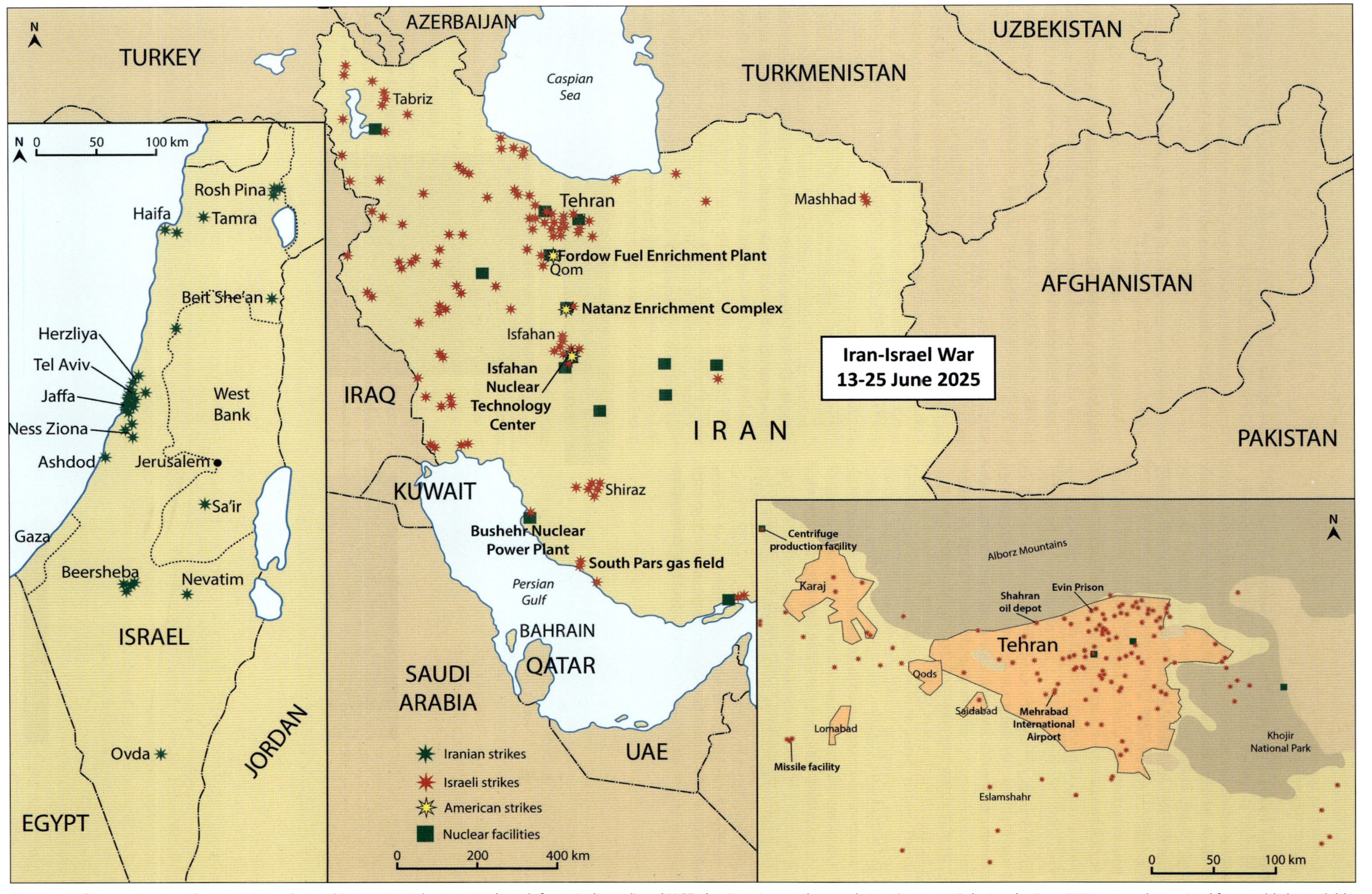

This map reflects Iranian missiles impacts inside Israel (approximately 40 to 70, though fewer indicated) and IASF plus American strikes inside Iran (some 900) during the June 2025 war as determined from publicly available sources. Israel censored reports of hits on military targets, and so the map may be incomplete. (Map by George Anderson)

7

ANOTHER RENEWED GAZA OFFENSIVE

The IDF operations in Gaza had continued during the Iranian crisis with more death, destruction, and mounting hunger. There was renewed optimism a ceasefire and possible end to the war with Hamas was near. The May mobilisation had been extended to 10 July 2025. On 30 June it had been reported the Army advised the government it would require two more weeks to accomplish its mission in the Strip as it issued new evacuation orders for the northern region. The two weeks passed with no declaration of goals achieved. It was winning all its battles but had not defeated the enemy. Achieving tactical objectives were more difficult given the much-diminished Hamas had gone underground and assumed attritional guerrilla methods. Its explosives were collected from unexploded Israeli ordnance and traps set using materials assembled locally. The IDF leadership recommended a diplomatic solution.

AID DISTRIBUTION CRISIS

A new truce proposal from the USA, announced on 26 May 2025, would have seen half the hostages released for a 60-day ceasefire leading to negotiations for a final resolution. Israel accepted this offer on the 29th, though extreme right-wing members of the government again threatened to resign. Given this was much the same deal the Israelis signed and then violated a year before, and firm Israeli demands for Hamas to disarm and disband were known, Hamas was less than enamoured with the proposal. Israel warned them to accept or face 'annihilation'; a threat appearing hollow after 18 months of combat. On the 31st Hamas gave a counter proposal which the USA mediator and Israel, who evidently had a different interpretation of 'negotiating', considered an unacceptable rejection of the 'generous' offer. (Israel and the USA clearly found even indirectly negotiating with the 'murderous barbarians' repugnant. Donald Trump, particularly, could not stop himself from uttering unhelpful, undiplomatic and inflammatory rhetoric.) Hamas wanted a permanent ceasefire with immediate Israeli pull-back and eventual withdrawal plus American guarantees that Israel would comply. That the Palestinians still considered America a reliable and impartial guarantor of Israeli compliance demonstrated the paucity of their leverage.

All this back-and-forth was during a period when the food crisis in the Strip was becoming acute. That months after the 2 March 2025 cutoff of all aid into the enclave people were starving was not surprising, but many still denied it. Netanyahu acknowledged that scenes of mass starvation would undermine any remaining support abroad for the war. Some of his far-right ministers continued opposing any aid entering the enclave.

In late May Israel agreed to permit aid to enter, distributed by an organisation approved by the military to bypass Hamas and existing assistance agencies. The IDF would regulate the flow that would be distributed by a new private American entity, the Gaza Humanitarian Foundation (GHF), and with security by a private American contractor. At least initially only four aid distribution sites in the south were planned whereas the UN and NGOs had operated some 400 throughout. The GHF effort would feed only about 60 percent of the population or 1.2 million people. This was demonstrably inadequate. It appeared intended to further condense the population away for areas to be cleared and possibly declared free-fire zones.

On 19 May Israel allowed five aid trucks to enter the Strip and this trickle slowly increased in following days. This was evidently a face-saving measure only as the need would normally require hundreds of trucks per day. The GHF began operating on 26 May, but its executive director resigned almost immediately pointing to impartiality and independence issues that were impeding the mission. The following day the distribution was so chaotic that an IASF helicopter fired warning shots as did IDF ground personnel with three persons reported killed – despite the fact security was supposed to be provided by an independent contractor. On 11 June the GHF accused Hamas of firing on a bus carrying its personnel, killing five and injuring more. The UN also pointed out that the IDF directed the trucks along unsecure routes, risking their interdiction. The few trucks headed north were looted and Israel seemed intent on keeping that area isolated.

People walked long distances to reach the handful of GHF distribution sites with no certainty of receiving anything. Chaos and violence at distribution sites soon set in, with casualties resulting. The IDF appeared to play a role in the violence.[1] As the number of killed amongst the desperate people around the sites exceeded 1,000, many nations urged Israel to return to prior distribution arrangements. By July all the foreign organisations in the enclave said the situation was dire, people expiring from malnutrition, and were removing their personnel so that they, too, would not starve. It was only in September 2025 that expanding beyond four stations was mentioned again. The UN said that ultimately 2,100 people were killed attempting to acquire the aid.

More truce proposals came and went, never satisfactory to both sides. Israeli and American warnings that these were best and final offers that Hamas must accept or face destruction made negotiations appear to be *diktat*. Resumption of full aid deliveries had become one of Hamas's primary objectives. Both sides seemed to be playing for time and the USA no longer the 'honest broker.' Hamas complained American mediators consistently skewed proposals emerging from negotiations to reflect Israeli preferences.

On 25 June Israel announced that it would again permit airdrops of aid into the Gaza Strip. This was roundly denounced as another face-saving measure given it was entirely inadequate as well as dangerous and costly, but the IASF began flying these the next day. Jordan and the UAE flew drops on the 27th, France and the UK joining later with German and Spanish contributions. Some residents said they resented having to run after descending bundles like dogs chasing a treat. On the 26th the government also said it would enact a 10-hour 'tactical pause' every day in three areas to open more corridors for aid trucks to enter. The NGOs previously operating in Gaza were to be permitted to resume their work and reopen distribution sites, Israel thereby tacitly acknowledging the GHF effort had been inadequate. (The organisation 'folded shop' a month later.) Israel was evidently bending to worldwide clamour, and demonstrations at home, over the expanding starvation it still insisted was not actually occurring. This government line was largely for local consumption, sustaining public support for the war.

The movement of aid trucks was the stuff of high diplomacy for two years. They were halted or released based on political motives, Israel accused of withholding humanitarian assistance as a (illegal) weapon of war. (IDF Spokesman)

A freeze frame from a predawn video taken at one of the GHF aid distribution sites on 1 June 2025 shows people fleeing after gunfire erupted (tracers seen passing overhead). The IDF was implicated in shooting events at and near the sites that took thousands of lives. (GHF)

Aid delivery into the besieged Gaza Strip included airdrops by the IASF (C-130J 662 of 103 Squadron shown) as well as foreign air forces. This was an expensive and low-quantity form of transporting food and medicine, and desperate people were killed by the descending bundles as they ran to retrieve them. (Ofer Zidon collection)

In the following days the IDF would point to enormous stacks of aid pallets collected at border crossings remaining undelivered. This ignored the warning that the prior distribution system could not be 'spun' back up immediately. The NGOs complained of IDF administration delays and the need to employ civilian clansmen to protect trucks against looters. It would be weeks before the famine could be turned around given the paucity of fuel and the altering landscape of destruction. Consequently, the volume of aid entering the enclave continued to remain far below that which those organisations insisted was necessary. As before, aid trucks passing through Israeli territory were occasionally attacked by residents that opposed permitting any assistance.

The Israeli organisation Coordination of Government Activities in the Territories (COGAT) inspected the contents of each delivery truck in a process taking up to 18 hours, this usually seeing some packing torn away after being X-rayed. Many trucks were turned away without explanation or for seemingly arbitrary and contradictory reasons, even though the consignment had been previously approved and the materiel was clearly of no military value. Some were sent back without inspection. If there was a record of the driver having engaged in smuggling contraband, the delivery could be rejected. Egypt built warehouses to store aid and support packaging and loading in what was an enormous operation. With delays in opening the crossings the truckers could spend weeks idle, thousands of vehicles lined up for kilometres. The NGOs saw all this as intentional obstruction. Israel insisted it facilitated aid deliveries and that there were no shortages.

TURMOIL

In Sderot, one of the towns hard hit on 7 October 2023, there was an observation deck on a hill with binoculars for people to watch smoke columns rising above the nearby Strip as bombs and shells fell with audible thuds. The 'Sderot cinema' was a popular attraction, some who viewed the show wondering when the last standing building they could see would fall. Much of the media inside Israel filtered the suffering in Gaza and followed the 'party line' with talking points provided by the government. (The word 'occupation' was to be avoided.[2]) Death tolls (other than IDF personnel) and starvation were rarely mentioned, and so the international outcry was derided as anti-Israeli and pandering to terrorists' defamation. Those that published contrary stories got threats of violence.[3] (This author found IDF Spokesman press releases during this period transitioning from a non-political character to one reflecting government narratives.) Stories and images contrary to this narrative were dismissed as staged, manipulated or fake.

Many in Israel still supported the war but two-thirds felt it should end. A survey showed only 21 percent of Jewish Israelis were troubled by reports of starvation in Gaza whilst 86 percent of Israeli Arabs were troubled. Another survey recorded 62 percent of Israelis agreed there were no innocent bystanders in Gaza. This attitude helped fuel the sense of dehumanisation of the Palestinians and willingness to look away from government excesses.

Efforts by the far-right in Israel to perpetuate the war in order to see Hamas destroyed, even as this extended the captivity of hostages, reportedly included corrupt acts. Two close associates of Netanyahu were arrested on 31 March 2025 accused of taking bribes to circulate reports to media denigrating Egyptian contributions to negotiations and praising Qatari mediation efforts. At the same time Netanyahu's corruption trials were delayed yet again due to demands on his time, potentially discouraging him from bringing the war to an end.

In March Netanyahu moved to oust the Shin Bet chief in what was seen as a largely political move, seeking an individual more aligned

In Gaza both opponents employed quadcopters for observation and attack (IDF operation shown). The latter included dropping grenades, or other explosives, and shooting various firearms. Some were one-way missions for the inexpensive UAV. (IDF Spokesman)

with the PM's tactics. Shin Bet was also believed to have initiated an investigation of the PM's office for inappropriately lobbying on behalf of Qatar. The Supreme Court placed a hold on the dismissal saying that Netanyahu was acting outside his authority. The Shin Bet chief, Ronen Bar, announced on 28 April 2025 that he would step down on 15 June, but Netanyahu was not satisfied. The government then worked to remove the Attorney General, but this was likewise blocked by the Supreme Court. All these were other elements of Netanyahu's self-inflicted government crisis from challenges to normal political behaviour since 2022 added more tension to the war the PM insisted was itself an existential conflict. Bar was replaced with Major General David Zini, Netanyahu's military secretary. Zini came with no intelligence background and so was a controversial choice, some believed ready to do Netanyahu's bidding with little debate.[4]

Trump warned Hamas on 2 July that the 60-day ceasefire proposal on the table was (again) the best and final offer. On 4 July the organisation offered adjustments to wording and the ceasefire appeared imminent. However, negotiations dragged on and some speculated Israel was stalling whilst the IDF continued its near-term work. As before, the truce would see the phased release of some remaining hostages, alive and dead, and a partial pull-back of the IDF whilst negotiations for an end to the war were undertaken. Aid would resume through normal channels. One sticking point was IDF insistence on retaining control of one of the southern corridors in the pull-back, a demand Hamas rejected. Israel eventually withdrew this proviso under pressure from the USA. Israel further stated it wanted to hold a 1.2km (0.75mi) zone across the border inside the Strip whilst Hamas proposed only 0.8km (0.5mi). The Americans warned Hamas that its guarantee of ensuring Israel negotiated an end to the war during the ceasefire could be withdrawn if an agreement continued to be delayed.

By 24 July the negotiators were exasperated and withdrew for consultation whilst people starved in the horror that was Gaza. The next day Trump, concluding Hamas had not been negotiating in good faith, said Israel should 'finish the job' of destroying the organisation through 'alternative options' for recovering the remaining hostages. Support for Israel's war had fallen to just 32 percent among American adults, though Trump was little influenced by such factors. A rocket flew from Gaza into Israel on the 26th. With continuing IDF casualties and hostage captivity approaching two years, opinion polls showed 74 percent of Israelis wanted an immediate end to the war and not the phased agreement being negotiated.

On 7 July 2025 it was revealed Israel was considering creating a 'humanitarian city' on the ruins of Rafah to house and more effectively control the Strip's population. Detaining some 600,000 persons there, it would allow easier checks for Hamas affiliation and processing for 'voluntary emigration.' Israel proposed that some international bodies operate the facility but, given that it appeared to be a concentration camp, none were identified or likely to step forward. The proposal ran counter to the outlined ceasefire then on the table that required a partial pull-back of the IDF.

On 13 August it was learned Israel was in negotiations with South Sudan about resettling Gazans there. The Sudanese denied this, and it emerged that Israel was in discussion with other countries to take these people, including Indonesia and some in Africa. (South Sudan was a war-torn region with challenges feeding its own citizens.) Those admitting such negotiations stated the accommodations were to be short-term and they expected to be compensated by Israel. Israel insisted such arrangements were strictly for volunteers, but surely anyone contemplating such a move had to consider whether Israel would actually permit them to return. Worldwide, and especially in

A D9 bulldozer is seen at work in the Gaza Strip on 16 November 2023. The Caterpillar product was modified for the IDF with armour and the added grating around the cab. The device on the rear had been used to dig deep ruts through miles of roads in West Bank Palestinian communities as evident collective punishment. (IDF Spokesman)

Arab countries, the reaction was loudly negative, warning of severe repercussions if Israel began shipping people out of the Strip.

Allegations emerged during the war of dismal if not reprehensible conditions in Israeli detention centres, common complaints being insufficient food and maltreatment, inadequate medical attention, and even torture. A prison set up in the Sde Teiman military camp, near Beersheba, became notorious. Israel dismissed all this as typical denigration of the State and maintained its treatment of prisoners met the highest legal standards.[5] However, a story emerged on 5 July 2024 of a beating and sexual assault of a detainee at Sde Teiman who had to be hospitalised with life-threatening injuries that included harm from sodomy with a metal rod and broken ribs. Portions of an illegally leaked video from within the facility were aired on 6 August that appeared to show the assault, partially substantiating claims of whistleblowers who had spoken out earlier of abuses at the prison. Ten soldiers were subsequently arrested on charges related to the incident, five later released. This caused an uproar with especially right-wing elements furious that IDF personnel were being prosecuted for anything related to handling incarcerated Palestinians who, one could infer, deserved whatever treatment they received. Two riots outside military facilities ensued. Claims were that the detainees were Nakba terrorists – 'the worst of the worst' – an allegation that was frequently made with little foundation to justify any measures taken. The Supreme Court moved to have the prison closed and the government agreed to do so.

The IDF's top lawyer, Military Advocate-General Major General Yifat Tomer-Yerushalmi, was accused of leaking the video to counter furious public claims her office was unfairly victimising the soldiers.

An investigation ensued that was leading nowhere until 31 October when she admitted to the leak and resigned. Netanyahu and many others in the government, plus society at large, were outraged and Tomer-Yerushalmi feared for her life. She was arrested on 2 November 2025 after going missing for several hours and the launch of a massive search. Defense Minister Katz immediately promised to strip her of her rank and throw her into prison, accusing her of a blood libel against IDF troops. Netanyahu declared it the 'the worst PR disaster in Israel's history', evidently because it undermined the reputation of the IDF and not because it showed almost indisputable evidence of the abuse Palestinians had been complaining about for decades.[6] A confrontation then emerged between the Attorney General, defending Tomer-Yerushalmi and so accused of a cover-up, and the Justice Ministry that insisted the Attorney General be disqualified and another investigator assigned, and the Attorney General's office itself investigated. The Ministry reached out to the Supreme Court for a decision. This debate was forming up as another 'constitutional crisis' fuelled by Netanyahu's efforts to limit the judiciary. The individual who was abused at Sde Teiman was released in the ceasefire's personnel exchanges (see later) and so the ability to get him to appear in court was questionable. There was high potential the charges against the soldiers would be dismissed.

GAZA CITY OFFENSIVE

Aid deliveries into September remained woefully inadequate and Hamas was insisting the humanitarian crisis be addressed before resuming negotiations. With images emerging of emaciated hostages, Netanyahu led his Cabinet to consider the 'full conquest'

Israel's Chief of Staff, Lieutenant General Eyal Zamir (left), meets with IDF officers on 8 August 2025. (IDF Spokesman)

of the Gaza Strip. On 8 August they voted to extend the war to ensure the elimination of Hamas and release of all of those held. This was over the objections of the new CGS, Lieutenant General Eyal Zamir, who warned of stress on the IDF and reserve system already reaching high levels, cost in more casualties, with no certainty of success whilst deepening the humanitarian crisis. The 10-hour meeting reportedly included much shouting at the general and requests he state clearly he would follow orders from his civilian masters. Instead of occupying the whole of the Strip, as the PM had advocated, the decision was to occupy all of Gaza City and thereby destroying Hamas and rescuing the civilians. Some 60 percent of the city and adjacent refugee camps had not been directly occupied and these Netanyahu described as final Hamas strongholds. The IDF then directly occupied 75 percent of the Strip, controlled 88 percent militarily, and with large areas under evacuation orders.

It was clear to most that the potential for this renewal of the offensive meeting the stated goals was virtually nil based on the past 22 months of combat. The likelihood of destroying Hamas and freeing all the hostages appeared low. Most expected the operation would expand in time to direct occupation of all the Strip. Given the vast devastation in the enclave, with most urban areas reduced to rubble, further bombing and shelling seemed only to stir the debris in hopes of eliminating some opposition members. There remained wide doubt Hamas could be eliminated. That the plan was also meant to ensure the continued viability of the Netanyahu government and delay of his corruption trial was also perceived as unstated objectives. Netanyahu insisted Israel was liberating Gaza from Hamas and wiping out a genocidal threat from thugs. Unsaid was the near certainty another resistance movement would arise in Hamas's absence if the occupation and blockade persisted.

More than 500 former Israeli security officials sent a letter to President Trump recommending he pressure the PM to end the war, observing that Hamas was no longer a strategic threat to Israel. That they reached out to a foreign chief executive for assistance demonstrated their lack of faith in local political avenues. The USA was reportedly leaning towards an 'all or nothing' deal to end the war and return all hostages.

The Gaza City operation was to commence by 7 October 2025 and take up to five months. The IDF announcing a 'tactical pause' to give time for the evacuation of noncombatants and offer room for continued negotiations. All inhabitants were ordered to evacuate and any that remained assumed to be hostiles. No aid would be permitted into the city, whilst that distributed elsewhere would be expanded. Hundreds of thousands of civilians had re-entered Gaza City during the January–March ceasefire. Some 800,000–1,200,000 people sheltering there then faced another displacement. Many refused to go. Relief organisations warned an evacuation of this magnitude in so short a time was impossible under the prevailing conditions, risking a further humanitarian catastrophe. The entire plan was met with almost universal condemnation, Trump being one exception in saying it was up to Israel how to conduct the war.

Hostage families called for a general strike in Israel on 17 August to protest the decision. This brought out nearly 500,000 persons and many businesses shut down. Another 'day of struggle' was staged on the 26th with 300,000 demonstrating in Tel Aviv. The government did not change course.

In preparation for the Gaza City offensive 60,000 reservists were called-up and the service of 20,000 more extended. On 20 August Netanyahu ordered the operation be hastened and attacks in the city had already begun ramping up, focusing on the environs. General Zamir warned publicly that clearing and demolishing the city could require a year of tough fighting with attendant strain on the Army. The security services continued to urge a negotiated end to the war.

Gaza City evacuation announcements included using speakers on quadcopters and these also dropping leaflets. Civilians were to move south of Wadi Gaza. The tactical pause over Gaza City was never absolute. Scores of bombing attacks on buildings in the area were slowly reducing large swaths of the city to ruin. The suspension was lifted on the 29th and the entire city declared a 'dangerous combat zone.' The next day the tactical pause was declared over and airdrop of aid in the north also terminated whilst truck-borne supplies were limited. By 5 September only 70,000 persons had relocated, and no aid distribution was occurring north of the Netzarim Corridor.

On 31 August Israel said it had killed the Hamas spokesperson, Abu Obaida. By this point the repeated advice from General Zamir to pursue a diplomatic solution was becoming heated and public. He made clear he believed Gaza City conquest would lead to taking the whole of the Strip and assuming full responsibility for the populace. Hundreds of reservists were hearing this and vowing not to report when called. Hamas released a propaganda video on 5 September, evidently filmed on 28 August, showing two hostages being driven around Gaza City to emphasise their vulnerability to the IDF operation. On 9 September Israel directed a full evacuation of the city and stated it planned to deliver 100,000 tents to house displaced people. Israel began levelling the city block by block. In the month since announcing the new offensive it damaged or destroyed 1,800 buildings with explosives, bulldozers and excavators. Some 78 percent of buildings in the Strip had already been damaged or destroyed.[7] Particular attention was paid to high-rise structures, usually brought down by aircraft-delivered bombs, with the explanation they were all used by Hamas cells to monitor IDF movements. By mid-September some 300,000 persons had evacuated the city.

Trump continued to swing between dismissing negotiations and urging Israel to finish the job of smashing Hamas, to promoting dialogue. His team had worked with Hamas representatives and on 7 September the Americans proposed Hamas release all hostages in exchange for some of the 14,000 Palestinians held by Israel and for a start in negotiations for ending the war. This was nothing new and Hamas had no reason to trust that Israel would comply. Even Trump's word that Israel would play along would seem to have held little credibility. He wrote in a tweet that Hamas should agree – 'last warning.' He made no similar warning to Netanyahu who said he was studying the proposal that had, in all likelihood, been coordinated in advance.

On 18 August Hamas said it had accepted a ceasefire proposal offered by mediators. Israel's initial response was that Hamas must agree to the State's maximalist demands, evidently disinterested in a phased approach. Knowing this would be unacceptable, the goal was evidently to perpetuate the war. They seemed to be emboldened by President Trump's shift saying Hamas must be destroyed and adding 'I think they want to die.' A week later he said an agreement to end the war seemed just weeks away. On 21 August Netanyahu ordered negotiations to resume, though not acknowledging the Egyptian/Qatari proposal Hamas had accepted. Instead, he said the goal was ending the war with decisive defeat of the enemy and release of all hostages, evidently believing the imminent Gaza City offensive would bring Hamas to heel.

On 9 September the Hamas negotiating team in Doha, Qatar, were considering the latest American ceasefire proposal. Qatar was urging them to agree, and an answer was expected within a day. Israel bombed their residential buildings with more than 10 jets and 10 pieces of ordnance.

This managed to kill five of the team, but not the principals. A Qatari security official also died. That the formation penetrated without being detected (as far as is known) or engaged would appear to highlight Israel's EW and cyber warfare capabilities. Qatar was understandably enraged and felt betrayed, calling the act state terrorism. They observed that Netanyahu has no limits.

The rest of the world was stunned. The message was that Israel did not want to negotiate an end to the war even if the ceasefire proposal had come from the American President. It did not care if one of its few supporters in the Arab world was alienated by a hostile act committed on its soil whilst performing a mediation role. Trump was evidently taken by surprise. Netanyahu said that the attack 'can open the door to an end to the war in Gaza' and was a gesture of peace. People were beginning to doubt the sanity of the Israeli leadership.

The Israeli PM said Israel accepted the American proposed principles for a ceasefire, knowing that Hamas could not respond. However, it was clear he considered Hamas to be murderous dogs and was willing to sacrifice chances for a ceasefire to kill all of them within reach. He suggested Qatar was harbouring terrorists by hosting the Hamas delegation where Israel was engaged in mediation.[8] This was clearly a contradictory position offered for public consumption by his followers yet driving an action. Qatar called the act barbaric and destroyed the chances of a negotiated peace with release of hostages. They believed Netanyahu had been wasting their time for weeks and so began reassessing whether they would continue involvement. (It was later revealed that the strike had been planned for more than two months.) Qatar was also a firm ally of the USA and had shown no hostile intent towards Israel. (Israel had informed the USA of the impending strike with too little time to pass this to Qatar and for them to react before the bombs fell.)

On 16 September the IDF declared its Gaza City ground campaign had commenced, though only an estimated 320,000 civilian inhabitants had yet evacuated. The start had evidently been moved forward given the international pressure. The armed forces warned the operation would extend over several months. It estimated there were 2,000–3,000 Hamas fighters in the city. Two divisions were committed to the mission and a third was expected to join. Katz declared that 'Those who remain in Gaza will be terrorists and supporters of terror.' The offensive appeared well underway by the end of the month when Israel reported 640,000–700,000 persons had evacuated.

An image played out thousands of times across many hundreds of miles shows an IASF bombing in progress inside Gaza. Tens of thousands of bombs were delivered in multiple countries and territories spanning two years with inevitable collateral damage and casualties. (Public Domain)

8

ENDGAME

Israel Katz said, 'Days when the heads of terror enjoyed immunity anywhere are over' and 'Anyone who raises a hand against Israel – his hand will be cut off.' If those harbouring Hamas terrorists did not expel them then Israel would come take care of it. It appeared to usher in a change in Israeli doctrine from containing and diminishing threats militarily via precision and low-key strikes within select problematic states or territories to going where the threats emerge or reside, even if that means actions like the Doha attack, to dismantle the enemy structure and kill its leadership. The IASF was the principal means for enacting this policy. Few could imagine that unrestrained attacks on virtually anyone within reach would lead to peace.

The 7/8 August Cabinet meeting that authorised the Gaza City offensive also issued a plan for post-war Gaza. This welcomed a foreign (Arab) force to police the enclave and to establish governance that excluded Hamas and the PA. However, on 18 September 2025 Minister Smotrich, spoke about the coming real estate bonanza in the Gaza Strip. He said he had been speaking with the White House about dividing up the land and that he had delivered an associated business plan. (Trump was a former real-estate developer focused on the 'deal.') 'We have done the demolition phase, which is always the first phase of urban renewal – now we need to build.' Minister Ben-Gvir added he had plans to build a neighbourhood in the Strip for Israeli police officers.

Anticipating a showdown at the UN over the continuing war, there were reports from insiders that the Israeli government was deliberating on annexing all or parts of the West Bank. A phased approach was an option discussed. One choice was taking the Jordan Valley, abutting the Jordan River, claiming it would be a security perimeter. (The threat from Jordan, across the river, was nil.) Annexing Area C and adjacent lands to further slice-up the territory would be another measure to make a Palestinian state nonviable. The occupation of remaining Palestinian areas – what Israel called a terrorist entity – was expected to continue to ensure security. Apart from the American administration, nearly everyone strongly advised against taking this step. Signers of the Abraham Accords warned the agreement could be suspended.

FINAL CEASEFIRE?

There was movement towards a plan for post-war governance of Gaza. Regional leaders offered feedback to include addressing settlements and sustaining the status quo in Jerusalem. However, with renewed talk in Israel of annexing all or some of the West Bank, Arab leaders warned that this would put the kibosh on ceasefire efforts to include any hopes for expanding the Abraham Accords. Trump voiced opposition to annexation.[1]

The Israelis emphasised that the PA could not have a role in governance without radical reforms. Their principal complaints with the PA were that the majority party, Fatah, was widely judged corrupt, the police did not work to suppress militants with sufficient energy, and Palestinians said bad things about Israel. They also resented what was called the Martyr's Fund that gave financial assistance to families of people detained or killed by Israeli forces, claiming this encouraged terrorism ('pay-for-slay').[2]

The surreal vision of air defences firing from within Tel Aviv and intercepts overhead is vividly illustrated in this time-lapse photograph. The expansive two-year war brought this home, and there was potential for more in the future. (Public Domain)

This image accompanied a May 2025 document from the Israeli government regarding Gaza redevelopment following the war. The fanciful depiction of the enclave in 2035, quite unlike any typical Arab city, likely intentionally reflected some of what President Trump also envisioned. Gazans were not consulted and the city depicted would not house the existing population. Where the water would come from for the river and lush vegetation is a mystery. (Public Domain)

Israel withheld tax revenue due the PA, weakening its financial stability and governmental functions. Israeli police and internal security services raided West Bank bookstores with printed materials judged inflammatory. Israel had criticised the PA for not holding elections, but it also obstructed elections and potential for Hamas winning full control was high. On 23 July 2024 Hamas and Fatah agreed to end their division and so enforce Palestinian unity, indicating the PLO was their sole representative. For Israel this meant Fatah was aligned with the terrorists. All these issues were internal to the PA, which did not threaten Israel (except its hegemony), and the Palestinians had similar complaints about Israeli attitudes towards them.

By fall 2025 Trump was saying that a ceasefire deal was close, suggesting Hamas's immediate agreement would be the clincher. Yet, on 18 September the USA vetoed a UNSC resolution (the only member to do so) calling for a ceasefire because it failed to condemn Hamas or recognise Israel's right to defend itself.[3] Qatar said it would continue mediating if Israel assured it would not again attack their country. Netanyahu agreed in principle but warned that if Hamas demurred, the war for their annihilation would continue. Doha and Cairo did approach Hamas with the latest ceasefire proposal.

On 24 September the American administration offered a 21-point ceasefire plan to end the war (with exaggeration described as a 'peace plan'). The plan contained nothing new, but with hope that timing was everything.

In Netanyahu's speech to the UNGA on 26 September he repeated the intent to destroy Hamas and called recognition of a Palestinian state 'shameful' and 'insane.' The speech was broadcast by the IDF via loudspeakers throughout the Gaza Strip. He also accused world leaders that opposed Israeli action of waging 'political and legal warfare against Israel.'

Trump was very upbeat about an agreement ahead of a 29 September meeting with Netanyahu. The White House sit-down appeared to reflect the optimism, but both men indicated it was up to Hamas capitulating for a deal to go forward. Still, the PM would need to persuade his far-right partners to agree with any plan. How Trump brought his opposite number around to accepting the agreement in principle was unclear, but some 'arm-twisting' was suggested.

The plan called for Hamas to disarm and Gaza to be demilitarised and 'deradicalized.' The group would hand over its weapons, their infrastructure would be destroyed, and members granted amnesty. An interim government of international character would have a leading board, without PA or Hamas participation, but with a Palestinian committee of apolitical technocrats. Ultimately a reformed PA was to govern. The 'Board of Peace' was to be chaired by Trump and include other heads of state. Israeli forces would withdraw some distance before Hamas released all hostages 72 hours after accepting the agreement. Israel would release 250 prisoners serving life sentences, 1,700 people detained indefinitely without charge (and the vast majority nominally noncombatants), plus 15 corpses. Aid would immediately be increased markedly, facilitated by opening the Rafah Crossing. The IDF would perform an initial pull-back and then await the disarmament before continuing in phased withdrawals to a security perimeter inside the border. Israel would not annex any part of Gaza. No one would be forced out of Gaza or denied ability to return. An International Stabilization Force (ISF) would deploy as the IDF withdrew, and begin vetting and training another Palestinian police force.

An Iranian long-range Arash 2 loitering drone is fired aloft from a simple transport/launch trailer. The control shelter for the system is seen beyond. Whilst fighting continued in Gaza, support front forces in several countries continued to fire such OWAs at Israel. (Public Domain)

A declared end to the war was to include the potential for a future Palestinian state – as enunciated 'a credible pathway to Palestinian self-determination and statehood.' On returning home Netanyahu immediately dismissed these words as nonbinding and vacuous.

An article in the ceasefire proposal promising that Israel would not again attack Qatar was removed, making it a 20-point plan. The President had Netanyahu speak on the telephone with Qatar's Prime Minister on the 29th and apologise for the death of a citizen during the 9 September Doha attack, though not the act itself, and said Israel would not conduct any future strikes.

On the 30th Trump gave Hamas three to four days to respond to the 'peace plan.' A negative answer would mean 'a very sad end' and 'all hell will break loose' according to the President. They considered it with assistance from Egyptian, Qatari and Türkish interlocutors. On 3 October Hamas said it was ready to discuss the details of the plan but, given it did not mention the disarmament terms, this appeared quite a conditional 'yes.'

Trump, eager to declare success, asked for Israel to immediately cease bombing inside Gaza as a sign of good faith. Israel made no direct reply and continued bombing. As always, it preferred negotiating whilst combat operations continued as a means of applying pressure to its opponent. But, there were reports on the morning of 4 October that strikes in Gaza City had ceased and Israel said that all offensive activities had been paused to permit Hamas to organise release of the hostages. Regardless, attacks and casualties continued. The IDF warned that the area north of Wadi Gaza remained a dangerous combat zone.

The sides prepared for an indirect negotiating conference ('proximity talks') in Sharm el-Sheikh for 6 October. Israel and the USA said they would not tolerate Hamas delaying tactics, implying it was not to be an actual negotiation. Trump urged the participants to hurry, not to lose perceived momentum. Netanyahu's government partners were still leery of the plan and opposed declaring the war ended without completely destroying Hamas. However, given the wider gains during the war, and if the hostages were released, Netanyahu had a fair chance of winning re-election if his government fell.

Israel proposed initial pull-back to a line 6.5km (4.0mi) from the border in the south, 2km (1.2mi) in the central zone and 3.5km (2.2mi) in the north – roughly where they were in August. They would effectively continue to occupy roughly half the territory and so stretched the definition of 'pull-back.' This was certain to be rejected by Hamas who in past negotiations had sought 1km (0.6mi) all around. The three-stage withdrawal tentatively agreed to showed a final line at a generous zone on the Gaza side of the border including above the Philadelphi Corridor and Rafah Crossing. So, Hamas was to release all the hostages and then rely on Israeli good will, backed by presumed pressure from the USA, to continue the withdrawal. This appeared to best a poor bargain, reflecting the meagre leverage Hamas still held.

On 8 October word emerged that Israel and Hamas had agreed on Phase One of the ceasefire plan with the hostage and prisoner releases expected on the 13th. Netanyahu's Security Cabinet voted on the 9th to accept Phase One conditions (only), and the wider Cabinet followed suit. On that day Hamas stated it required a formal statement from the Israeli government that the war was over to proceed. It never got it.

The ceasefire went into effect on the morning of the 10th and the 72-hour clock for hostage release began winding down. The initial withdrawal started that day and took 24 hours. This was to a 'Yellow Line' on the planning map that was to see the IDF exit Gaza City and the Netzarim Corridor but remain in direct occupation of 53 percent of the Strip. As usual, Israeli operations, including bombing, continued to the last moment. Markedly more aid began to enter on the 11th, the agreement being 600 trucks per day. The USA deployed 200 military personnel, establishing a coordination centre in Kiryat Gat, southern Israel, to 'monitor the ceasefire' and 'support stabilization efforts.' This physical symbol of USA commitment, with no initially specifically defined role, was reportedly important for both parties in achieving agreement.

The living hostages to be released were fairly well known and expected to be readily accessible. The deceased was another matter, it having become clear that some of the remains would take effort to recover from the detritus of war and some might never be found. The Palestinians gave Israel a list of people they wanted released in return, but Israel decided exactly who to exchange. This excluded some of the most notorious prisoners and some that might be charismatic leaders of Palestinian unification. Many Israelis still protested granting freedom to those accused if not convicted in military courts of heinous terrorist acts – with 'blood on their hands.' In the exchanges, Israel deported 142 individuals, released into areas other than where they were taken into custody, to impede any resumption of militant activities.

Trump travelled to the region to witness the beginning of hostage releases on 13 October and gave a speech before the Knesset where he declared the war over. Netanyahu himself had not uttered those words. Trump also called for Netanyahu to be pardoned.[4] The President was possibly more popular than Netanyahu at that moment, the populace seeing Trump and not Netanyahu as the one bringing the ceasefire to fruition. Throughout the region there was some gratitude for Trump's efforts to end the fighting, though this having been sustained to a large degree through American weapons delivered to Israel and Trump urging Netanyahu to carry on.

Trump then went to Egypt ostensibly for the signing of the agreement at Sharm el-Sheikh, though only Phase One had been agreed to. This was a bizarre spectacle with 20 leaders of noncombatant nations celebrating a ceasefire agreement between Hamas and Israel who were not present to sign. The event included an international 'Peace Summit' to set the course for Gaza's future. There 'The Trump Declaration for Enduring Peace and Prosperity' was signed by Trump, the President of Egypt, the Emir of Qatar and the President of Türkiye. This was a statement of goodwill with no specific actionable content. All was symbolic world commitment to make the ceasefire lasting and a first step such that the war resuming was unlikely. It was notable that the President of the UAE and leader of Saudi Arabia were not present, both deeply committed to a Palestinian state and wholly dissatisfied with Netanyahu. It was all theatre for a premature Trump's self-praising 'victory lap' supporting his vocal campaigning to be awarded the Nobel Peace Prize. The White House hailed it, with much hyperbole, as the Trump Peace Agreement and as a 'historic dawn of a new Middle East.'

Trump's unabashed ambition to receive the Nobel Peace Prize meant he sought wins to bolster his résumé. He claimed the ceasefire deal ended the entire Middle East conflict going back 3,000 years, a preposterous assertion. Netanyahu submitted a recommendation to the Nobel Committee to consider Trump in clear pandering to the man's vanity. Even before the UNGA Trump said that he deserved the award, having ended six or seven long-running wars in just the past seven months – an eye-rolling falsehood. The 2025 prize awarded on 10 October was not to Donald Trump.

There was, in fact, still much to do. Detailed negotiations on further phases of the agreement moved slowly and with little word of progress. The ISF had not been formed or even defined nor the rebuilding program fully committed to by donors. A 17 November vote of the UNSC to support the plan lent it international legitimacy. Hamas and the PIJ, however, rejected international guardianship without addressing core Palestinian issues. They wanted the ISF only at the borders. By that point the UN estimated rebuilding would require $70 billion over 10 years and would begin by removing 61 million metric tonnes of debris plus tonnes of unexploded ordnance (more than anywhere since the Second World War). The estimate was that five percent or more of ordnance deposited in the Strip did not explode, amounting to thousands of individual unexploded

World leaders attending the 'Summit for Peace' in Sharm el-Sheikh, Egypt, on 13 October 2025 pose for a photo shoot. The event was more of an ego-boost for Donald Trump, celebrating the first phase of the Israel-Hamas ceasefire he helped orchestrate, than to accomplish anything of real substance. (Public Domain)

munitions. In the four weeks following the ceasefire 320 individuals were killed by this hazard. It would take years to clean up, with ordnance expected to be found for generations to come.

Within a day of the ceasefire commencing Israel was complaining that Hamas was tardy in delivering deceased hostage bodies, extending beyond 72 hours. One handed over was discovered to not be a hostage. On 15 October Israel moved to obstruct half the daily aid trucks until this was rectified. It also limited fuel and gas deliveries plus meeting essential humanitarian needs whilst threatening to delay opening the Rafah Crossing. That locating and recovering all the deceased hostages would be challenging was understood before the process began, possibly requiring weeks. Collective punishment was unlikely to hasten the effort. American mediators worked to resolve the issue and urged Israel not to take extreme measures.

Hamas confessed it would need help finding additional deceased hostages, particularly special equipment. Israel offered to assist, though the situation on the ground remained hostile and some areas inaccessible. An offer from Türkiye, for one, was more welcome. Israel believed the organisation had information on the location of at least six more remains and shared that via mediators. It also said it understood five had gone missing entirely. Regardless, bodies continued to be delivered and Israel began lifting restrictions on aid. The trucks passed through the Kissufim and Kerem Shalom gates whilst Rafah remained closed. By November food distribution in the north was still unsatisfactory, trucks not driving there directly. There continued to be complaints of Israeli needless obstruction. Israel was releasing 15 additional detainees/prisoners for every set of remains. In time they handed over 90 remains of deceased Palestinians.

There was unease that Hamas was delaying its disarmament, although the negotiations were still ongoing. Regardless, Trump insisted Phase Two had begun and warned the USA would disarm Hamas if they did not do so willingly. He declined to explain how this would be achieved. However, he implied he was holding Netanyahu back from reacting in his usual manner.

Displaced Gazans began immediately to move back north. People were warned not to approach IDF troops.

Israeli personnel fired on people who came too close and did not respond to warnings. By December 350 people had been killed by such fire, more wounded. Translating a line drawn on a map into a defined boundary on the ground, amongst ruins and debris, was challenging. The actual position of the Yellow Line was unclear to civilians and likely soldiers as well. The IDF began placing yellow concrete blocks along the line to aid identification, but these were occasionally shifted.

Hamas emerged from cover to reassert its control in the areas free of Israeli troops. Its internal security organisation, the Rada'a, began to re-establish order. This included exacting retribution on those seen as having collaborated with 'The Occupation.' The focus was clans and gangs that worked with the IDF and escorted aid deliveries. Videos of summary executions caused viewers to shudder. (Hamas had always governed in part by intimidation and Mafia-style methods, violence being one tactic.) Trump growled that

The initial IDF pull-back under the Phase One ceasefire agreement left the majority of Gaza under IDF direct control. (Map by George Anderson)

if Hamas did not stop killing people he would see to it that they were stopped, though adding it would not be American personnel to enforce this threat. Some of the organisations the IDF employed during the war were operating from beyond the Yellow Line and crossing to 'do business' before retreating to the nominal protection of the IDF. It soon became clear Israel continued to support militias undermining Hamas's authority and keeping Gaza in turmoil. So, it was acknowledged that immediately disarming Hamas without the ISF in place could promote chaos.

There was an incident on 19 October in which two IDF personnel, behind the Yellow Line, were killed by fire from Rafah. Israel immediately responded with several airstrikes and again halted aid deliveries. Hamas insisted the perpetrators were from a deviant group. There were isolated pockets of militants who might have been unaware or growing desperate and remained ready to fight. In areas still under IDF control the Army was dealing with pockets of diehards. In early November they had an estimated 200 fighters trapped in tunnels inside Rafah for whom they were negotiating safe passage via Egypt. These men may have been responsible for the attacks on Israeli personnel, and IDF efforts to eliminate them and their tunnels were assessed as violations of the ceasefire by Hamas. However, Israel wanted the body of a dead soldier from 2014 released concurrently. The remains were delivered on 9 November. The Army continued building demolitions and displacing people in areas it occupied. By 10 December the UN counted 360 killed in more than 350 IDF attacks since the ceasefire began. On the 13th the IDF killed another Hamas commander and 'architect 'of 7 October in a targeted strike that also took three other lives whilst wounding 29. Israel claimed it was not a ceasefire violation because they were hitting an individual 'actively engaged in terrorism.'[5]

The return of hostage corpses continued into December when just one remained to be found. Israel insisted Phase Two of the ceasefire could not begin until this one last set of remains was handed over and elimination of the holdouts. The Rafah Crossing remained closed, though Israel welcomed Gazans leaving through the gate. Israelis grumbled it appeared Hamas was intentionally drawing-out the process to irritate their enemy. They released drone video on 28 October showing a staged 'discovery' of a deceased hostage for the Red Cross to observe. Some remains were not those of hostages or were of corpses already handed over. Another IDF soldier was killed by enemy fire on the 28th. Israel's aggravation was expressed in a flurry of airstrikes that day that killed at least 104 persons. Israel partially reopened the Rafah Crossing on 1 February, though not to aid trucks that entered through two other points. The government was considering expanding the Yellow Line, reoccupying some areas to include the Netzarim Corridor, and restricting aid. Hamas immediately suspended handing over remains. Both sides soon declared their commitment to the ceasefire. More fire at IDF positions on 19 November prompted further IASF strikes. On 22 November Gazans pointed to nearly 500 IDF violations of the ceasefire that had left 342 dead and 875 injured. On 31 January airstrikes killed 31 people bringing deaths since the ceasefire to exceed 500. Israel said this was in retaliation for eight fighters emerging from tunnels in Rafah the day before. The last remains were returned on 26 January.

Hamas was suggesting its arms could be stored for a period. The situation remained precarious. The White House scrambled to shore up the ceasefire, sending senior officials to Jerusalem for talks with Netanyahu and others. Someone called it 'Bibi-sitting', urging him to understand that no amount of bombing was going to help the situation.

Gazans struggle to make temporary homes amongst the destruction wrought within their community. (EPA/Haitham Imad)

On 4 November it was learned the USA was drafting a resolution for the UNSC regarding forming the International Stabilization Force. Nations offering to provide resources insisted it fall under a UN mandate, but Israel was resisting a United Nations role. Expectation was the ISF would operate until the end of 2027 at which point the UN would assess whether to extend its mandate. There was discussion of deporting fighters to a third country, with Türkiye one option. That such details were undefined at the time the ceasefire went into effect reflected the haste with which it was pushed through. Türkiye had been expected to play a significant role in the ISF. However, given its issuance of arrest warrants for Israeli senior officials on 7 November, their participation was likely to be nixed by Israel.

Until the ISF was in place reconstruction was on hold.[6] Since much of the financing and labour for reconstruction would be Arab, the proposal that work begin in areas occupied by the IDF was moribund. In the meantime, COGAT was not permitting in building materials. Clear plans for governance structure were not released until the end of December. As negotiations on Phase Two passed two months, despair began to take hold. Although famine had been arrested, refugees suffered in their tents as winter set in and began to perish. The UN warned of imminent economic collapse in the devastated enclave, and the West Bank was little better. Israel insisted they were doing everything necessary yet threatened to deregister NGOs from operating in Gaza unless they complied with objectionable new requirements.

Trump rolled-out the Board of Peace on 22 January 2026 with himself as permanent chairman, with a few luminaries as members, and extended invitations to numerous countries. Nations seeking to have a permanent seat would need to contribute $1 billion. There seemed little enthusiasm, especially as it appeared to conflict with the role of the UNSC. Trump particularly invited Russian President Vladimir Putin and Netanyahu and stated the Board would address many conflicts worldwide. Netanyahu objected to Türkiye and Qatar being represented. The Board's composition and expanding scope suggested its true functional role in the rehabilitation of Gaza would be minimal if not counterproductive. The Trump notional plan for rebuilding Gaza was also presented, evidently with no Palestinian input.

The durability of the ceasefire had to be demonstrated over time. Certainly as the plan, yet to be fully implemented, made no mention of the West Bank and Jerusalem, it was hardly a blueprint for an end to the conflict and anything approaching a peace treaty as the White House asserted. There remained a long and treacherous road ahead.

FALLOUT

Consequences inside Israel from the war was evident in the Knesset. On 11 November 2025 Ben-Gvir succeeded in bringing a long-sought bill before the parliament to expand the death penalty in Israel. Previously it had applied to Nazi war criminals and treason, and only used once. If passed, the law would extend to convicted Arab terrorists and nationalistically motivated murderers. A military court could impose the sentence by a simple majority vote rather than the previous unanimous vote.

Another piece of legislation would allow the government to shut down foreign news outlets without a court order. During the war Israel had taken the latter path to remove outlets it felt published stories overly slanted to an anti-Israeli viewpoint. The 'Al Jazeera Law' was one outcome of this, the Qatari-based media network having been ejected from Israel in 2024, justified because of the national emergency. If the bill passed this could be done by government decree without cause stated. Netanyahu had for years angrily criticised the Israeli press of playing into the hands of the state's enemies and

weakening the country by publishing pieces critical of his governance (and him). Reporters and editors were threatened with physical violence by activists on the right. On 1 December the government began moving legislation to make the independent media regulators political appointees, presumably to 'control the message' by punishing outlets perceived as crossing a line. Press freedom appeared at risk.

The growing power of Jewish orthodox parties in right-wing governments has seen a steady decline in the influence and presence of Israeli women in positions of authority. This trend appeared likely to continue with a bill that would expand the role of rabbinical courts in settling domestic disputes. Femicides were up as gun ownership expanded given a relaxation of permitting requirements.

There was a preliminary vote on a bill in October 2025 calling for Israeli sovereignty over the West Bank. Although it passed, it did not move forward and was meant to embarrass Netanyahu's coalition. A 3 November preliminary vote endorsing Trumps full Gaza plan, to include those beyond Phase One, was boycotted by the governing coalition as it was clearly meant to discomfit them. On 8 February 2026 the Security Cabinet voted to extend Israeli enforcement powers in West Bank Areas A and B, allow more proactive land purchases (appropriation without consent), plus allow the Jewish neighbourhood in Hebron to expand without consulting the Palestinian municipal government. These further unilaterally undermined the Oslo Accords.

Another action was to announce on 11 November that 89 Gazans undergoing medical treatment in Israel and Israeli-controlled areas, and their companions, would be expelled to Gaza within a week. For some this would surely lead to their deaths and was illegal. The Supreme Court had blocked a similar move in March 2024.

When the USA leaned towards selling F-35s to Saudi Arabia, Israeli pressured President Trump to link the sale to normalisation of relations and abandoning the Palestinian cause. This apparent easing of firm USA support for Israeli interests also included arms and economic deals with Saudi Arabia in May 2025 without also insisting the Kingdom normalise relations with Israel. Trump demurred, this suggested easing of firm USA support for Israeli interests when conflicting with American interests.

A new fight in Israel emerged over the character of the investigation into the failures leading to 7 October 2023 to ensure it was fair and impartial on one side and controlling the process and possibly the outcome on the other. On 23 November 2025 several defence officials and officers were relieved and reprimanded based on the military's own review.

On 8 December the Israeli police raided the UNRWA headquarters in East Jerusalem over a complaint of unpaid property taxes which, under UN convention is not to be applied. The police seized property, cut communications and replaced the UN flag flying over the compound with an Israeli flag. Subsequent Israeli legislation authorised water, power and communications to UNRWA facilities to be cut. The state moved to expropriate the agency's land and facilities in East Jerusalem, and the building was demolished on 21 January 2026. Earlier that year it began forcibly shuttering UNRWA operations to include schools in Jerusalem and planned more expropriations.

Israel appeared to be heading to a darker place thanks to the seemingly endless conflict propelling individuals with such leanings to national authority.

> If you gaze long enough into an abyss, the abyss will gaze back into you. Be careful when you fight the monsters, lest you become one.
>
> Friedrich Nietzsche

RESOLUTION?

The final death toll in Gaza was beyond 70,000 and with about 170,000 injured as reported by the Gaza Health Ministry. At least 460 deaths were due to malnutrition and, by the end, a quarter of the population was slowly starving. Publicly, Israel claimed over 17,000 Hamas fighters killed, 2,300 captured and 8,000 more wounded. However, actual MoD estimates from a classified database were 8,900 enemy fighters killed or likely killed as of May 2025.[7] Nearly two million people (95 percent of the population) had been displaced, many multiple times. Israel had given up some 2,100 dead with 841 military personnel dead throughout the war, 405 inside the Gaza Strip. Approximately 20,000 service members were wounded, 900 total in Lebanon, or around 1,000 per month. Throughout the entire two-year conflagration approximately 80,000 people died and 193,000 were injured.

Some outsiders, particularly Israel and its supporters, expressed doubt as to the veracity of the Health Ministry's numbers and speculated they could be inflated for propaganda purposes. Israel pointed out the counts sometimes emerged surprisingly close to the events, suggesting they were created from whole cloth. The IDF offered none other than rounded numbers of 'terrorists' killed. Unlike previous bouts of combat in the Strip, Israel prohibited internationalist journalists from operating independently in the enclave, though providing a few 'embeds'.[8] (Those who did report from there were already in the enclave when the war began.) However, international aid groups operating in the territory concluded the Health Ministry figures were largely accurate, if not underreporting. The count excluded what were likely 11,000 bodies under the rubble of collapsed buildings, the recovery of which was delayed until after the war. They also did not distinguish between combatants and noncombatants.

Regardless, few could contest that tens of thousands had been killed given the scale of IDF actions and destruction delivered. During the week of 7 September 2025 the former CGS, General Halevi, remarked that one in 10 of the Gaza Strip's 2.2 million inhabitants had been killed and injured, or more than 200,000. (The Gaza Health Ministry was then reporting 65,000 dead and 164,000 wounded.) In a statement by the recently retired head of A'man, General Haliva, he used one of the Hamas casualty figures. His statement suggests him, at least, believed them and added they were all necessary deaths to bring the Palestinians to heel. He proposed 50 deaths for each life taken on 7 October 2023 (equal to 60,000), even if they are children. This remark also suggests inflicting such casualties was one objective of the war. On 30 January 2026, in a briefing to journalists, the IDF acknowledged the war had cost approximately 70,000 Gazan lives, excluding those missing, and that Health Ministry figures were essentially correct (then reporting 71,667 deaths and 171,343 wounded).

The IDF insisted it had lowered from six or seven the ratio of collateral civilian casualties accepted as common in urban combat and had done more than any other military in history to achieve this.[9] Apart from this being a statement likely devoid of hard data backing it up, the greatly disproportional casualty figure argue against it. This is one indication of the 'all restraints lifted' declaration the MoD made when initiating the Gaza campaign. Certainly the concurrent war in Ukraine and others in the prior quarter century were not directly comparable. Israel fought in one of the most densely populated urban areas on Earth, engaging an irregular foe, with goals demanding considerable destruction placing all residents in harm's way. Consequently, measures taken to reduce civilian casualties find no comparison. These included dropping more than seven million leaflets and making over 70,000 telephone calls,

The Israel Air and Space Force mission support centre is seen in operation during the 10 January 2025 airstrike on Yemen. With scores of complex long-range strikes for the IASF during the extended war, this was likely a common scene. (IDF Spokesman)

sending over 13 million text messages, and 13 million voicemails, employing drones with loudspeakers, and airdropping a huge speaker emitting a message whilst descending under parachute. All these warned civilians to evacuate areas ahead of intense fighting. Actual mass movements were tracked by drone and satellite imagery plus cellphone tracking. Tactical pauses were implemented where necessary. Still, the civilian casualties were distressingly high.

In Gaza some 82 percent of the buildings (approximately half a million) were severely damaged or destroyed, including some 92 percent of residential buildings (436,000 homes).[10] Some 98.5 percent of cropland and greenhouses had been damaged and/or rendered inaccessible. (Agriculture had provided 44 percent of food in the Strip before the war.)

It was seemingly a virtuoso performance by the IASF. Across two years of nearly constant combat it had executed tens of thousands of sorties and delivered unprecedented quantities of ordnance with very few losses. Every aircraft and every aircrew member participated in an unparalleled operations tempo. Just keeping the aircraft in the air over such a period, likely by deferring maintenance, was a remarkable feat by maintainers. The UAVs flew some 60 percent of the flight hours over Gaza and hit 50 percent of the targets with ordnance. Early in the campaign in Gaza the USA was providing some drone services for intelligence, surveillance, and reconnaissance purposes.[11] The sounds of drones over the fronts was omnipresent, part of the 'soundtrack' for the war.

Israel also continued improving capabilities and introducing new ones during the long war. Among these was clearing the external store delivery capability of the F-35I and so increasing overall combat load above weapons carried strictly in the weapons bays. The IASF became the first operator to employ such configurations in combat.

Air defences, both ground-based and air-to-air, had knocked down hundreds of UAVs in a campaign that had yet to be detailed at time of writing. Israeli aircraft alone, using AAM, had accounted for 288 UAVs by August 2024. Carriage of Python 4s on F-16 wingtip launchers was cleared to provide the option for four medium-range, advanced infrared-guided AAM to be employed in confronting swarms of the UAVs.[12] Carriage of older, less effective weapons such as Sparrow, on aircraft devoted to strike missions as self-defence indicated a worrying draw-down in stores of the leading missiles or an effort to preserve them.

Software upgrades of one or more systems prior to the war had improved abilities to engage UAV swarms.[13] Some targets were defeated by electronic means.[14] Rafael also reported that, in cooperation with the government, it had accelerated fielding of a laser defence system ('Iron Beam') that succeeded in shooting down

'scores' of drones (clarified as 40 intercepts). This was believed to be the first combat use of such a system. Range was said to be 8–10km (5–6mi) and each intercept consumed only $45 of resources. Recharge time meant that batteries of several fire units were required.

Allied aircraft helping defend Israel from the threats faced similar issues. The Americans used comparable systems but also innovated. Among the weapons used by USA aircraft was the AGR-20 Falco Advanced Precision Kill Weapon System. This was a 2.75in air-to-ground rocket with a laser guidance and control section attached at the front and so required a system to 'laze' the target. The rocket had a unit cost of $15,000–20,000 and the guidance/control section added a few thousand more. Fighter aircraft were successful in shooting down Houthi drones with the rocket. No doubt cannon fire was also employed. However, scores or hundreds of drones could overwhelm air defence systems – crews reloading whilst the UAVs flew by to their targets – and so there was a requirement for high-capacity air-to-air systems. For short-range ground-based systems American defenders employed the canister-launched Coyote expendable UAS to engage swarms with swarms for C-UAS. Guided by radio from a ground station equipped with radar, they simply crashed into the target or detonate the 2kg (4lb) warhead via proximity fuse. Another was the C-RAM (counter-rocket, artillery and mortar), a radar-directed 20mm gatling gun system derived from the shipboard Phalanx. Electronic warfare techniques were also employed, though also a short-range option. This appeared the best prospect for the future. The hope was that OWA swarms would be a 'passing fad', soon rendered so ineffective that it would fade from the military scene.

Loss of UAVs dominated IASF attrition (Table 2). The UH-60A mishap in the Gaza Strip on 11 September 2024 occurred during landing and took the lives of two Unit 669 personnel onboard and seriously injured four others.

A Houthi OWA drone is seen on a cockpit monitor over the Red Sea just prior to being shot down by a French Navy Panther helicopter, likely firing 7.62mm rounds. (EUNAVFOR ASPIDES)

A flight test USAF F-15E is flying with six seven-round pods of Advanced Precision Kill Weapon System II (APKWS II) rockets for 42 total rounds. This proved effective against drones and became a low-cost solution to downing the cheap little aircraft, non-manoeuvring, in high numbers. (USAF)

Table 2: IASF Attrition[15]

Date	Aircraft	Location	Circumstance
7.10.2023	Yas'ur	Gaza Envelope	ground fire
29.10.2023	Hermes 900	Lebanon	SAM
5.11.2023	Hermes 450	Lebanon	
18.11.2023	Hermes 450	Lebanon	SAM
26.2.2024	Hermes 450	Lebanon	
11.3.2024	UH-60	Nevatim	ground collision
9.4.2024	Hermes 900	Lebanon	SAM, wreckage bombed
14.4.2024	C-130	Nevatim AB	Iranian missile strike
18.4.2024	Skylark (Army)	West Bank	crash ?
22.4.2024	Hermes 450	Lebanon	SAM
14.5.2024	SkyStar aerostat	Galilee	anti-tank missile
1.6.2024	Hermes 900	Lebanon	SAM
11.9.2024	UH-60A	Philadelphi Corridor	accident, salvageable? 2 fatalities
9.10.2024	? helicopter	southern Syria	accident ?
22.10.2024	Hermes 450	Lebanon	SAM (fifth shootdown)
31.12.2024	Yas'ur	Tel Nof AB	blown over in wind storm
9.4.2025	? UAV	Lebanon	malfunction
14.6.2025	Heron TP	Iran	
17.6.2025	Hermes 900	Iran	
19.6.2025	Eitan	Iran	
19.6.2025	Eitan	Iran	
19.6.2025	Heron TP	Iran	
19.6.2025	Heron TP	Iran	
23.6.2025	Hermes 900	Iran	
23.6.2025	Hermes 900	Iran	
26.6.2025	Heron TP	Iran	
?.6.2025	RA-01 (assumed)	Iran	2 reported shot down
16.1.2026	S-70A	West Bank	fell from sling under CH-53

grey font = damaged

A Hermes 900 is seen after being shot down in Iran during June 2025. Beside it was an unfired Mikholit missile. (Tom Cooper collection)

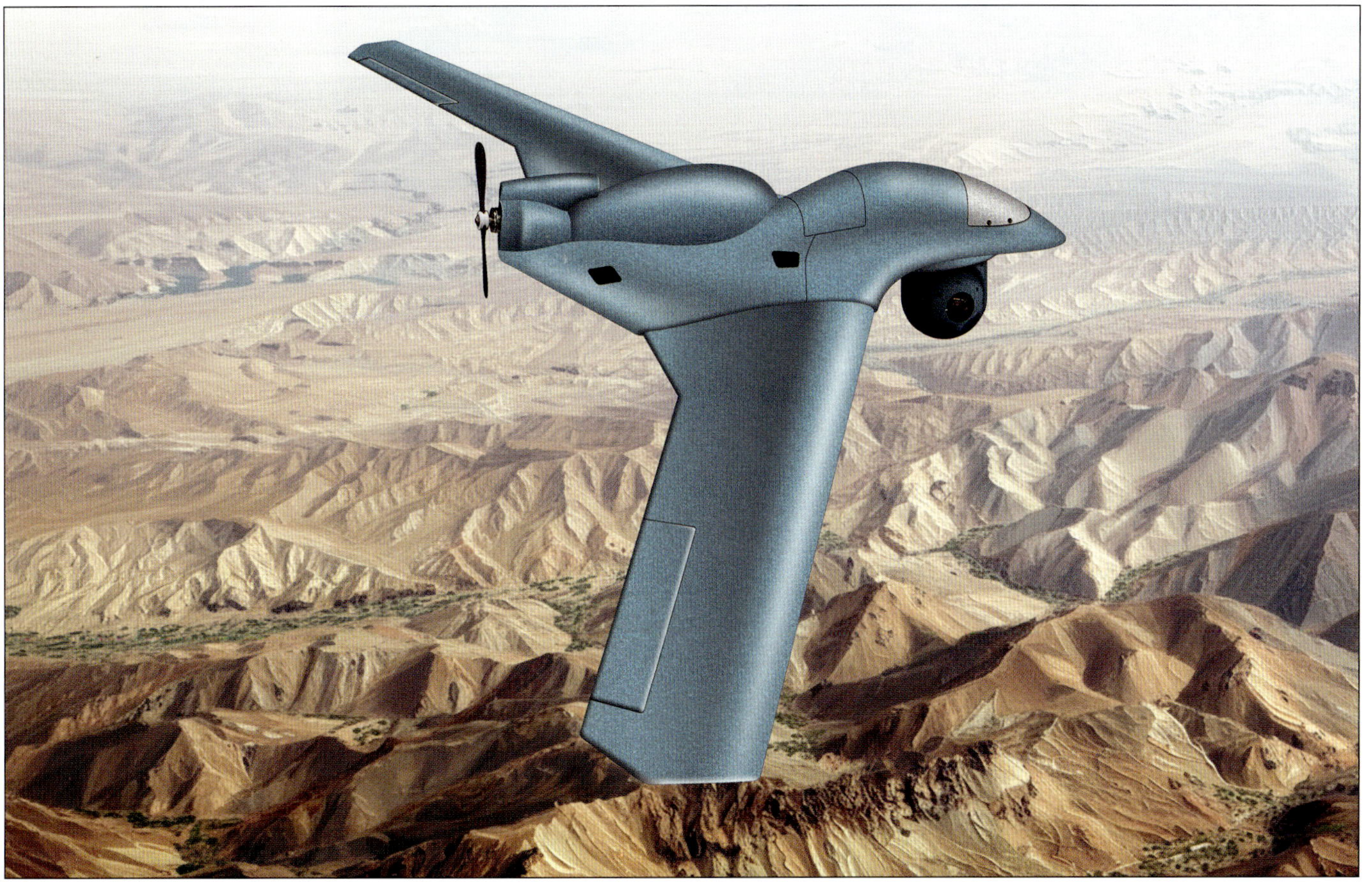

During the war word emerged via a leaked classified USA document about a stealth Israeli UAV, reportedly designated RA-01, which was employed over Iran for surveillance and targeting. Little was known of the secret system, and the artwork is somewhat speculative but based on images from the ground and wreckage recovered in Iran of at least one vehicle. (Artwork by Anderson Subtil)

Ground-based air defence systems had to adapt to meet the unprecedented scale of attacks. The ABM systems had provided good coverage, but the details on hit-to-miss ratios were unavailable at time of writing. This had been the largest ballistic missile and ABM contest yet and it does appear Israeli defences were running short of interceptors towards the end.

A two-year war on seven fronts subjected Israel to more attacks and damage than ever before, with dismaying casualties and 200,000 citizens displaced for many months (53 communities in the south and 42 in the north). The war also brought in actors from beyond those in states adjacent to Israel, especially Iran supporting Iraqi militants and the Houthi, and Western nations helping to protect Israel from those adversaries to prevent the war widening to a regional conflagration. It was by no means clear Israel was any safer after the unprecedented violence. Threats had been reduced and pushed back, but not eliminated. With nothing fundamentally resolved, and Israel more aggressive, they were bound to strengthen anew and Israel remain the most dangerous place for Jews. Even if Hamas disappeared, another such organisation would emerge in its place if nothing else changed. Vast stores of armaments had been captured and destroyed on multiple fronts. But, as in the past, these could be replenished and new fighters trained.

The sense was that the basic factors fuelling the century-old conflict had to be transformed soon or the situation would deteriorate further as each war brought more death and destruction. Recent history had demonstrated the status quo was untenable. However, any final decisions over borders, settlements and Jerusalem were certain to set off a political and societal firestorm inside Israel for which no conceivable government seemed unwilling to initiate, and certainly not one led by Benjamin Netanyahu. The 2026 elections in Israel would be one indicator of national sentiment.[16] Given lingering animosity, it may be another generation and thousands more lives sacrificed before positive factors align again for peace to advance.

All involved were ensuring the conflict perpetuated itself, not appreciating that sacrifices made for peace can be as meaningful as those made in war. For all who believe they have enjoyed benefits from war, there are many more who suffered only destruction and death, both friend and foe.

Medium-range ballistic missiles were shown to be inefficient as a tactical weapon and modestly effective as an intimidation tool. This Iranian rocket, posed for launch from a TEL with tractor still attached, were difficult targets to locate, and elimination of substantial numbers a high workload endeavour. Sufficient ABM assets could greatly diminish their impact. (Public Domain)

An Arrow 3 ABM interceptor fires on 16 June 2025, responding to an inbound Iranian ballistic missile. (Israel MoD)

A Royal Air Force Typhoon is preparing to depart on another sortie from Akrotiri, Cyprus, to confront Houthi depredation in the Red Sea. Operation Poseidon Archer was conducted with the USA from January 2024. (Public Domain)

Substantial damage was sustained by this building in Bat Yam, Israel, as seen on 15 June 2025, inflicted by an Iranian ballistic missile impact. This was but one of many such consequences of the war that was more costly than any other in Israel's history. (Public Domain, Yoav Keren)

ADDENDUM (AS OF 11 MARCH 2026)

2026 WAR IN IRAN

The USA and Israel spent months after the war complaining Iran was revitalising its ballistic missile production and fielding plus restoring its nuclear sites. Given that Israel and the United States had demonstrated they were existential threats to the Republic, it was no surprise they would seek to rejuvenate their best military resources as a sovereign right. The June 2025 ceasefire had no terms proscribing such actions.

Another round of negotiations between American and Iranian diplomats were conducted with the usual results. The Americans insisted Iran cease all uranium enrichment, greatly curtail its ballistic missile program, and stop supporting proxies threatening Israel and undermining American foreign policy interests. Oman had been mediating the negotiations and the Foreign Minister stated significant progress was being made. Iran had agreed not to stockpile enriched uranium. This did not deflect the Americans from a course of confrontation. There was significant public unrest in Iran during early January 2026 over the very poor economy, brought on in large measure by American and Western sanctions. Many thousands of citizens were killed by government internal security personnel and repressive measures imposed. President Donald Trump threatened to intervene, but nothing happened apart from the Pentagon increasing military assets within reach of Iran. The particular Iranian foreign policies the USA criticised represented vital characteristics of the theocratic government and Islamic revolution. They could be expected to fight with all they had to survive. Yet Trump expressed puzzlement why Iran did not capitulate to his demands. The nation was certainly at its weakest in decades.

President Donald Trump was photographed on 1 March 2026 at his Mir-a-Lago, Florida, residence as he oversaw the initiation of war with Iran. He was singularly responsible for starting the war. (Public Domain, Daniel Torok)

In the early morning hours of 28 February 2026 Israel and the USA collaboratively struck Iran in a major military effort – Operation Epic Fury for the USA and Operation Roaring Lion for Israel. This followed months of joint planning, and these allies anticipated the campaign requiring weeks.

SHIFTING JUSTIFICATION

Trump claimed, without presenting evidence, that Iran was developing an intercontinental ballistic missile capable of reaching the United States. This was refuted by individuals in the intelligence community speaking on condition of anonymity. He insisted Iran represented an imminent threat to the American people, without specifying. The claim made, once again, that Iran was on the verge of having a nuclear weapon was even more questionable in February 2026 than it was in June 2025. The President confessed that Iran did not have access to its stockpile of highly enriched uranium. How much of all such statements were fiction or based on intelligence data was unclear. (That Donald Trump often contradicted himself and his staff, made illogical statements, fabricated information on the spot, and playing loose with facts was readily evident. His supporters insisted this was a way to throw-off his adversaries. It was, however, unhelpful when communicating with the American public and allies.) He also said he 'had a feeling' Iran was preparing to pre-emptively attack Israel and possibly the USA – an assertion no publicly available evidence supported and would appear to have been very unlikely. (Netanyahu later repeated this claim.) Secretary of State Marco Rubio hinted that the USA was sure Israel would attack Iran and that this would bring Iranian strikes on American assets in the region and so joined in. This would suggest Israel manoeuvred a willing President Trump into the war. Rubio denied this, but it seemed unlikely Israel would have gone to war with Iran again in so short a time given the uncertain outcome of June 2025. Trump then offered incredulously that if the United States did not act Iran would have 'taken over' the Middle East. The President later said simply, after days of shifting justification for going to war, 'something had to be done about Iran.' (That most of Trump's statements about the decision-making leading to war began with the pronouns 'I' or 'me' instead of 'we' is telling.) Presidential legacy may also have been another motive. Secretary of Defense Pete Hegseth (he preferred Secretary of War) asserted Iran started the war with its actions across past decades.

Trump made no effort to build a consensus at home on going to war, did not seek war authorisation from Congress, did not try to bring together a coalition of allies, and did not warn other nations of what was to come. He evidently had little concern with the consequences of war outside the combat area including impact to the world economy. His statements suggested he believed all would accept these unwelcome impositions given the 'good' that would ultimately ensue. He wrote that anyone who thought differently was a 'fool.' Apart from collaborating with Netanyahu, he alone decided to commit the USA to a war with an uncertain outcome that would get thousands of people killed. His utterances and those of Hegseth suggested they considered employing the US military in combat as 'cool' and justified in correcting what they perceived as conditions in the world inimical to American interests. Grounds were always found to argue the actions did not obviously contravene international law. In their expressed view it was a new world order of military intimidation and economic coercion wherein the mightiest dictated terms. An effort in Congress on 5 March to constrain the President's authority to wage war was defeated.

Donald Trump made no secret one of his goals was regime change in Iran, what he called a rogue and evil terrorist regime. The President certainly felt empowered to undo foreign governments he personally assessed as corrupt, illegal and opposed to American hegemony, national interest, and the whims of Donald Trump. On 2 January 2026 the United States had conducted a special operation to snatch the President of Venezuela, Nicolás Maduro, and his wife Cilia Flores from Caracas after pronouncing them corrupt drug-trafficking narco-terrorists. No effort was made to support this claim before world legal bodies. Afterwards Trump declared the USA would be 'running' Venezuela. He also imposed sanctions on Cuba, particularly obstructing oil deliveries to the island with humanitarian consequences, whilst calling for regime change.

On 2 March Secretary Hegseth stated the goal in Iran was not regime change, but later the White House clarified it was not a primary objective. Trump urged Iranians to 'take over your government.' Regime change via air attack alone appeared doubtful to many. There seemed to be as many Iranians supporting the theocratic government and Islamic revolution as opposed. A civil war with a torrent of blood and refugees could result. The outcome was by no means certain. (On 11 March the Iran's chief of police warned that protesters encountered on the streets would be treated as enemies of the state and risked being shot.)

Bringing economic and military coercion to bear on a country to induce regime change violates USA and international law.

ONCE AGAIN TO WAR

Several waves of attacks struck Iran daily. On the afternoon of 4 March Israel said it was executing its 11th wave of strikes. Initial 'decapitation' strikes succeeded in killing many senior leaders. Israel and the Pentagon claimed to have eliminated some 40 such individuals, among these the Chief of Staff Lieutenant General Abdoorahim Mousavi and, more significantly, the 86-year old Supreme Leader Ayatollah Ali Khamenei. Many civilian relatives, evidently sheltering in the targeted compound, were also killed or injured. (Israel took credit for the deed.) Those remaining said they would fight on, especially given the existential peril to their governance and the revolution. Shiite senior leadership called for Muslims to wage a jihad against the attackers, issuing a fatwa to that effect – an Islamic clerical legal ruling.

Whilst deliberations were underway in Iran to select a new Supreme Leader, Israel said it would be gunning for the replacement. In the meantime, a three-member leadership council was in charge. Trump proclaimed he should have a say in the composition of the next Iranian government. Mojtaba Khamenei, 56, son of the assassinated Ayatollah, was announced on 8 March as the next (third) Supreme Leader. With quite junior clerical credentials and lending an appearance of a dynastic descent (contrary to tenants of the revolution), it was a controversial choice. He was reported injured in the airstrike that killed his father and many family members. Perceived as a 'hardliner' likely to follow is father's policies (having run his office), Trump promptly declared the choice unacceptable, 'a big mistake', and he 'is not going to long.' Khamenei made no public or electronic media appearances for many days after being selected.

Iranian air defences were also early targets. By the second day Israel claimed to have 'dismantled' this in central and western areas of the country to gain air superiority. The USA claimed air superiority the next day. On 4 March Trump declared Iran's navy, air defences and air force were destroyed, but Hegseth remarked the allies were still days from claiming air superiority. On 7 March Netanyahu mentioned Israel and the USA had almost complete control of the skies. The IDF stated the attackers were still targeting air defence systems. An Israel F-35I pilot shot down a Yak-130 trainer with an

A Tomahawk cruise missile is seen being fired from the USS *Frank E. Peterson*, a guided missile destroyer, on 28 February 2026. (US Navy)

air-to-air missile on the 4th. As late as 5 March Iran insisted it was still shooting down American and Israeli UAVs.

It was essential that the ballistic missile threat be eliminated as quickly as possible. The Americans were dropping deep-penetration GPS-guided 2,000lb bombs on underground missile shelters. Israel stated it expected to substantially reduce the ballistic missile launch capability by the 3rd and so diminish the threat to Israel and other nations – launches decreasing daily. By the 6th the USA was reporting the volume of missile fire had decreased by 83 percent (also given as 90 percent). At that time Iran reported it was using cluster munition warheads.

One target of the USA was the Islamic Republic of Iran Navy as this represented a threat to American warships and an Iranian power-projection means. Within a day the Pentagon claimed to

The Iranian Supreme Leader, Ayatollah Ali Khamenei, is shown on 6 October 2024 awarding the Fatah medal to Amir Ali Hajizadeh whilst other senior military personnel look on. Khamenei was intentionally targeted and killed in a 28 February 2026 Israeli airstrike on a Tehran compound. (Public Domain)

An IASF F-35I completes undercarriage retraction during climb-out on 4 March 2026 for a mission to Iran. Aircraft 944 has the markings of 116 Squadron. (IDF Spokesman)

have sunk nine Iranian vessels and heavily damaged the naval headquarters. On the third day it said the Navy was decimated. By 6 March up to 30 vessels were said to have been destroyed. On the 4th the US Navy (USN) submarine USS *Charlotte* (SSN-766) sank the frigate INIS *Dena* off Sri Lanka, in the Indian Ocean, with a torpedo – the first such sinking by the US Navy since the Second World War. This claimed the lives 87 sailors with 61 more missing, and 32 survivors were recovered by Sri Lanka in what Iran called an atrocity. On the 2nd the Iranian drone carrier IRIS *Shahid Bagheri* was hit and dead in the water. The vessel was a rework of the South Korean container ship *Perarin* and had an angled flight deck with ski-jump. It was attacked again on the 6th and set afire by two missile strikes (weapons unstated).

These preliminaries allowed nuclear sites to be targeted with less risk. The first such facility was struck on the 3rd, the fuel enrichment plant at Natanz. Israel also bombed a facility in which they said Iran was developing the components for nuclear weapons. However, there were no other mentions of attacks on what would presumably

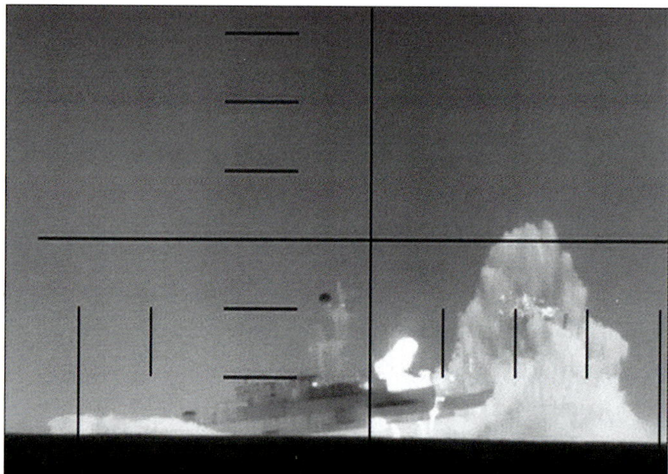

The Iranian frigate IRIS *Dena* is seen in a 4 March 2026 photo from a submarine periscope taking a torpedo hit in the stern that has lifted the ship from the water. It subsequently sank with at least 87 crewmen losing their lives. (US Navy)

Israeli 253 Squadron F-16Is were photographed on 4 March 2026 en route to strike targets in Iran with heavy JDAM bombs and all the external tanks that could be mounted, but no evident AAM. (IDF Spokesman)

be primary targets. Perhaps all others were considered rendered inoperable in June 2025.

On the 4 March Trump hinted that the most intense round of bombing, the 'big wave', was still to come and said he anticipated a four to five week campaign. Hegseth mentioned up to eight weeks. The next day the Pentagon said it was striking progressively deeper into Iran. On the 6th it added that over the past 72 hours USA forces had hit more than 100 targets 'deep inside Iran.' On 5 March Israel also said it was moving to the next phase of 'broad-scale wave' strikes after the 'surprise attack phase' of 2,500 attacks. This was highlighted with more heavy strikes inside Tehran that targeted national infrastructure with impact on civilians. Oil storage and fuel distribution resources there began to be bombed on the 7th. The oil refinery also appeared to have been hit. (The next morning the skies over Tehran were darkened by smoke and toxic black rain fell.) On 7 March Mehrabad IAP was burning after the IASF struck 16 aircraft it said were used to ship weapons to Hezbollah. The next day the IASF claimed to have attacked a number of the IRIAF F-14A fighters at the Isfahan airport. Hundreds of thousands had fled Tehran in a growing internal displacement crisis. On the 6th Israel reported it had flown in excess of 7,000 hours and hit more than 750 targets since the start of the war. The morning wave on the 7th was executed by more than 80 fighter-bombers.

The usual bombing errors occurred with tragic results. An elementary school for girls was destroyed, this probably mistaken as a portion of the adjacent IRGC Naval headquarters complex struck at the same time. Iran said 168 students and 14 teachers were killed. Analysis pointed to the USA as the most likely responsible party. Trump blamed Iran, suggesting inaccurate ordnance. Hegseth said only Iran targets civilians indiscriminately. Evidence quickly emerged that the nearby base was hit with BGM-109A Tomahawk Land Attack Missiles, and the school likely included in the same attack. Trump hastened to point out several other countries operated Tomahawks (though not Iran and Israel, as he said) or it may have been a Tomahawk look-alike (though the images were unmistakable). This evidently suggested Iran attacked its own Naval HQ and elementary school to justify claiming the USA bombed the school, or that Australia, Japan, The Netherlands or the UK set-up the United States for blame in a war crime. It was more likely Trump was just trying to sow confusion or was himself confused. News of the DoD investigation's findings began to leak on the 11th. The US Central Command developed target coordinates, passed to the Navy, based on outdated information provided by the Defense Intelligence Agency. Was the war planned too hastily?

At least one hospital and other medical facilities were also substantially damaged by bombs. Throughout the country civilian casualties rose quickly to the hundreds – more than a thousand by 6 March. Red Crescent counted tens of thousands of civilian structures damaged such that a housing crisis loomed. An American attack on a desalination plant, which may or may not have been in error, risked depriving thousands of civilians of water. Iran subsequently attacked a Bahraini desalination plant.

IRANIAN RESPONSE

Iran reacted with Operation True Promise 4 that included firing ballistic missiles and OWAs at American bases in the region and engaging Israel as it had done in June 2025. As senior leadership and command & control nodes were degraded, the IRGC adopted their Mosaic strategy of decentralised authority. Junior officers were empowered to make targeting and strike decisions. This held risk of miscalculations of national significance.

The Iranian drone carrier *Shahid Bagheri* is seen dead in the water and then after two missile strikes that set it ablaze. (US Central Command)

Targets lay in Bahrain, Iraq, Jordan, Kuwait, Oman, Qatar, Saudi Arabia, and the UAE. It was soon revealed that Russia was providing targeting and drone tactical information to Iran. Russia denied this. Ukraine offered to help with its anti-drone experience. On 5 March alone Kuwait reported intercepting 178 ballistic missiles and about 384 drones. Bahrain reported on the 6th 86 missiles and 148 drones intercepted. On the same day the UAE intercepted nine ballistic missiles and 109 OWAs. On the 10th they counted 1,700 total projectiles since the war began of which 90 percent had been intercepted. Qatar shot down two Iranian Su-24s on the 2nd inbound to an American base. On the 9th the IRGC said it was devoting 60 percent of its fire to USA regional targets and the rest to Israel. Three USAF F-15Es were mistakenly shot down on 1 March by Kuwaiti air defences, the aircrew ejecting safely. Whilst projectiles were being intercepted, some got through. American assets began to suffer and personnel became casualties. Seven service members died in the first 10 days and around 140 were wounded (eight severely), though the Pentagon discouraged reporting casualties. The strikes appeared to target communications, radar and intelligence infrastructure important in coordinating the offensive. Also targeted were air defence systems such as radar and command & control resources. A USA naval base in Bahrain, home to the Fifth Fleet service centre, were among the locales damaged. The USA embassies in Kuwait, Iraq and Saudi Arabia were also hit.

The Pentagon was not enumerating successful hits on its resources in the region, but commercial satellite imagery allowed news organisations and researchers to gain insight into Iranian successes which appeared to be significant. THAAD elements throughout the Middle East were clearly being degraded. (On 10 March South Korea noted apparent preparations to move the THAAD battery on its territory, possibly to the Middle East.) Satellite image provider

Planet Labs began to delay release of imagery of Iran and the Gulf States for 14 days, up from four days, possibly at the request of the Pentagon. As before, the Israelis withheld information about successful strikes inside the country apart from highlighting urban areas hit and civilian casualties as a point of outrage. An apartment building in Israel took a direct hit, killing nine. A total 12 individuals inside Israel had been killed by 11 March.

Iran said the host countries for American basing also deserved punishment. A few days into the war national assets were being targeted to include the energy industries. This added civilian casualties to the few USA military personnel killed and wounded. Other damage was caused by falling debris. Iran had hit a tanker and Qatar said there were strikes on its energy sector. The Gulf States began to consider taking offensive action themselves. The Iranian President apologised on 7 March, but the IRGC hastily added it would desist only if the American bases were not used for attacks inside Iran. The contradictory statements appeared to indicate either a lack of communication between the bodies or conflicting decisions. The caveat was unacceptable and the Iranian attacks continued.

Air travel throughout the region was disrupted. The USA was tardy planning for evacuation of its nationals, requiring days to catch up. GPS jamming across the region by both sides was affecting military and commercial navigation alike.

On 6 March Saudi Arabia said it had intercepted 16 drones en route to one of the largest oil fields in the Middle East. Consequently, oil and gas production was shut down across the region. Sailing through the Strait of Hormuz was suspended as a precaution. Approximately 20 percent of the world's crude passed through this chokepoint. Iran threatened on 2 March to attack any vessels attempting passage. Tankers could not safely sail and there was limited onshore storage capacity. World gas and oil supply declined. The prices for these commodities surged and stock markets tumbled in the largest disruption of the supply chain ever. So, the war affected the entire world – conditions that could prevail for weeks beyond the war. The USA began lifting sanctions on the sale of oil from Russia to help ease the shortage.

The US Navy said it would escort ships through the Strait once the assets could be re-tasked. The planning began immediately, evidently and remarkably not a scenario anticipated. Iran mysteriously stated that it welcomed this development and later said ships from Arab countries that expel Israeli and American ambassadors could sail safely through the Strait. Tump said of the Strait he was 'thinking about taking it over', ignoring that this lay in the territorial waters of three nations. (The President had previously moved to rename the Persian Gulf the Arabian Gulf, but backed off under the incredulous backlash.) Without a ceasefire, the shippers were unlikely to risk their vessels, crews and cargo. It was doubtful even the USN could eliminate every minelaying ship, clear every mine, sink every explosive boat, down every drone, destroy every shore-based anti-ship missile, etc. The Americans were likely promising more than they could deliver in the crisis of their own making.

On 7 March the IRGC reported attacking a tanker. On 11 March three commercial vessels were struck by assailants unknown, adding to the 10 previously attacked. There was a report on the 10th that Iran had begun laying mines in the Strait. Trump demanded they be removed immediately or 'a lever never before seen' would be engaged and Iran would suffer significant consequences. Tehran gave no response. The USN had decommissioned its four minesweepers in the area the prior September and had not brought any to the area prior to the war – something else evidently overlooked. Three Littoral Combat Ships, with minesweeping as one mission, were in the region

but their effectiveness was in doubt. It looked like the Americans might need to seek assistance to clear the mines, if they existed, from the nations Trump had been offending for the past year. Belatedly, the Navy began a search-and-destroy for minelayers, sinking 16 in the first day – so it seemed the Iranian Navy was not eliminated after all. The Iranians used about any vessel capable to sow mines, even fishing boats, so this was a large task. They had 5,000–6,000 mines of various types. They had mined the Strait in the 1980s.

After Israel and the USA began an expanded wave of strikes on 5 March the Iranians replied on the 9th with what it called a new phase with strikes on energy infrastructure across the Middle East. The IRGC also stated its missiles would henceforth carry only warheads weighing more than a ton, with rate of fire increasing. It also accused Saudi Arabia of preparing to participate directly in the war with fighter-bombers and aerial refuelling tankers. The Saudis denied this. By this point any goodwill the Iranians had built-up over the past years with its Arab neighbours had been sacrificed. On 10 March it said it had arrested 30 individuals accused of spying for the enemy.

Western militaries with assets in the region acted to defend these resources and their allies by intercepting Iranian projectiles. With the USA not having coordinated with other nations beforehand, there was understandable reluctance on the part of nations to collaborate on the war effort. Spain and France refused, calling the operation contrary to international law. Trump vowed economic retaliation. It was only 2 March before the UK agreed to permit the USA to use bases in the country and on the island of Diego Garcia provided the aircraft were being deployed for defensive purposes such as eliminating missiles and drones. When bombers started operating from RAF Fairford, questions were raised. The Iranians may have anticipated this with a 1 March drone directed at RAF Akrotiri on Cyprus. The drone originated in Lebanon, likely launched by Hezbollah. A hangar housing American reconnaissance aircraft was hit with minor damage. The next day two drones were destroyed by Greek F-16s as they approached Cyprus from Lebanon. On the 5th a British pilot flying an F-35B from Akrotiri shot down two Shaheds over Jordan with ASRAAM missiles.

Spain said it would send the frigate *Cristóbal Colón* to the island to help defend it. France was sending an aircraft carrier and 10 other vessels to the eastern Mediterranean and would allow the USA to use an air base only if not supporting the war. The Netherlands also said it would send a frigate. The UK prepared a carrier to sail to the eastern Mediterranean for the same purpose. This drew a mocking retort from Trump about joining the fight after it was already won. Apart from declaring the war won being premature, he obviously chose to misunderstand the United Kingdom's intent. Britain did send Wildcat helicopters equipped for counter-drone operations and the guided missile destroyer HMS *Dragon*. Australia also said it would send an E-7A Wedgetail AEW aircraft and a supply of AIM-120 air-to-air missiles to the UAE. Türkiye deployed six F-16s and air defences systems to Northern Cyprus.

The Americans and Israelis also bombed the headquarters of the Popular Mobilisation Forces in Diyala, Iraq, killing 18 militants. Whether this was in response to offensive action by the group or as a pre-emption was unclear. Iraq said it would defend itself but otherwise remain neutral. Türkiye also appears to have been targeted and NATO assets were being used to destroy inbound projectiles. Iran denied targeting Türkiye. It had drones with up to 1,500km (930mi) range.

There were reports the American Central Intelligence Agency was planning to arm anti-Iran Kurdish opposition groups to begin

A B-52H lifts off on 3 March 2026 from an undisclosed location for another mission to targets in Iran. (DoD)

another front against Iran, helping to spark an uprising. In Iraqi's Kurdistan this was denied and Iran headed off the eventuality by initiating friendly contacts with the Kurds. Yet the IRGC began a campaign of attacks on these groups inside Iraq and warned of consequences if fighters crossed from Kurdistan. On 7 March Donald Trump ruled out sending in the Kurds. The Kurds said they would do what was in their best interest, disregarding Trump's shifting positions.

On 5 March two drones hit Azerbaijan's IAP and a school, injuring two individuals. Iran insisted the drones were not theirs and suggested it was a false-flag operation by Israel who had close ties to the South Caucasus nation. Baku, also closely aligned with Türkiye, was certainly leery about being drawn into the war.

LEBANON BATTERED AGAIN

The IDF had prepared from the outset for possible military action along its northern border, calling up approximately 100,000 reservists. It still held five locales across the frontier in Lebanon. Hezbollah weighed-in on the night of 1/2 March with six missiles

and drones aimed ineffectually at an Israeli military base. This brought the expected response of airstrikes in the south and Beirut. The targets in the city lay principally in the southern Dahieh district which Minister Smotrich said would soon look like the ruins of Khan Yunis. A strike on a hotel during the 8th was said to have killed a number of Quds Force commanders of the Lebanon Corps and Palestine Corps. (Iran said they were diplomats.) Israel did agree not to attack the IAP or its access road. The Lebanese government reacted angrily, accusing Hezbollah of betraying the country and sparing no harsh words for Israel, either. The government insisting the Hezbollah cease operations and surrender its weapons immediately. The Army was directed to act accordingly. No one 'held their breath' awaiting such an outcome.

Ground operations began on the 2nd to expand the five cross-border outposts to achieve a more 'enhanced forward defence posture.' The stated intent was to prevent attacks on Israeli border communities via Hezbollah ground incursions. However, given that anti-tank fire had claimed several casualties, and these had up to 8km (5mi) range, Israel felt it had to clear up to this limit. This suggested

The US Navy aircraft carriers provided a goodly portion of the air power brought to bear on Iran during the war. Carrier Air Wing 9, with F-35Cs and F/A-18s on deck, prepares to sortie from the USS *Abraham Lincoln*, CVN 72, on 28 February 2026. (DoD)

another security buffer zone across the length of the border. They insisted it was not the beginning of a major campaign, but Israel certainly did not want to evacuate border communities again.

On 6 March Israel stated it had struck more than 500 targets all across Lebanon in 27 waves of strikes. There was a sense they wanted to 'finish the job' of crushing Hezbollah and General Zamir said the IDF would 'completely dismantle' the organisation. However, if it could not be done during the last war this was evidently unachievable. The effort was once again at the expense of Lebanon where, by that date, 123 people had been killed and hundreds more injured. By the 11th 570 Lebanese were dead along with two Israeli soldiers. Nearly 100,000 people had relocated from southern Lebanon into the capital in anticipation of more extensive fighting and after Israel warned them to 'flee for your lives.' Throughout the country nearly 760,000 were displaced. On the 10th the Lebanese government was appealing to the international community for help enabling the Army to disarm Hezbollah. Legislation declared Hezbollah's actions illegal. President Joseph Aoun sought direct talks with Israel to permanently end the decades of deadly conflict on its territory. It was, however, unlikely any outside nation would step foot in the Lebanon quagmire and attempt to assist in disarming the largest non-state military in the world if it was uncooperative.

On the night of 6/7 March the IDF conducted a raid near the village of Nabi Chit which they said was to recover the body of an airman missing for decades. Ron Arad, an F-4E navigator, had been captured in 1986 after ejecting from his aircraft and never heard from again. New intelligence on the location of his remains was said to have emerged from Ahmad Shukar, a former Lebanese security official reportedly kidnapped in December 2025. Brought in by four helicopters, the soldiers were engaged by Hezbollah gunmen and locals in a firefight with responding airstrikes. When the Israelis disappeared at dawn 41 people were dead and 40 wounded, none Israeli. They reportedly found nothing of Arad.

During the first two days of the war in Iran, Israel closed all crossings into Gaza. It later reopened them in a very limited capacity. This had the expected humanitarian consequences. West Bank settler violence also ticked up whilst the military constrained all movement of the Palestinian residents.

ATTRITION MATH

How many air defence missiles Israel and the USA had been able to replenish since June 2025 is unclear, but it was unlikely to have been a great many given even accelerated production rates. But, with a renewed all-out campaign of Iranian attacks, it was a race to see who ran short of ordnance first. The same played out in the Gulf States, hoping the USA and Israel would severely degrade Iranian capabilities before they could no longer adequately defend their airspace. In the first days of the war alone Iran fired some 500 rockets and 2,000 drones. On 9 March Trump said Iran was down to around 10 percent of their missiles and 25 percent of their drones, if he could be believed. Still, the Iranians perhaps planned to hold out for the weeks necessary for the attritional math to work in their favour. Persisting in attacks on neighbouring states was hoped to persuade those nations to pressure Trump to relent. Keeping the Strait closed deepened the world economic impact and so more pressure on the Americans. The Pentagon made clear it felt it had a logistics advantage and the USA prepared to ship 12,000 bombs to Israel on an emergency basis not requiring Congressional approval. In just the first two days of the war the USA expended $5.6 billion of munitions and later burned about $1–2 billion per day. This would eventually bring domestic pressure to end the budget drain. The IASF flew 50 airlift missions bringing 1,000 tonnes of munitions and equipment into the country.

On 6 March Trump called for an 'unconditional surrender' by the Iranians, with 'total immunity', and for the citizenry to rise up. He claimed 60 percent of Iran's missiles and 64 (or 60) percent of the launchers had been destroyed. Israel's Foreign Minister, Gideon Sa'ar, said on the 9th that in the past week his country had suffered more attacks from Lebanon than Iran. To that time the Americans alone having hit over 3,000 targets. As for possibly deploying ground forces into the country, the President said it had not been

This map depicts American and Israeli strikes in Iran, Israeli strikes in Lebanon, and Iranian strikes across the Middle East. It was based on information available from public sources, and a 'snapshot' as the war was still underway, and so may be incomplete or inaccurate. (Map by George Anderson)

discussed. This was a remarkable admission that all scenarios of how the war could play-out had not been contemplated. Certainly taking custody of the cache of highly enriched uranium, wherever it was, would likely require some such action. Trump had also said he was surprised at Iran lashing out at the Persian Gulf states. He may have thought Iran, after Khamenei was eliminated, would immediately *kowtow* to American's will as Venezuela was perceived to have done after Maduro was removed. However, Iran was an entirely different 'kettle of fish.'

The war was initially popular in Israel and likely to help Netanyahu's re-election campaign. There was a chance he would call for early elections whilst enjoying the surge that could dissipate if things went sour. Israel considered eliminating Iran as a threat, and the harm Iran caused in Gulf States, could lead to improved relations whilst those states worried about an empowered Israel seeking to extend its hegemony.

WAR'S END?

On 9 March Trump said the war was a 'short-term excursion' and 'pretty much' complete, but also that the USA would persist until 'ultimate victory.' After more than 5,000 strikes he summed the war as essentially won, but the USA needed to 'win more.' Hegseth was telling the media 'this is only just beginning' as his boss speculated the war could be over in days as Iran had 'nothing left in a military sense' and suggesting the USA and Israel were running out of targets. Yet, drones and missiles continued to fly and Hegseth said the 10th marked the most intense period of American attacks yet. Israel was saying at the time they foresaw two more weeks to achieve their goals.

To that point 2,452 Iranian citizens had perished, 1,122 of them military plus another 613 undetermined, according to the Human Rights Activists News Agency. The White House was signalling that when the President determined Iran no longer represented a threat, or 'feel it in my bones', that this would be considered 'unconditional surrender' even if the Republic's leaders did not utter those words. However, it was unlikely Netanyahu would be satisfied with Trump declaring the war over without regime change in Iran. Trump had said he did not want to come back every five or 10 years to repeat the exercise, and this was Israel's intent as well. So, there was incentive not to call the war over too soon.

BIBLIOGRAPHY

Abou-Ghazala, Yahya, Diamond, Jeremy, Salman, Abeer, Mezzofiore, Gianluca, Al-Sawalhi, Mohammad and Araújo, Madalena, '"Death and Hunger": Videos, Expert Analysis and Witnesses Point to Israeli Gunfire in Gaza Aid Site Shooting', CNN, 5 June 2025, online post

Bob, Yonah Jeremey and Evyatar, Ilan, *Target Tehran, How the Mossad is Using Sabotage, Cyberwarfare, Assassination and Secret Diplomacy to Stop a Nuclear Iran and Realign the Middle East* (New York, New York: Simon & Schuster, 2023)

Bull, Odd, *War and Peace in the Middle East, The Experiences and Views of a U.N. Observer* (London, England: Leo Cooper, 1976)

Burns, E.L.M., *Between Arab and Israeli* (London, England: George G. Harrap & Company, 1962)

Cohen, Elkana, *Oct 7, The War Against Hamas Through the Eyes of an Israeli Command Officer* (Hoboken, New Jersey: Viva Editions, 2024)

Dagan, Nehemia, *Lessons from 5,000 Feet* (eBookPro Publishing, 2025)

'Deaths of Palestinians in Israeli Custody', www.phr.org.il, accessed 18 November 2024

Frantzman, Seth J., *The October 7 War, Israel's Battle for Security in Gaza* (New York, New York: Wicked Son, 2024)

Graham-Harrison, Emma and Abraham, Yuval, 'Revealed: Israeli Military's Own Data Indicates Civilian Death rate of 83% in Gaza War', The Guardian (online), 21 August 2025 (accessed 6 October 2025)

Hasson, Nir, Kubovich, Yaniv and Peleg, Bar, 'It's a Killing Field': IDF Soldiers Ordered to Shoot Deliberately at Unarmed Gazans Waiting for Humanitarian Id', Haaretz (online), 27 June 2025, accessed 3 November 2025

Hutchison, E.H., *Violent Truce: A Military Observer Looks at the Arab-Israeli Conflict 1951–1955* (New York, New York: The Devin-Adair Company, 1956)

Katz, Yaakov and Bohbot, Amir, *Whilst Israel Slept, How Hamas Surprised the Most Powerful Military in the Middle East* (New York, New York: St. Martin's Press, 2025)

Lappin, Yaacov, 'The IDF's Learning Curve Following October 7 and its Global Implications', The Jerusalem Institute for Strategy and Security, 9 September 2025 (online post)

M., Guy, *The Rescue, October 7 Through the Eyes of Israel's Para-Rescue Commandos* (e-book: Wicked Son Book, 2025)

Mezzofiore, Gianluca Qibiawa, Tamara and Araújo, Madalena 'US Used About a Quarter of its High-end Missile Interceptors in Israel-Iran War, Exposing Supply Gap', CNN, online post, accessed 24 December 2025

Morris, Benny, *1948, A History of the First Arab-Israeli War* (London, England: Yale University Press, 2008); *1948 and After, Israel and the Palestinians* (Oxford, England: Clarendon Press, 1994); *Israel's Border Wars 1949-1956* (Oxford, New York: Oxford University Press 1997); *Righteous Victims: A History of the Zionist-Arab Conflict, 1881–1999* (New York, New York; Alfred A. Knopf, 1999)

Netanyahu, Benjamin, *Bibi, My Story* (New York, New York: Simon & Schuster, 2002)

Saifi, Zeena, 'Global Outrage Has Grown After Two Years of Bombardment in Gaza, In Israel, it is a Different Story', CNN, 5 October 2025

Saifi, Zeena and Bordeaux, Thomas, 'Satellite Images Reveal Wide Destruction in Gaza City as Israel Steps Up Assault', CNN, 12 September 2025

Shahak, Israel, *Open Secrets, Israeli Nuclear and Foreign Policies* (London, England: Pluto Press, 1997)

Shlaim, Avi, *Genocide in Gaza, Israel's Long War on Palestine* (Belfast, Ireland: The Irish Pages Press, 2024)

Shkedy, Elyezer, *Who the F*uck is Michael?!: An Israeli Air Force Chef's Uncompromising Code for Achieving Greatness* (Hoboken, New Jersey: Viva Editions, 2025)

Spence, John, 'Israel Has Created a New Standard for Urban Warfare. Why Will No One Admit It? | Opinion', *Newsweek* (online), 26 March 2024

Taghvaee, Babak, 'Crushing Iran's Nukes', *Air Forces Monthly*, August 2025, No.449, pp.32–39; 'Phantoms of Shahrokhi', *Air Forces Monthly*, September 2025, No.450, pp.32–37.

Yannay, Yael, *Avi Lanir, A Short Life Story* (Noam Lanir, 2025), e-book

Yingst, Trey, *Black Saturday, An Unfiltered Account of the October 7th Attack on Israel and the War in Gaza* (Fox News Books, digital edition October 2024)

ENDNOTES

Foreword

1   Armed Palestinian and related groups have been referred to as terrorists, guerrillas, irregulars, militants, radicals, and freedom fighters. These forces targeted civilians and infrastructure much more frequently than military because of their comparative weakness for conventional warfare against a standing army with extensive defensive/offensive means. Where they were seeking an insurgency and popular uprising, they could be considered guerrillas. However, many operations were blatant terrorism in the form of indiscriminate fire and murder inspiring only revulsion and condemnation. It is a matter of perspective. This account uses the terms interchangeably based on the author's assessment of the nature of the associated events.

Chapter 1

1   The Jewish nation of the Bible had been conquered before the Roman occupation. The Romans repressed the Jews because of their rebellious behaviour and most of these people were displaced. There remained a modest number of Jews living in the area subsequently known as Palestine (in various linguistic forms) for nearly two millennia. The Holy Land changed rulers several times in this intervening period and so had always been under foreign occupation.

2   The Western Wall in Jerusalem is the last remnant of Judaism's destroyed Second Temple. It forms one part of the Temple Mount, an elevated plateau on which Muslims built the Al-Aqsa Mosque and the Dome of the Rock shrine.

3   The holocaust was the systematic murder of six million Jews during the Second World War by Germany and its collaborators.

4   Transjordan formally annexed the West Bank on 24 April 1950. This aroused a clamour of Arab anger that was only quieted by the Arab League asserting that Jordan held the area in trusteeship until the 'Palestine question' was settled. The League of Arab States was a long-standing association of Arab nations to coordinate policy and provide mutual assistance.

5   Benny Morris, *1948, A History of the First Arab-Israeli War* (London, England: Yale University Press, 2008), provides examples and summarises this on pp.405–406 as perhaps 800 civilians and prisoners of war murdered, eclipsing Arab massacres.

6   Benny Morris, *1948 and After, Israel and the Palestinians* (Oxford, England: Clarendon Press, 1994), pp.83–92, with details derived from period Haganah documents.

7   Among the surveillance efforts was a programme in which dozens of agents, training to speak Arabic fluently and to practice Muslim customs, were planted in Arab communities. They married and fathered children, living as Muslim men, whilst reporting on activities. When the programme was ended after many years the women and children were told the truth and that they would relocate to live a Jews, it was understandably cataclysmic for them. Yael Yannay, *Avi Lanir, A Short Life Story* (Noam Lanir, 2025), e-book, search for 'astonishing human drama'.

8   Benny Morris, *Israel's Border Wars 1949-1956* (Oxford, New York: Oxford University Press 1997), pp.99–102, 427 and 430–430.

9   See Odd Bull, *War and Peace in the Middle East, The Experiences and Views of a U.N. Observer* (London, England: Leo Cooper, 1976), E.L.M. Burns, *Between Arab and Israeli* (London, England: George G. Harrap & Company, 1962, and E.H. Hutchison, *Violent Truce: A Military Observer Looks at the Arab-Israeli Conflict 1951–1955* (New York, New York: The Devin-Adair Company, 1956)

10 Benny Morris, *Righteous Victims: A History of the Zionist-Arab Conflict, 1881–1999* (New York, New York; Alfred A. Knopf, 1999), p.295 and *Israel's Border Wars*, pp.424–425, referencing period documents, and Burns, *Between Arab and Israeli*, pp.303–304 note 33 and Avi Shlaim, *Genocide in Gaza, Israel's Long War on Palestine* (Belfast, Ireland: The Irish Pages Press, 2024), p.217.

11 Burns, *Between Arab and Israeli*, p.191, the author stating he was 'credibly informed' of this plan.

12 East Jerusalem was not officially annexed by Israel until a 1980 law declaring it Israel's 'eternal and indivisible' capital. Most countries did not recognise this annexation.

13 Two major divisions of the Islamic faith are Sunni and Shia, with the latter a small minority. Their disagreements are the root of much discord and even violence. Iran is mostly Shia and there are large percentages of Shia in Yemen and Lebanon, all countries with leadership or dominant military factions that challenged Israel militarily as a foundation of their strength and appeal. Both Muslim factions suffered from fundamentalist divisions stoking violence.

14 Hamas was a Palestinian arm of the Islamic Brotherhood that opposed the government in Cairo.

15 These 8,000 lived on 25 percent of the Strip that had 1.4 million in the rest of the total 365km² (141mi²), yet was 40 percent of the arable land and consumed disproportionate quantities of water. Israel levelled the settlements before leaving.

16 The USA and Israel had encouraged Fatah to stage a coup.

17 Punishing a populace for actions of its government is unjust. By 2023 only a minority had voted for Hamas in 2006.

18 The IDF comprised a core of full-time personnel, conscripts serving a few years, and a vast pool of reservists who could be called to fill out standing brigades and activate others.

19 Claiming such operations are self-defence against an adversary resisting occupation and oppression is inadmissible under international law.

20 Yonah Jeremey Bob and Ilan Evyatar, *Target Tehran, How the Mossad is Using Sabotage, Cyberwarfare, Assassination and Secret Diplomacy to Stop a Nuclear Iran and Realign the Middle East* (New York, New York: Simon & Schuster, 2023), e-book, search for 'launched the drone'.

21 Bob and Evyatar, *Target Tehran*, e-book, search for 'I'm against it'.

22 Civilian population transfer into occupied territory violates the Geneva Convention that Israel ratified in 1951. The principal points of applicable law were the prohibition on the acquisition of territory through force, the obligation to respect the right of peoples to self-determination, and the obligation to refrain from imposing regimes of alien subjugation, domination and exploitation inimical to humankind, including racial discrimination. Israel has argued that the status of the territories is historically disputed, not having been a part of a recognised nation-state, and settlements are spontaneous acts of civilians and not policies of the State. In fact, Israeli governments have offered incentives for citizens to move to the Territories. Also, during the British administration Palestine was depicted as such on maps, had its own currency, issued Palestine passports, and most of the governance and policing was performed by locals. No one questions that India, under similar circumstances at the time, was not a distinct country.

23 The municipal area of East Jerusalem was repeatedly expanded into appropriated land for new Israeli housing. As occupied East Jerusalem had been unified with the West, annexed and declared their 'eternal capital', Israel insisted this did not constitute additional annexation of Palestinian land but rather 'natural growth'. 'Jerusalem is not a settlement' they would say and not, in their view, occupied territory even if the environs were extended into such land.

24 Persistent claims that the UN has been forever anti-Israel (except, presumably, the 1947 partition vote) ignores that members of the diplomatic corps are in constant flux, the individuals reflecting their nation's policies, and the only organisational imperative is adherence to the UN Charter. That Israel has been repeatedly admonished via Resolutions for violations of the Charter is because it has many times been in violation and disregarded Resolutions. Member states bring complaints before the body that must be heard. That some of these have been a form of 'ganging-up on Israel' cannot be denied. Israel has also lodged a great many complaints with successful outcomes, lobbied for voting blocks and relied on a USA veto in the UNSC. In the 1975 Sinai II agreement the US pledged to defend Israeli interests in UN votes.

25 Benjamin Netanyahu, *Bibi, My Story* (New York, New York: Simon & Schuster, 2002), e-book, search for 'fish to fry'. Also, a leaked IDF presentation predicted 500 dead in such an operation, causing many to recoil. This may have been what Netanyahu referred to, acknowledging understanding in 2014 that a ground invasion to eliminate Hamas would cost tens of thousands of civilian lives and leave wide destruction. Search for 'wholesale destruction of Gaza'.

26 Netanyahu had been subjected to repeated investigations and court cases for a decade.

27 The IDF had been assessed as the eleventh strongest in the world.

Chapter 2

1   Seth J. Frantzman, *The October 7 War, Israel's Battle for Security in Gaza* (New York, New York: Wicked Son, 2024), e-book, search for 'got wind of Hamas'.

2   Yaakov Katz and Amir Bohbot, *Whilst Israel Slept, How Hamas Surprised the Most Powerful Military in the Middle East* (New York, New York: St. Martin's Press, 2025), e-book, search for 'not a single Israeli spy'.

3   Israel reported it found the drug Captagon on the bodies of some of the fighters. This synthetic amphetamine allows an individual to stay alert for long hours whilst also enhancing aggressiveness. Captagon had been used elsewhere by irregular forces in recent years.

4   Post-war the IDF decided to allow approximately 10,000 reservists to keep weapons at home to respond more readily in a similar emergency. The IASF also adjusted force allocations to ensure more rapid response.

5   Frantzman, *The October 7 War*, e-book, describes an artillery unit on the northern front who picked up and moved to the Gaza frontier, using transport, without authorisation. Had Hezbollah launched a major operation concurrent with Hamas, as some feared, this could have degraded the IDF response. But, such was the nature of the IDF, with more informality than in other leading armed forces. Search for 'put the M109s'. Another such event was a reconnaissance battalion training in Galilee that also moved south and summoned its reservists on its own initiative. Katz and Bohbot, *Whilst Israel Slept*, e-book, search for 'scrambled the entire battalion'.

6   Some Israelis declared, seemingly with an element of pride (connecting with ancestors via shared trauma), that they had survived a pogrom. A pogrom is a riot against a specific ethnic group, inspired by a government for repressive purposes. Hence, the Hamas attack, also referred to as Black Sabbath and limited to a small fraction of the populace, does not fit the definition. The subsequent war was also referred to as Israel's Second War of Independence, which is equally inflated and nonsensical.

7   A similar event on 7 October was tank fire directed at a house where terrorists were holding hostages. Besides the enemy, 12 of the 14 Israelis were killed. Ordered by a brigadier general, it is not clear this was in response to the Hannibal Directive. Frantzman, *The October 7 War*, e-book, search for 'controversial decisions' and 'ordered a tank'.

8   Despite proclamations by the IDF and its pundits, Israel had always applied disproportionate military responses to provocations as a form of deterrence. The most superficial review of IDF history shows the opposite has always been the practice. In recent times this was expressed as the Dahiya Doctrine in which civilian areas would be considered military bases if fire originates there and disproportionate force applied to the point of destruction. Even after more than seven decades experience demonstrating the strategy never deterred the enemy for long, it was continued.

9   Elkana Cohen, *Oct 7, The War Against Hamas Through the Eyes of an Israeli Command Officer* (Hoboken, New Jersey: Viva Editions, 2024), e-book.

10   Shlaim, *Genocide in Gaza*, p.299, gives some personal accounts.

11   Given the ongoing war in Ukraine, there was a worldwide shortage of 155mm artillery shells. The USA had shipped out 200,000 of these rounds stored in Israel for its potential use, but the IDF requested 50,000 be returned. The first aircraft of a replenishment airlift arrived on 13 October. Ceramic ballistic plates for vests and small unit drones were in particular short supply.

12   According to international law, 'human shields' are those persons forcibly placed alongside military targets during combat, not those who just happen to be living where military operations may be conducted. A great many IDF installations were within civilian communities and so targeting them risked collateral damage and casualties. No one accused Israel of using Israeli residents as human shields.

13   Katz and Bohbot, *Whilst Israel Slept*, e-book, provides accounts of property owners intimidated into accepting their stashes. Search for 'forcing them to hide'.

14   The IDF employed a device known as Switchblade that tracked friendly forces and permitted a commander to know the location of adjacent units. This did not always function or was not consulted, or the 'fog of war' undermined its value.

15   This tragic event on 15 December 2023 appears to demonstrate both the readiness to fire on anyone and a sense of vulnerability. The soldiers interpreted SOS signs on a building and Hebrew voices within as Hamas ruses. The approaching shirtless men, shouting in Hebrew and one waving a white cloth, should not have been interpreted as a threat.

16   Cohen, *Oct 7*, e-book, describes this process throughout the book. Other sources describe the same.

17   Frantzman, *The October 7 War*, e-book, search for 'within 200 meters' and Katz and Bohbot, *Whilst Israel Slept*, e-book, search for 'couple dozen yards'.

18   Frantzman, *The October 7 War*, e-book, search for 'generally misfire' and 'approximately 450'.

19   The notion that Biden could have halted Israel's excesses by withholding munitions ignores support of Congress who would have pushed through deliveries and overridden his veto. Israel said that Biden was withholding some authorised munitions, the assertion probably as a way to energise supporters in Congress. The Administration denied this, saying some materiel was still in the process of preparation and shipping.

20   In 2014 Netanyahu's popularity rating dropped from 85 to 38 percent after ending the war in Gaza without destroying Hamas.

Chapter 3

1   The Houthi, a.k.a. Ansar Allah, was an Islamic political-military organisation backed by Iran that had seized power in a portion of Yemen during a civil war. They were anti-American because the USA backed their enemy Saudi Arabia. Their anti-Israel stance was largely to distract the populace from their human rights abuses and general poverty.

2   Trey Yingst, *Black Saturday, An Unfiltered Account of the October 7th Attack on Israel and the War in Gaza* (Fox News Books, digital edition October 2024), e-book, search for 'mission was called off'.

3   Most of the Druze were not Israeli citizens, considering themselves Syrian Arabs. However, some integrated into Israeli society and were conscripted into the IDF.

4   Israel Shahak, *Open Secrets, Israeli Nuclear and Foreign Policies* (London, England: Pluto Press, 1997), e-book, Chapter 7, states that the 1994 peace treaty between Israel and Jordan allowed for Israeli use of Jordanian airspace for defensive purposes in an emergency. This reference also suggests that the accord permitted Israel to operate from an airfield in eastern Jordan under such circumstances.

5   Researchers examined Planet Labs PBC satellite imagery of the vast base following the strike and counted evident impact damage.

6   An Israeli firm had developed TIKAD, a quadcopter attachment that minimised the recoil of shooting.

7   This was the Heritage Minister, Amihay Eliyahu, who likely had no direct knowledge of the IDF's nuclear capabilities.

Chapter 4

1   During his funeral, four IASF aircraft performed a low fly-by and reverse of the missing-man formation, presumably not to honour the man.

2   Türkish work by the end of 2025 to install radar inside Syria caused Israel angst.

Chapter 5

1   A leaked military intelligence document dated 13 October 2023 outlined a plan to push the entire population into northern Sinai and officials proposed Egypt's World Bank debt be forgiven if it accept the people.

2   Evangelicals (or at least a portion called Christian Zionists) believed that the 'second coming of Christ' would occur only when ancient Israel was reestablished, the temple in Jerusalem was rebuilt, and all the world's Jews converged there. This suggests present-day Israel holding sovereignty over all of the former Palestine and more.

3   On 20 December 2025 Trump unveiled Project Sunrise, a concept to rebuild Gaza over 20 years into a modern luxury destination and tech centre. Projected to cost $112 billion, he sought investors. This appeared more focused on earning money and less so housing two million mostly poor people in the most rapid and practical manner. It was bound to meet resistance and slow reconstruction.

4   The High Court subsequently ruled the government's ban unlawful.

5   These people and supporters believed ancient Hebrew ancestors having lived there granted them inalienable rights to all such land regardless of all that transpired in subsequent millennia. Those tribes had been as busy as all others conquering and enslaving surrounding peoples and so assessing which lands were 'originally' Jewish (all previously held by someone else) is a convoluted topic. To those holding these views it does not matter. That a Hebrew tribe at one time inhabited the Golan Heights was enough to stake a claim long after the territory was occupied in June 1967. Any discrimination against Jews by Islamic rulers of Palestine hundreds of years ago was also considered part and parcel of present-day grievances demanding recompense. (Islam arose in the seventh century CE and its Arab conquerors won Palestine from the Byzantine Empire the same century.) Such territorial claims in present-day jurisprudence is novel.

6   Many Israelis repeat this despite their past governments having made innumerable public statements and signing numerous agreements and treaties with these people so named and acknowledging their right to self-determination in occupied lands to include naming the West Bank.

7   This is a quotation from a Netanyahu speech.

8   At this time, during Passover, Jewish worshipers ascended to the Al-Aqsa compound to openly pray whilst security forces kept all others at bay. By long-standing agreement only Muslims were allowed to pray there and so this was another measure to alter the status quo and diminish Arab authority in areas under Israeli occupation.

9   There was evidently an expectation that at least senior officers in the IDF hold to the 'party line.' One reserve Brigadier General expressed the view that if he publicly espoused the two-state solution he could expect to be stripped of his rank. Nehemia Dagan, *Lessons from 5,000 Feet* (eBookPro Publishing, 2025), e-book, p.538.

10   This report was in a July 2025 issue of the *Maariv* daily newspaper.

11   This was a report on the Army Radio on 18 August 2025.

12   There was a USA law prohibiting security assistance to countries who are credibly accused of human rights abuses. The State Department report was classified and so withheld from public review. Its existence was revealed via leakers.

13   Thereafter Netanyahu was careful about where he travelled. The USA under the Trump administration, for one, was certainly not going to arrest him. He had travelled to Hungary without incident. His 25 September 2025 flight to the USA to speak before the UNGA was circuitous across the Mediterranean, evidently to avoid airspace of nations that might seek to arrest him. More than 100 UNGA diplomats from more than 50 countries in attendance at Netanyahu's speech left the chamber.

14   Cohen, *Oct 7*, e-book, search for 'buildings belonging to UNRWA'.

15   Most or all governments lie when it serves their purpose. The record is clear that Israel had dissembled multiple times since its founding for various reasons. More recently, a Fox News video correspondent said the IDF had lied to him, and he did not take anything at face value. Yingst, *Black Saturday*, e-book, search for 'at face value'.

Chapter 6

1   If Iran had used covert operatives to kill Israeli nuclear scientists with hidden bombs the Israelis would have called it state terrorism. That Israel employed fighter jets to drop the bombs is little different if the target is illegitimate under the laws of war. Israel had also killed Iranian nuclear scientists with hidden bombs.

2   Online claims were that this was achieved with drones flown by a Mossad team.

3   Babak Taghvaee, 'Phantoms of Shahrokhi', *Air Forces Monthly*, September 2025, No.450, p.35, suggested no contacts. Online reports were that some of the drone shoot-downs were by F-4Es.

4   Most missile warhead stages reach hypersonic velocities in its final phase of flight and any additional speed would require a boost motor, which seemed unlikely to have been adopted. Decoys are another complication, but it is unclear these were employed.

5   Babak Taghvaee, 'Crushing Iran's Nukes', *Air Forces Monthly*, August 2025, No.449, p.36, without attribution. On p.37, in a caption, the account gives

this as more than 600 IASF tanker sorties, but this is unreasonable as it would be more than eight long-endurance sorties per day for each of the six Boeing 707 tankers, assuming all were operational.

6   These numbers are from Yaacov Lappin, 'The IDF's Learning Curve Following October 7 and its Global Implications', The Jerusalem Institute for Strategy and Security, 9 September 2025, online post. However, the numbers vary in accounts for an average 550 inbound missiles. Another analysis stated that defences destroyed 201 of 574 missiles with 57 hitting populated areas and that the rate of success increased over the 12 days with eight percent in the first week, 16 percent in the second, and 25 on the last day. The THAAD was responsible for nearly half of the intercepts. Gianluca Mezzofiore, Tamara Qibiawa and Madalena Araújo, 'US Used about a Quarter of its High-end Missile Interceptors in Israel-Iran War, Exposing Supply Gap', CNN, online post, accessed 24 December 2025.

Chapter 7

1   Testimonials from IDF personnel who witnessed or participated in such actions were recounted in Nir Hasson, Yaniv Kubovich and Bar Peleg, 'It's a Killing Field': IDF Soldiers Ordered to Shoot Deliberately at Unarmed Gazans Waiting for Humanitarian Aid', Haaretz (online), 27 June 2025, accessed 3 November 2025. There was also analysis of sound recording of gunfire at a site which identified the weapon as an FN 7.62mm machine-gun commonly mounted on IDF armoured vehicles. Yahya Abou-Ghazala, Jeremy Diamond, Abeer Salman, Gianluca Mezzofiore, Mohammad Al-Sawalhi and Madalena Araújo, '"Death and Hunger": Videos, Expert Analysis and Witnesses Point to Israeli Gunfire in Gaza Aid Site Shooting', CNN, 5 June 2025, online post, accessed 3 November 2025.

2   The word does not appear in Netanyahu's autobiography. Images and discussion of settler violence plus Israeli operations in the West Bank were scrubbed from the Internet.

3   Zeena Saifi, 'Global Outrage Has Grown After Two Years of Bombardment in Gaza, In Israel, it is a Different Story', CNN, 5 October 2025. This journalist repeated a Reporters Without Borders 2025 World Press Freedom Index assessment that 'Press freedom, media plurality and editorial independence have been increasingly restricted in Israel since the start of the war in Gaza'.

4   Zini's brother, Bezalel Zini, was charged in February 2026, along with 10 others, with running a smuggling ring bringing goods into Gaza to be sold at exorbitant profit. He was also part of a semi-official group of reservists called the Uriah Force, made up predominantly of right-wing extremists, who brought bulldozers and other heavy equipment into the Strip for wholesale demolition. This evidently provided cover for the alleged smuggling.

5   A study by an Israeli human rights group determined that at least 98 Palestinians had perished in Israeli custody since October 2023 from physical violence and medical neglect. 'Deaths of Palestinians in Israeli Custody', www.phr.org.il, accessed 18 November 2024. When the war began Israel ceased providing information to the Red Cross of Palestinians taken into custody and would not permit them access to detention facilities.

6   Hamas would remark, after examining the remains of deceased detained Palestinians released during the ceasefire, that some were still in restraints and showed evidence of abuse and torture. People hastened to dismiss this as propaganda, riding the storm of controversy that made such statements more readily accepted.

7   Zeena Saifi and Thomas Bordeaux, 'Satellite Images Reveal Wide Destruction in Gaza City as Israel Steps Up Assault' CNN, 12 September 2025. The conclusions were based on reviewing satellite imagery.

8   Qatar began hosting Hamas leadership in 2011 at the request of the USA to simplify interactions.

Chapter 8

1   In 2020 Trump had come within a hairs' breadth of recognising Israeli sovereignty over 30 percent of the West Bank.

2   Israel compensated its citizens and businesses impacted by terrorism and acts of war, and gave benefits to service personnel killed or wounded in combat plus family members. Israel worked with the US Congress to draft and pass the Taylor Force Bill that reduced American funds to the PA until the payments to those judged deceased terrorists and their survivors were curtailed.

3   Article 51 of the UN Charter recognizes a right of self-defence provided the force used is necessary and proportionate.

4   Only the Israeli President, Isaac Herzog, had the authority to issue a pardon. Of course, the PM had yet to be convicted of a crime for which

a pardon could be granted. A pardon would be deeply unpopular inside Israel, stories of corruption on many peoples' lips over many years. Trump's appeal was a clear case of interfering in the internal affairs of another country, but he was insensitive to such nuances. In November Trump sent a letter to Herzog again asking that Netanyahu be pardoned. On 20 November Netanyahu himself sent a missive to Herzog seeking clemency 'in the public interest.'

5   Such IDF actions had 'torpedoed' ceasefires in the past.

6   Only in mid-February 2026 did the Board of Peace formalise plans to build a 5,000-person military base in the Strip to house the ISF.

7   Emma Graham-Harrison and Yuval Abraham, 'Revealed: Israeli Military's Own Data Indicates Civilian Death rate of 83% in Gaza War', The Guardian (online), 21 August 2025, accessed 6 October 2025.

8   The government asserted that journalists' reports endangered Israeli personnel, and the Supreme Court upheld this. They defended the policy even after the ceasefire.

9   John Spence, 'Israel Has Created a New Standard for Urban Warfare. Why Will No One Admit It? | Opinion', Newsweek (online), 26 March 2024, offered that 'Israel has implemented more precautions to prevent civilian harm than any military in history' and by doing so impeded its progress. The assessment was based on his personal exposure a few months into the war but lacks data supporting the assertion. The claim in Elyezer Shkedy, Who the F*uck is Michael?!: An Israeli Air Force Chef's Uncompromising Code for Achieving Greatness (Hoboken, New Jersey: Viva Editions, 2025), e-book, of 24:1 targeted individual-to-civilian killed by airstrikes in 2010 (search for 'from 1:1 to 12:1'), if true, appears to have been reversed in the 14 years since realized. Spencer concluded that Israeli measures were creating only one to two civilian deaths for every combatant death (a ratio of 1:1.5) compared with a world average of 1:9. The 1:2 ratio is also mentioned in Katz and Bohbot, Whilst Israel Slept, e-book, search for 'less than 1:2', though this book was written before the war was half over. Eighteen months later the numbers were starker and testimonials from even IDF personnel told a different story. The MoD's 8,900 estimate also stated that five of every six casualties inflicted were civilian, 1:5. This was among the highest of modern conflicts and especially as executed by one of the most advanced militaries in the world. The Lebanese figures presented in Chapter 4 of this book indicate a 1:14 ratio on that front, within Iran (Chapter 6) 1:7, and on the West Bank likely more than 1:15.

10   Such numbers, like much else, was a subject of controversy. Those shown were arrived at by analysts examining satellite photographs. However, IDF analysts arrived at different (reduced) numbers.

11   Lappin, 'The IDF's Learning Curve Following October 7 and its Global Implications'.

12   The 288 by AAM and the Python IV information are details provided the author by a knowledgeable and 'connected' Israeli researcher.

13   Lappin, 'The IDF's Learning Curve Following October 7 and its Global Implications'.

14   The responsible unit was identified as the 5114th Battalion of the Spectrum Warfare Center.

15   Guy M., The Rescue, October 7 Through the Eyes of Israel's Para-Rescue Commandos (e-book: Wicked Son Book, 2025), e-book, search for 'report of a helicopter', states that he had heard about a helicopter shot down on 7 October by a terrorist with a MANPADS whilst in a hover just above the ground. A MANPADS engagement in such circumstances is virtually impossible, so it may have been an RPG. This was likely the Yas'ur damaged by ground fire, that event also reflected in Frantzman, The October 7 War, e-book, 'search for commandeered by Lieutenant' and 'struck by fire', saying the pilot was forced to land. Guy M. mentions another helicopter hit on the 8th, search for 'our helicopter got hit', and events not mentioned in other sources found by the author and may be consigned to rumour. Guy M. responded to an e-mail on 18 October 2025 stating that the accounts in his book were not necessarily chronological or historically accurate, it being principally his personal experiences and recollections.

16   As the elections beckoned, Netanyahu played up his strong association with Trump. He had Israel recognise the break-away Somaliland as an independent state (the only nation to do so) with the price evidently being the 'country' joining the Abraham Accords as another 'feather in the cap' of Netanyahu's re-election campaign. However, the religious parties threatened to bring down the government over the Haredi service deferment issue and 36 former security chiefs wrote that the PM was solely responsible for the failures leading to the 7 October 2023 disaster.

ABOUT THE AUTHOR

William J. Norton is retired from a flight test engineering career that spanned 40 years, including 20 as a US Air Force officer. He has held numerous positions in many organisations on dozens of aerospace programs spanning all aircraft types. He has penned scores of technical papers, 20 books, and a multitude of magazine articles. The Arab-Israeli conflict has been a repeated topic of these publications. Bill holds a Masters in Aeronautical Engineering and has taught courses at the college-level. He is a civil pilot with numerous ratings, restored and operated a DHC-1 Chipmunk, and built and flight-tested a Rutan Long-EZ. Bill is married to the lovely and talented Anya Victoria Eriksson.